This book belongs to

Mr Maxwell
8-1-85

BLACK'S NEW TESTAMENT COMMENTARIES

GENERAL EDITOR: HENRY CHADWICK, D.D.

THE GOSPEL ACCORDING TO ST. MARK

A COMMENTARY ON
THE GOSPEL ACCORDING TO
ST. MARK

SHERMAN E. JOHNSON, Ph.D.

DEAN EMERITUS OF THE CHURCH DIVINITY SCHOOL
OF THE PACIFIC, BERKELEY,
CALIFORNIA

ADAM & CHARLES BLACK
LONDON

FIRST PUBLISHED 1960
SECOND EDITION 1972
REPRINTED WITH CORRECTIONS 1977
A. AND C. BLACK LIMITED
35 BEDFORD ROW LONDON WCIR J4H

© 1960, 1972, 1977 SHERMAN ELBRIDGE JOHNSON

ISBN 0 7136 1257 6

PRINTED IN GREAT BRITAIN BY
BILLING & SONS LIMITED,
GUILDFORD, LONDON AND WORCESTER

TO
CAROL AND MARCIA

I am reminded of the genuine faith that first dwelt in your grandmother Lois and your mother Eunice, and which I am persuaded is also in you. 2 Tim. i. 5.

PREFACE

THE aim of this commentary is, first, to present the point of view of the evangelist St. Mark and to try to indicate what his words meant to him. This is not only the current fashion in study of the gospels, but it is properly the first step to be taken before asking those questions which are of paramount interest to the general reader: what Jesus actually taught, what happened in the course of his ministry, and what these events mean in their context. A generation ago the commentators made a great contribution by dealing with such issues in the light of the Jewish and Hellenistic background of the NT. Recently this type of study has been put to one side by many scholars who have concentrated their attention on the message of the evangelists. I have, however, given some attention to the original events and their background, for all this is involved in the process by which the stories and sayings groups were developed into the finished gospel.

Everyone acquainted with NT studies will recognise at once my vast indebtedness to earlier commentators, particularly Rawlinson, Montefiore, Branscomb, Lohmeyer and Grant. I have been greatly helped by suggestions from my colleagues, Professors E. C. Hobbs and M. H. Shepherd, from my wife, and from my students, Dr. Frederick G. Bohme and Mr. J. P. Engelcke. The unfailing courtesy and help of the general editor of the series, Professor H. Chadwick, is gratefully acknowledged.

The present translation is based on the text of Nestle, with a few variations. No attempt has been made to deal with textual matters except where the problems concern interpretation of historical issues. Nor has it seemed possible to bring out the unique flavour of the evangelist's style; to reproduce his historical present or other peculiarities would result only in a parody. The aim is to express Mark's meaning, so far as possible, in simple modern English.

SHERMAN E. JOHNSON

Church Divinity School
of the Pacific,
Berkeley, California

CONTENTS

ABBREVIATIONS

AJT	*American Journal of Theology.*
ANET	J. B. Pritchard (ed.), *Ancient Near Eastern Texts relating to the OT* (2nd ed., Princeton, 1955).
Arndt-Gingrich	W. F. Arndt and F. W. Gingrich (eds.), *A Greek-English Lexicon of the NT* (Cambridge, 1957).
ATR	*Anglican Theological Review.*
Bacon, *Mark*	B. W. Bacon, *The Gospel of Mark* (London, 1925).
Bacon, *Story*	B. W. Bacon, *The Story of Jesus* (London, 1927).
BC	K. Lake and F. J. Foakes Jackson, *The Beginnings of Christianity*, Part I (London, 1920–1933), 5 vols.
Bishop	E. F. F. Bishop, *Jesus of Palestine* (London, 1955).
Branscomb	B. H. Branscomb, *The Gospel of Mark* (London, n.d.).
Cadbury, *Peril*	H. J. Cadbury, *The Peril of Modernizing Jesus* (New York, 1937).
Carrington	P. Carrington, *The Primitive Christian Calendar* (Cambridge, 1952).
FTG	M. Dibelius, *From Tradition to Gospel* (London, 1935).
GG	B. S. Easton, *The Gospel before the Gospels* (New York, 1928).
GM	R. H. Lightfoot, *The Gospel Message of St. Mark* (Oxford, 1950).
Gospel of Thomas	A. Guillaumont and others, *The Gospel According to Thomas* (Leiden, London and New York, 1959).
Grant	F. C. Grant in *The Interpreter's Bible*, vii (New York, 1951).
Grant, *EG*	F. C. Grant, *The Earliest Gospel* (New York, 1943).
Grant, *Gospels*	F. C. Grant, *The Gospels: Their Origin and Their Growth* (New York, 1957).
HPC	J. Weiss, *The History of Primitive Christianity* (New York, 1937).
HTR	*Harvard Theological Review.*
IB	*The Interpreter's Bible.*
JBL	*Journal of Biblical Literature.*
JOT	S. E. Johnson, *Jesus in His Own Times* (London, 1958).

JTS	*Journal of Theological Studies.*
KGSM	R. Otto, *The Kingdom of God and the Son of Man* (London, 1943).
Klostermann	E. Klostermann, *Das Markus-Evangelium*, Handbuch zum NT (4th ed., Tübingen, 1950).
Knox, *Sources*	W. L. Knox, *The Sources of the Synoptic Gospels*, i (Cambridge, 1953).
Kraeling, *Atlas*	E. G. Kraeling, *Rand McNally Bible Atlas* (Chicago, 1956).
Lohmeyer	E. Lohmeyer, *Das Evangelium des Markus* (Göttingen, 1951).
LXX	Septuagint version.
Marxsen	W. Marxsen, *Der Evangelist Markus* (Göttingen, 1959).
McCasland	S. V. McCasland, *By the Finger of God* (New York, 1951).
McNeile-Williams	A. H. McNeile, *An Introduction to the Study of the NT* (2nd ed., revised by C. S. C. Williams, Oxford, 1953).
MR	T. A. Burkill, *Mysterious Revelation* (Ithaca, N.Y., 1963).
Moore, *Judaism*	G. F. Moore, *Judaism* (Cambridge, Mass., 1927–1930).
OL	Old Latin version.
OSSP	W. Sanday (ed.), *Studies in the Synoptic Problem by Members of the University of Oxford* (Oxford, 1911).
Problem	J. M. Robinson, *The Problem of History in Mark* (London, 1957).
1QH	Dead Sea Hymns of Thanksgiving.
1QS	Manual of Discipline.
Rawlinson	A. E. J. Rawlinson, *The Gospel According to St. Mark* (London, 1927).
RB	*Revue Biblique.*
SB	H. L. Strack and Paul Billerbeck, *Kommentar zum NT aus Talmud und Midrasch* (Munich, 1922–1928).
Sherwin-White	A. N. Sherwin-White, *Roman Society and Roman Law in the NT* (Oxford, 1963).
TG	S. E. Johnson, *The Theology of the Gospels* (London, 1966).
TWNT	G. Kittel (ed.), *Theologisches Wörterbuch zum NT.*
ZAW	*Zeitschrift für die alttestamentliche Wissenschaft.*
ZNW	*Zeitschrift für die neutestamentliche Wissenschaft.*

INTRODUCTION

I. THE GOSPEL FORM

IT was an event of incalculable importance when a Christian, known to us only by the common Roman name of Marcus, undertook to write the earliest of our four gospels. So far as anyone knows, no book of just this kind had been previously attempted. A document usually designated by the symbol Q no doubt already existed. This was mainly a collection of Jesus' sayings, perhaps prefixed by a brief account of the preaching of John the Baptist and the temptation of Jesus, and concluding with the parable of the Talents or Pounds. It included no account of the Crucifixion, and its single miracle tale, that of the healing of the Centurion's Servant, was to illustrate Jesus' teaching. Although it proclaimed Good News, it was not a complete gospel like the four in the NT canon. Q was more like a collection of 'words of the wise', and the existence of the later *Gospel of Thomas* makes it possible that there were such writings. A narrative of Jesus' arrest and Crucifixion had probably also been written. There is every reason to think that Mark, and no one else, invented the gospel form.

It is sometimes thought that Mark took as his model an outline of mission preaching preserved in certain speeches attributed to Peter and Paul in Acts.[1] The best example of such a summary of Good News is found in x. 36-43, but this and other speeches (ii. 22-36; xiii. 23-41) could equally well be understood as summaries of the written gospels.[2] We know much about the content of early Christian preaching but little about its rhetorical outline except as it can be conjectured from the remaining literature. If Mark had any models, they must be sought elsewhere. They were probably several, not merely one, and the framework chosen by Mark to organise his fragmentary material

[1] Cf. C. H. Dodd, *The Apostolic Preaching and Its Developments* (London, 1936); cf. his *New Testament Studies* (Manchester, 1953), pp. 1-11.
[2] D. E. Nineham, *Studies in the Gospels* (Oxford, 1955), pp. 223-239.

and to express the Church's faith in Jesus as Son of God and Son of Man is probably his unique creation.

A gospel is not a biography, although there is enough resemblance for Justin Martyr to speak of 'the memoirs which are called gospels' (τὰ ἀπομνημονεύματα τῶν ἀποστόλων, *Apol.* i. 67; ἀπομνημονεύματα, ἃ καλεῖται εὐαγγέλια i. 66; cf. i. 33).[1] The interest of the gospels is not in the human side of Jesus' life, his appearance, habits, ways of speech and methods of teaching, but in the message that man's true life depends upon reconciliation to God through him. Their central theme is not 'This is an interesting man, important in world history; you can learn something from his virtues and his failings'; instead, 'God has come into history through this man, bringing release from sin, false teaching, sickness and death; repent and believe in the Good News!' It was inevitable, of course, that when this News took the form of a narrative, it should include materials biographically significant.

The gospels thus appear superficially to be lives of Jesus. But only Luke, with his historical interest, writes a kind of biography. Matthew modifies Mark's gospel form to produce a manual of instruction of leaders and people. John preserves Mark's original purpose of proclamation but transforms everything in the light of his own theology. The data for a full and rounded picture of Jesus' personality were simply not transmitted, even though through the gospel tradition we can learn a great deal about him.

The gospel form seems inevitable to the modern reader, but this is because he has always had the gospels, and the western literary tradition is rich in history and biography. But the accidents of history might have been such as to prevent the writing of any gospel or other life of Jesus in ancient times, or to postpone this kind of activity so long that a different kind of book should emerge. Even in the Graeco-Roman world few men had a Plutarch—or even a Suetonius—as their biographers. Philostratus composed a life of Apollonius of Tyana, who was both a wonder-worker and philosopher, but it is mainly a collection of anecdotes. So great a figure as Epictetus is known to

[1] Cf. K. L. Schmidt in Εὐχαριστήριον . . . *für Gunkel* (Göttingen, 1923), pp. 50-134.

2

us mainly from the lecture notes taken down by his pupil Arrian. In the Jewish world, out of which Jesus came, biography was almost non-existent. The Maccabean kings are known to us from the Books of Maccabees, which are sacred histories on the model of the OT historical books, and from Josephus, who, beginning as a Jewish military man from a priestly family, ended his life as a Hellenistic historian. Fortunately he had enough vanity to write an autobiography. What a boon it would be if someone had composed lives of Rabbis Shemaiah and Abtalion, Hillel and Shammai, Gamaliel the Elder, Johanan ben Zakkai and Akiba, or if someone like Luke had recounted the early history of the Pharisees or the Essenes. But the religious Jew took little historical note of himself or his associates; he was concentrated on the Law of God, the Word of God in the Bible and the oral tradition. Stories were told of a few martyrs, as in the Maccabean period (see, e.g., 4 Maccabees), but for the most part all that was recalled of a man were his crisp and wise sayings. This was almost what happened to the story of Jesus. His words were preserved early and with considerable care; fewer pains were taken to remember the events of his life, except for the last days of it.

Mark's gospel has its own form. Its two parts, i. 1-viii. 26 and viii. 27-xvi. 8, are different from one another but related in such a way that the gospel is a unity. The first half is located almost entirely in Galilee (as far as vii. 23). Jesus proclaims the Reign of God, and by his victory over demons and illness, and his forgiveness of sinners, does what he says God will do in establishing his Reign. Although he has dangerous enemies, he is powerful and triumphant. Here we find most of the epiphanies of his divine glory (except for the Transfiguration, ix. 2-8), and all his exorcisms and the healings (except ix. 14-29; x. 46-52). The Caesarea Philippi scene (viii. 27–ix. 1) introduces a new dimension. Jesus has previously spoken mysteriously of himself as the Son of Man. Now he reveals that the Son of Man must suffer and die, although he will return. No longer is he triumphant and successful; miracles seldom occur now; his vocation is to be servant and slave of all, and a true disciple must follow him in his humility (x. 42-45).

What is Mark saying when he structures his gospel in this

3

specific form, and what function do the miracles serve in the first part of his book? The epiphanies, exorcisms and healings are similar to stories of heroes or 'divine men' like Apollonius of Tyana, told in the Hellenistic world. Philo in his *Life of Moses* portrays the lawgiver in much the same way. Jews and Christians were not isolated from the culture of their own time, and Mark may have taken over a collection of miracle stories that portrayed Jesus as a divine or semi-divine figure. Elijah and Elisha in the Books of Kings were wonder-workers, and they served partially as models for Mark, but in the gospel Jesus, like Philo's Moses, is much more divine.

Three solutions may be proposed.

(1) Mark, naïve and clumsy, wrote his gospel without realising that the two parts did not fit together. The care with which he linked his story together excludes this; he had a theological purpose.

(2) Mark's opponents proclaimed a Christ who was super-human in his ministry and they themselves claimed similar powers. These were like the 'super-apostles' or 'false apostles' of 2 Cor. x-xiii. Because the gospel was written to combat these men, Mark portrays the Twelve as stupid, disobedient, and cowardly. The miracles are set up only to be discredited.[1] This theory fails because the disciples sometimes do fulfil their mission—like all Christians, they are often but not always weak—and because Mark takes delight in the miracles of Jesus.

(3) The most reasonable solution is that Mark was not combatting an error but expressing a positive message. The triumphs of Jesus against demons and illness, his Baptism, Transfiguration, and walking on the water, and his humility and suffering on the Cross, were all part of the same glory.

Mark, then, appears to have been a creative theologian who lived in a Gentile Christian community that was not completely out of touch with Judaism but was developing a culture of its own.

---

[1] This is the hypothesis of T. J. Weeden, *Mark: Traditions in Conflict* (Philadelphia, 1971).

II. The Place of Mark in Early Christian History

The Gospel of Mark was written at a turning-point in early Christian history. The new faith had spread among Jews in all parts of Palestine, some Samaritans had been reached by it, and there were new churches in Syria and Cilicia. Greek-speaking followers of Stephen went as far as Phoenicia, Cyprus and Antioch, and in the latter city 'men of Cyprus and Cyrene' began to convert Gentiles also (Acts xi. 20). If the epithet *Christianoi* ('partisans of Christ') was fastened on the Antiochene group at this time (Acts xi. 26), it would have increased their consciousness of being separate from Judaism.

The Apostle Paul was at least partly a product of this movement, but his ministry in Asia Minor and the mainland of Greece directed the movement into new channels, both geographically and theologically. The towering significance of his thought was not yet perceived; he was but one apostle among many, and Gentile Christianity developed in partial independence of his work. He and other missionaries no doubt had many ideas in common, so that much of what seems to be Pauline influence in Mark and other gospels belongs to the common store of early Christian thought. Long before he came to Rome there were Christians there—any movement with spiritual power would certainly spread to the capital city. Juvenal's remark, that the Orontes had flowed into the Tiber (*Satires* iii. 62), is often quoted; and, as Tacitus said, 'in Rome . . . everything ugly and shameful from every part of the world finds its centre and becomes popular' (*Annals* xv. 44). There may have been Christians in Egypt before A.D. 70, but in small numbers, because Claudius in his letter to the Alexandrians disapproves of visits to Egypt by Syrian Jews.

The earliest gospel also stands at the point of transition from the primitive Palestinian message of Jesus' life and teaching to the relatively more deliberate interpretation of his significance which we find in the later gospels. To a large degree Mark lets the tradition speak for itself, so that, as J. Weiss says, we receive the 'impression of the unique, partly foreign, partly human, but completely enigmatical greatness of his personality'. By contrast, Jesus is the rabbi-Messiah in Matthew, the Saviour in

5

Luke, and in John, God in human form. Nevertheless, Mark shows a shift away from the interest in Jesus' teaching towards concentration on his Person, in the direction of the Fourth Gospel.[1]

Since the historical perspective has shifted, there is a tendency to find allegorical meanings in the parables and sayings of Jesus; cf., e.g., ii. 20; iv. 14-20; xii. 1-11; and possibly xiv. 58. This process, which in Mark is only in its beginnings, is developed further in Matthew (e.g. xxii. 7), and finds its culmination in the Fourth Gospel.

The early Palestinian Christians seem to have believed that Jesus became Messiah or Son of Man after his Resurrection, but for Mark he is already Son of Man on earth (ii. 10), and sayings containing the phrase 'I am come' have begun to appear (ii. 17; cf. i. 38).

Mark is a boundary gospel in still another way. The Church is just at the point of emerging from Judaism as a new, self-conscious community. It still regards itself as the eschatological Israel of the end-time, and the Twelve are still the intimate disciples of Jesus who look forward to reunion with him in the new age; there is not yet much consciousness of their future rôle as apostles (the word is used only once, vi. 30) and foundation stones of the Church. At the same time, chap. vii sharpens Jesus' criticism of the Law and draws out its implications—the Way for Christians is not that of the synagogue—and, although there is not much time, the Good News must be preached to all the nations (xiii. 10).

Mark is thus more than a digest of Jewish-Christian traditions; it is a gospel for a Church which contains a significant proportion of Gentiles. But the evangelist, instead of being in direct contact with Paul, is heir to the general tradition of Gentile Christianity. Thus we are to understand his use of the technical terms 'gospel' (εὐαγγέλιον), 'to proclaim' (κηρύσσειν), 'the Word' (ὁ λόγος), and 'to believe' (πιστεύειν); his idea that the death of Christ frees men (x. 45); the intimate connexion between the Cross and the Resurrection (e.g. in the passion predictions, viii. 31; ix. 31; x. 34); the rhythmic prose of xiv. 38

---

[1] J. Weiss, *HPC*, pp. 691, 701.

INTRODUCTION: EARLY CHRISTIAN HISTORY

with its contrast between flesh and spirit; the use of εὐχαριστεῖν in viii. 6; xiv. 23;[1] the catalogue of vices in vii. 21-23; and perhaps even the apparent contacts between the Transfiguration story (ix. 2-8) and 2 Cor. iii. 7-v. 5, though here perhaps we should think of the diffused influence of Paul.[2]

The message of the non-Pauline Gentile Church is perhaps best observed in the Antiochene traditions of Acts, in such speeches as Acts xiv. 15-17; xvii. 22-31, and in books like the first epistle of Clement. This teaching tradition was based on the missionary propaganda of the diaspora synagogue and contained monotheistic ideas drawn from Stoicism and other popular philosophies.[3] Its tremendous influence can be seen from the fact that, although Paul wrote a letter to the Romans warning against the legal method of winning salvation, and although the Gospel of Mark was centred in Jesus as Son of Man, there is no sign in Clement or Hermas that the Church in Rome had made these ideas truly its own. Clement is dominated by the monotheism of the synagogue and the thought of the OT as the moral Law; Hermas' teaching is a simple puritanical moralism, and where he echoes Mark it is in a garbled form (Hermas, *Sim.* v. 2).

The first gospel, however, shows few traits of the characteristic Gentile-Christian propaganda. For obvious reasons Mark finds it unnecessary to emphasise monotheism, God's creation of the world, or the sin of idolatry, and even repentance, the Holy Spirit, the general resurrection and the resurrection of Jesus are not prominent. Other ideas appear, but in undeveloped form. The 'blood of the covenant' is mentioned (xiv. 24) but not the New Covenant. Jesus' followers constitute the 'elect' (xiii. 20, 22, 27). The way of asceticism does not have the prominence that it receives in Luke-Acts, and it is connected with the eschatological situation (x. 29-31). There is only the slightest suggestion that old cults and rituals are replaced by a

[1] Cf. W. L. Knox, *Some Hellenistic Elements in Primitive Christianity* (London, 1944), pp. 3-5.
[2] Older scholars, such as B. W. Bacon, held that Mark was directly influenced by St. Paul; cf. *The Gospel of Mark* (London, 1925), pp. 221-271. For a criticism of this position, see M. Werner, *Der Einfluss paulinischer Theologie im Markusevangelium* (Giessen, 1923); Grant, *EG*, pp. 188-206.
[3] Cf. J. Weiss, *op. cit.* pp. 850-863.

7

new worship (xiv. 58). Baptism is already related to Jesus' death (x. 39) and the bestowal of the Holy Spirit (i. 10), and Christian ideas have influenced the account of John's baptism (i. 4). The words of institution at the Last Supper are developed slightly, but there is not yet a command to repeat the celebration (xiv. 24-25). The moral commands of the OT and the teaching of Jesus are of course assumed as valid, and there is some sense of the problem of man's weakness and the need of grace (x. 26-27; xiv. 38).[1]

The Gospel of Mark thus stands at a theological turning-point. This does not provide an absolute date for it, for the point of transition from Jewish Christianity to Gentile, from primitive to revised eschatology, and from group-consciousness to Church-consciousness, would not have occurred simultaneously in all parts of the Empire. The question of date will be considered later, but here it should be said that the earliest gospel also seems to mark a watershed in the external history of the Church. A long series of troubles in Palestine has led to the first Jewish revolt, and the gospel is written when tension is still at a high pitch. Unlike the later evangelists, Mark does not look back at the event with the perspective of several years (cf. Matt. xxii. 7; Luke xxi. 20). There are suggestions that a few of the Twelve have died a martyr's death (x. 39), but some of their number are still alive (ix. 1). One motive for writing the book is surely that of collecting the primitive traditions that already are in danger of being lost. At the same time, the evangelist—unlike Luke, for example—has no interest in the literary art of the Hellenistic world, or any need for it. Like the letters of Paul, his book is a tract for the times, written as briefly and vividly as possible, in order to arouse the readers before it is too late; indeed the time may be very short.

In one important respect the Gospel of Mark differs from most of the NT books. Important parallels to the Essene literature are to be found in Luke-Acts, the special material of Matthew, the letters of Paul, the Epistle of James, and even to

---

[1] This summary of the non-Pauline Gentile *kerygma* is based on R. Bultmann, *Theology of the NT* (London and New York, 1951), i. 63-183. The attempt to distinguish between St. Paul's teaching and that of other Gentile Christians of his time is, of course, a highly subjective enterprise.

some degree in the Fourth Gospel;[1] but not in Mark, with the exception of the OT quotation in i. 3 and the divorce section (x. 2-9), and doubtfully in a few other places. This may be because much of Mark's tradition comes from Galilee, while other parts of the NT were written by Christians in closer touch with Jerusalem and Judaea, where Essenes were more numerous.

III. MARK'S THEOLOGICAL MESSAGE

The theology of Mark is essentially a Christology; almost all the ideas of the gospel are related to the unique position of Jesus in history, and there is no direct treatment of the basic themes of the OT. But the term 'Christology' must be understood in its widest sense, for Mark does not speculate on the essential and eternal relation of Jesus to God, as Paul has begun to do in Philippians and Colossians; rather, the interpretation of our Lord's nature is by way of function and dramatic action. Except that Jesus is given some titles or designations such as 'Son of Man' and 'Son of God', we are never told who he is; instead we see what happens when he appears. His entrance into the religious scene of Palestine means that 'the time is fully come' (i. 15), and Mark regards this moment as a unique and brief season, still going on when he writes, whose climax will be the coming of the Son of Man in glory (xiii. 26; xiv. 62). As soon as Jesus begins to herald the Kingdom of God in Galilee, the demons retreat in terror and are vanquished, the sick and insane are healed, and a new and authoritative teaching—a Word with power—reinterprets and partly abrogates the Mosaic Law.

The Good News collides not only with the demonic world but also with the Jewish authorities and their followers, and to some degree with the original disciples of Jesus. Mark sees our Lord's rejection, and his crucifixion and resurrection, as an essential part of the conflict, foreseen and somehow predestined. Full understanding of Jesus' teaching and work eludes the Twelve, even when they are told the truth plainly; thus they

[1] See, e.g., K. Stendahl (ed.), *The Scrolls and the NT* (New York, 1957); S. E. Johnson, *HTR*, xlviii (1955), 157-165; W. F. Albright in W. D. Davies and D. Daube (eds.), *The Background of the NT and Its Eschatology* (Cambridge, 1956), pp. 153-171.

share in the blindness of Israel and when they follow to Jerusalem they are only partial followers. One leaves the gospel with the impression that only after the Resurrection have they begun to understand and to watch for the coming of the Son of Man. The so-called idea of the 'messianic secret' thus dominates the presentation of Jesus' life and teaching in the earliest gospel.

Mark expressed in several ways his belief that the nature of Jesus was a secret not understood until after the Resurrection. (a) The demons recognised him and were forbidden to make him known (i. 25, 34; iii. 12). (b) He tried to avoid publicity for his miracles (i. 44; v. 43; vii. 36; viii. 26) except in one instance when the man healed may have been a Gentile (v. 19-20). (c) He often withdrew from the crowds (i. 35, 45; iii. 7; iv. 35; vi. 31; vii. 24; viii. 27; ix. 30). (d) He refused to give a sign to 'this generation' (viii. 12). (e) On more than one occasion he gave private teaching to the disciples (iv. 33-34; vii. 17-23; ix. 28-31; xiii. 3-37), and the parables were not understood because they were intended to be esoteric (iv. 10-13). (f) This came about because of the wilful 'hardness of heart' of the Jewish people or at least that of their leaders (e.g. iii. 5; vii. 6-7) and was a judgement of God upon them, or at least a part of his plan (xiv. 27, 49). (g) Jesus refused to let the secret of his nature be known until the Son of Man should be risen from the dead (viii. 30; ix. 9).

Wilhelm Wrede concluded from this that belief in Jesus as Messiah arose only after the Resurrection, and that the entire theory of the messianic secret had been imposed upon the gospel materials by the evangelists.[1] This is an unnecessarily extreme position. Mark is probably responsible for the notion that the demons, being spiritual beings, could perceive that Jesus was Son of God, and also for the curious idea that the parables were intended to conceal, not to illuminate, Jesus' message. He shared with St. Paul the conviction that the Jewish nation by and large had not accepted the Gospel because of the divine predestination, and he no doubt exaggerated Jesus'

---

[1] W. Wrede, *Das Messiasgeheimnis in den Evangelien* (Göttingen, 1901). An excellent criticism of this is given by Rawlinson, pp. 259-262; cf. Grant, *IB*, vii. 644.

desire for privacy. It would be perverse to suppose that our Lord never taught his disciples in private, but again Mark has over-emphasised the extent of private teaching.

It is easy to see how the theory of the messianic secret arose. How could such a teacher, who brought Good News to the world, have been rejected by his own people? And why were the earliest disciples so bewildered by the Crucifixion? Surely God must at least have permitted this to happen. In addition, the original context of much of the teaching, including the parables, was already lost, and some of this material was difficult for even the evangelist to understand. Finally, the tradition itself contained genuine elements that pointed in the direction of the messianic secret. It is well attested that Jesus refused to give signs. In all probability he drew attention away from his healings, for they were only one part of his vocation; his principal purpose was to announce the Kingdom of God (i. 38). Quite naturally he sought quiet and time for prayer (i. 35). He was extremely reluctant to have the term 'Messiah' applied to himself, for it would almost certainly be understood in the conventional sense, and his vocation and office were much more than this. Yet the disciples, even before the Resurrection, must have considered him the Messiah, for the Resurrection alone would not have led them to this conclusion but only to the faith that God had preserved him from death. The element of judgement on the nation also has an historical basis. Jesus' teaching and activity brought him into controversy with the religious leaders of his time. Many of them were unwilling to understand him, and he in turn rejected their authority.

Thus Mark believed that the true nature of Jesus was not apprehended during his ministry. But what the disciples fail to perceive, according to the evangelist, is not just a doctrine about him but the fact that the time of salvation is near and has broken into the world, at least in the sense that the final conflict is under way. The Galilean ministry and the eschatological discourse of chap. xiii are all of a piece. Tribulations and the victories of the Good News are both taking place—in the words of Luther's chorale, it is a wondrous battle in which life and death are joined —but the end is not yet; the ministry of Jesus, climaxed by the Cross, decisive though it is, is the event of the interim.

GOSPEL ACCORDING TO ST. MARK

Mark's favourite terms for Jesus, 'Son of God' and 'Son of Man', are to be understood in the light of this basic conception of history. Mark's concept of the Son of Man evidently derives from Daniel vii. and from Ps. cx. 1. The Son of Man will return on the clouds of heaven with all the power of God. The phrase does not exclude the humanity of Jesus but it calls attention to something quite different: that he who seems to be the rabbi and prophet of Galilee is also one who is here incognito (cf on ii. 10) to play a decisive rôle in human history. Jewish Christians who read Daniel would recognise the phrase 'Son of Man', but the term 'Son of God' gives to Gentile readers of the gospel a further explanation of Jesus' nature (cf. on i. 1, 11). Though a distinction is drawn thereby between Jesus and God (or 'the Father', xiii. 32), the relation of Jesus to God is completely filial; therefore he can save and heal those who are in need, and even his Crucifixion is heroic in character (cf. on xv. 34, 39). If Jesus can be called 'Messiah' at all, he must be understood as Son of God and Son of Man, and there must be no confusion of him with the conventional image of the anointed Son of David, who belongs to the purely national hope of Judaism.

The earlier idea of the Son of Man is modified in one important particular: the Son of Man must suffer (viii. 31), i.e. he is at the same time the Servant of Second Isaiah, who was wounded for our transgressions and by whose stripes we are healed (Isa. liii. 5). His death was a 'means of freeing many' (x. 45) and the Last Supper represents the giving of his Body and Blood to his people (xiv. 22-24). Here the evangelist is dependent upon very early traditions and there is no good reason to doubt the substantial accuracy of the Words of Institution; but the connexion of the Servant theme with that of the Son of Man is perhaps the most profound and dramatically powerful part of Mark's doctrine of the messianic secret. Jesus was not only incognito as a teacher in Galilee, but even his apparent defeat and degradation are the means of his victory.

The Resurrection is the guarantee of this victory, but this leads forward to the risen Lord's expected appearance in Galilee. The events of Jesus' ministry, both past and future, are also bound up intimately with the two principal rites of the early Church. Jesus' Baptism—in which his disciples must

12

share—proclaims his sonship to God, and it has its counterpart in the Transfiguration, which in turn anticipates the glory of the Son of Man. The miraculous Feedings and the Last Supper likewise look forward to reunion with Jesus in the Kingdom of God.

One who reads the Gospel of Mark superficially may not perceive at once how much these themes dominate it, for the book is mainly made up of earlier traditions. But when the evangelist's own work is separated from the traditional material the peculiarly Marcan point of view stands out. Jesus' original proclamation was the Kingdom of God; even though he occupied a unique position in relation to it, this was secondary to the message of what God was now doing. Mark by no means obscures the message of the Kingdom of God—for him Jesus' teaching, healing and forgiveness are all indications of its nearness—but he does not seem to use the term itself except where he has found it in the tradition. It may be quite otherwise with his concept 'Son of Man', which to him gives meaning to the whole gospel story. Thus he combines the gospel *of* Jesus, i.e. the Good News which Jesus preached, with the gospel *about* him, so that for Mark the term 'gospel' has a twofold meaning. Jesus' controversies with the Pharisees regarding the Law, which were originally a debate within Judaism, now begin to be a controversy against the Law, in which the protagonists are the Church and the Synagogue. Still more, the conception of the risen and coming Christ is partly projected back into the earthly ministry. The process which culminates in the Gospel of John has thus begun.

IV. MARK AS A ROMAN GOSPEL

The tradition that Mark was written in Rome is closely bound up with that of its author's relationship to St. Peter. A late and highly developed form of this is found in Eusebius. In one passage (*H.E.* vi. 14. 5-7) he quotes Clement of Alexandria's *Hypotyposes* as saying that Peter's hearers urged Mark to write down what Peter had said, and he did so, distributing to them copies of the gospel; and that when Peter heard of this, he neither strongly disapproved nor encouraged this activity. Eusebius elsewhere (ii. 15. 1-2) gives a still more legendary account: the hearers put great pressure on Mark to write, Peter learned of this 'by revelation of the Spirit', and authorised that the book be read in churches; almost, as it were, 'Imprimatur. Petrus, apostolus, pontifex maximus.' This in itself shows how traditions can grow.

Clement of Alexandria's story may be ultimately based on the famous statement of Papias (*H.E.* iii. 39. 15):

> This also the presbyter used to say: Mark, having been Peter's translator (ἑρμηνευτής), wrote accurately, not however in order, as much as he remembered of the things said or done by the Lord. For he had neither heard the Lord, nor had he followed him; but later, as I said, [he had followed] Peter, who used to make up his instructions as need arose (πρὸς τὰς χρείας ἐποιεῖτο τὰς διδασκαλίας), but not as though he were composing an ordered account (σύνταξιν) of the dominical sayings; so that Mark committed no error in writing some things as he recalled them. For he was concerned for one thing only, not to omit any of the things he had heard, or to falsify anything in them.

From Papias' account, one would naturally suppose that at the time when the gospel was written Peter could no longer be consulted. Nothing is said about Rome, but in view of other traditions that the great apostle met his death there, the capital city is not excluded as a possibility.

Another account, possibly from the second century, is contained in the so-called anti-Marcionite prologue:

> . . . Mark related, who was called 'Stumpfinger' because for the size of the rest of his body he had fingers that were too short. He was the interpreter of Peter. After Peter's death the same man wrote this gospel in the regions of Italy.[1]

Another possibility is that Mark wrote in Alexandria, as Chrysostom said (*Hom. in Matt. i*). The new fragment of Clement of Alexandria, published by Morton Smith, indicates

---

[1] Translation by R. M. Grant, *ATR*, xxiii (1941), 231-245; cf. literature there cited. The tradition may be known to Hippolytus, who calls Mark κολοβοδάκτυλος, *Refut.* vii. 30.

that a form of the gospel containing two peculiar passages was extant in that city in the second century.[1] The tradition that Mark was martyred in Alexandria is first found in St. Jerome.

The gospel could conceivably have been written in Galilee, which is the land of revelation, and it is promised that Jesus will meet his disciples there (xiv. 28; xvi. 7).[2]

The traditions in favour of Rome, like others regarding the origins of NT books, are tenuous, but are to be preferred.

(1) In First Peter, which is probably a Roman document of the later first century, Mark is associated with Peter ('Mark my son', v. 13).

(2) Even though several forms of Mark may have been current in Alexandria, this is no proof that the gospel was written there. Nothing is known of Christianity in Egypt before the second century.

(3) An evangelist whose tradition was mostly Galilean might think of Galilee as having special theological significance although he had not lived there. Mark's knowledge of the region is imperfect. The geography of vii. 31 is not clear, and he calls Bethsaida a village (viii. 26) though it was a city. He evidently confuses the members of the Herodian family, and he may not understand the references to the Pharisees and the Herodians (viii. 15; xii. 13). Mark regards the hearing before the high priest as a trial (xiv. 64), and assumes that a wife could divorce her husband (x. 12), as she could do under Roman, not Jewish, law. He explains the customs of the Pharisees (vii. 3-4) and gives translations of Aramaic words, even *Abba* (xiv. 36). One of these words ($\beta o\alpha\nu\eta\rho\gamma\acute{e}s$, iii. 17) is difficult to reconstruct precisely, and in most cases his transliterations are at best approximate. It appears, therefore, that although many of his traditions go back to Aramaic he is not perfect in that language.

(4) His Latinisms cannot be used as an argument for the Roman origin of the gospel, since Latin words were used in Greek—and even in Hebrew—in various parts of the Empire.

---

[1] M. Smith, *Clement of Alexandria and a Secret Gospel of Mark* (Cambridge, Mass., 1973).

[2] This is suggested by W. Marxsen, *Der Evangelist Markus* (2nd. ed., Göttingen, 1959, p. 41), but since he argues that for the evangelist Galilee is more a theological concept than a place (p. 59 f.) the argument has little force.

Nevertheless, they are numerous and are sometimes avoided by Matthew and Luke in the parallel sections, e.g.: κεντυρίων (xv. 39, 44, 45); σπεκουλάτωρ (vi. 27); φραγελλοῦν (xv. 15); κῆνσος (xii. 14); κοδράντης (xii. 42); πραιτώριον (xv. 16); συμβούλιον ποιήσαντες (xv. 1); ποιῆσαι τὸ ἱκανόν (xv. 15). More doubtful are συμβούλιον διδόναι (iii. 6); φαίνεται =*videtur* (xiv. 64); ῥαπίσμασιν αὐτὸν ἔλαβον (xiv. 65); and ἐπιβαλών (xiv. 72). It must be said, furthermore, that a tradition in the Jerusalem Talmud (Jer. Kidd. 58d) gives the same equivalent as xii. 42: one *quadrans* equals two *perutas* (i.e. λεπτά). Thus, as Bacon remarks, there is no proof that Mark explains Greek words by Latin ones.[1]

(5) Although Mark was supplanted in popularity by Matthew early in the second century, there are signs that it early achieved a secure place in the Church in Rome. We have already noted Hermas' probable use of the gospel, and Bacon shows that 1 Clem. xv. 2 quotes Isa. xxix. 13 almost exactly as it is given in Mark.[2]

(6) Mark's dating of the Last Supper, which conflicts with that of John and probably with the tradition on which Mark drew, may have been due to the fact that already the Church in Rome had its own date for celebrating the Lord's Resurrection.[3]

(7) Finally, if one asks which of the great sees of Christendom is most likely to have produced a gospel of this character, Rome seems to be the most natural answer. The Gospel of Mark appears to be known to Hermas, one of the earliest Roman writers. The great fire of Rome (A.D. 64), with Nero's persecution that followed, provides the best possible background for the gospel, with its emphasis on discipleship and martyrdom.[4]

V. The Author

Papias' statements concerning the authorship of the gospel can be summarised as follows:

(1) Mark was Peter's translator. This does not imply that the Apostle wrote anything; it can mean either that he acted as

---

[1] B. W. Bacon, *Is Mark a Roman Gospel?* (Cambridge, Mass., 1919), pp. 54-58. [2] *Ibid.* p. 107. [3] *Ibid.* pp. 90-98. [4] Grant, *EG*, p. 56.

interpreter, translating into Greek as Peter spoke in Aramaic, or that he wrote down in Greek what he had heard Peter say. The latter seems more likely, since Papias says that he wrote 'some things as he recalled them'.

(2) He had not heard Jesus speak, nor was he one of his original disciples.

(3) Mark did not write 'in order'. Peter indeed had not delivered a fully arranged account of Jesus' life, but, like most preachers, mentioned sayings and incidents as occasion arose; and Mark wrote down what he could remember of these. Papias may contrast this lack of order with the obvious topical arrangement of Matthew.[1]

(4) Mark was as accurate as he could be under the circumstances; he tried not to omit anything and did not deliberately falsify.

The anti-Marcionite prologue adds that Mark was known as 'Stumpfinger', and that he wrote in Italy after Peter's death.

Papias was perhaps concerned to show that the written gospels then in circulation (c. A.D. 130) were, after all, dependent on oral tradition received at second hand, and not to be preferred to the tradition that he himself had received. Matthew's gospel was scarcely any better than Mark's: 'Matthew compiled the sayings (λόγια) in the Hebrew language, but everyone translated them as he was able' (H.E. iii. 39. 16). Therefore Papias used to consult those who had known the 'elders'—esteemed Christians of an earlier generation—and inquire 'what Philip, or what Thomas or James, or what John or Matthew or any other of the Lord's disciples; and the things which Aristion and John the Elder, disciples of the Lord, say. For I supposed that things from books were not of as much benefit to me as the utterances of a living and abiding voice' (H.E. iii. 39. 4).

The prologue to Luke (i. 1-2) assumes a similar situation. Before the third evangelist wrote, 'many had undertaken to draw up an account (διήγησις) of the matters that have been accomplished among us', but others, who were 'eyewitnesses

---

[1] B. W. Bacon, *Studies in Matthew* (New York, 1930), p. 5.

and servants (ὑπηρέται) of the Message' had delivered them in tradition (παρέδοσαν).

It is often asked whether Mark, the author of the gospel, can be identified with a man of the same name who is mentioned in the NT. When Peter escaped from prison he went to the house of Mary, whose son had a Jewish name John and was also known by the Roman name of Mark (Acts xii. 12). When Barnabas and Saul returned from Jerusalem to Antioch after bringing the famine relief, they were accompanied by John Mark (xii. 25). He was also with them on the journey to Cyprus as their assistant (ὑπηρέτης, xiii. 5), but left them in Perge of Pamphylia and returned to Jerusalem (xiii. 13). Barnabas wished to take John Mark on the next journey, but Paul considered him a deserter, and the two apostles parted, and Barnabas and Mark went to Cyprus (xv. 37-41). Acts does not mention Mark again, but in Col. iv. 10 Mark the cousin (ἀνεψιός) of Barnabas joins in salutations, and evidently the same Mark is mentioned in the companion letter, Phm. 24. 2 Tim. iv. 11 also represents Paul as asking for the services of Mark. Whether or not the latter is a genuine fragment of correspondence, it evidently refers to the same person, for he is mentioned along with Luke, as in Colossians and Philemon. The NT materials associate him more with Paul than with Peter; but Peter may have met him at his mother's home in Jerusalem, and the reference in 1 Pet. v. 13 to 'Mark my son' argues for a traditional connexion between Peter and some man named Mark, even though the epistle is probably pseudonymous.

John Mark, the servant of the apostles, might more easily be identified with the evangelist if the editorial parts of the gospel— the final work of the man who put the traditions together— were more Palestinian and in close touch with Judaism. But it is only in the sections attributable to Peter and in the old pericopes that the Jewish background is apparent; the evangelist himself does not know Palestine well, he is almost hostile to Judaism, in short it is easier to consider him a Gentile Christian of Rome than a cousin of Barnabas from Jerusalem.

The Gospel of Mark, as we have seen, stands at the point of transition and no longer belongs to the first generation. The author was influenced to some degree by the theology of the

Gentile Church. At the same time, he wished to hand down the earlier traditions. In particular, his thinking was dominated by the Son of Man theology, and he composed his gospel so as to lead up, not only to the Passion, but to the discourse in chap. xiii. He also pictured the Kingdom of God as an inbreaking power, in decisive conflict with the demonic realm. Sometimes the evangelist imposed these and other ideas on his source material, but he nevertheless derived them from certain elements in the gospel tradition. He was evidently in close touch with Peter and other Galilean Christians, and was caught up by their tradition of the nature and activity of Jesus, and carried along by it. Therefore the earliest gospel is not a mere compilation of earlier accounts, nor on the other hand an artificially constructed scheme. Although the order of events is sometimes determined by dogmatic ideas and teaching devices, the evangelist has gathered from his anonymous informants a broad outline of the life of Jesus and a sense of the dramatic movement of his ministry. This may explain the combination of art and apparent artlessness, of simple verisimilitude and theological reflection, which tends to make the gospel difficult to analyse.

VI. THE DATE

The earliest conceivable date for the gospel is in the forties, shortly after the composition of the 'Little Apocalypse', but if we are correct in understanding the great fire in Rome and the martyrdom of Peter as part of the background, a date earlier than A.D. 64 is excluded. The question then arises whether Mark wrote at the outbreak of the first Jewish revolt, at its height, or after the destruction of the Temple.

The predictions of chap. xiii are vague enough to permit the dating given by Rawlinson, i.e. A.D. 65–67. As he remarks: 'The expectation of a personal Antichrist (xiii. 14; contrast Luke xxi. 20 . . .) suggests a date earlier than the Fall of Jerusalem in A.D. 70, and it is more probable than not that the Jewish War has not yet broken out, since the persecution of the Church (which has happened already) is interpreted as being only the *beginning* of the "travail pangs" of the New Age (xiii. 8), and *the end is not yet*' (pp. xxix f.).

On the other hand, the Antichrist may be represented by the standards bearing the emperor's portrait, which have already appeared in Judaea. The unique terror of the war, it can be argued, is well known, but it is also known that the conflict is nearing its end, and the Lord has shortened the days (xiii. 19-20); furthermore, false prophets have arisen in Jerusalem (xiii. 21-22; cf. Josephus, *B.J.* vi. 5. 2-3). It is therefore possible to think of the gospel as having been written after the destruction of the Temple but before the conclusion of hostilities in Palestine. Although Titus celebrated his triumph in 71, the fortress of Masada did not fall until April in 73. At any time in this period the evangelist might expect that the woes would end with the triumphant coming of the Son of Man.

Bacon goes so far as to draw a parallel between the martyrdom of John the Baptist and an incident that took place in the year 75. Bernice, the sister of Agrippa II, was living with Titus in Rome, and two Cynic philosophers denounced them for this. One was flogged and the other beheaded.[1] It is barely possible that Mark included his story because of its obvious parallel to this well-known scandal. The gospel can scarcely have been composed later than this time, but it is written when a few Christians have succumbed to 'the cares of the world and the delight of riches' (iv. 19); not everyone is awake and alert, as he should be.

VII. The Structure of the Gospel

Older studies of the Gospel of Mark were controlled by the desire to use it as directly as possible to reconstruct the story of the life and teaching of Jesus. More recently the interest has shifted to the gospel itself, in the realisation that one should stand, if one can, where the evangelist and his readers stood, and determine the purpose of the book and the methods employed to carry it out. This is undoubtedly the first necessary step which must precede any attempt to understand the meaning of the separate pericopes.

[1] Dio Cassius, *Hist.* lxv. 15; Bacon, *Mark*, pp. 73 f. Knox, *Sources*, i. 43, argues that Mark may, however, have written at a time when Christianity had not yet been condemned by Nero's government.

Recent commentators have therefore devoted much study to the structure of the gospel.

Ernst Lohmeyer divided the gospel into several main sections, largely on a geographical basis, but within these he saw a distinct tendency of the evangelist to group the individual pericopes into threes. At the same time, he noted elaborate interconnexions between the several parts; e.g. iii. 7-13 and iii. 20-35 correspond in structure. Like other commentators, he observed that Mark inserts one section into another in order to indicate the passage of time, e.g. iii. 22-30; v. 25-34; xi. 15-18; xiv. 66-72.[1] The form of the gospel is determined by the ideas of Galilee as the land of revelation and the coming of the Son of Man.[2]

The approach of Austin Farrer is based on two observations: that the evangelist uses the OT typologically, and that he organises his book in cycles and numerical schemes. For example, Farrer calls attention to the presence of thirteen miracles, with 'negative' (i.e. exorcistic) and 'positive' miracles alternating. The 'Little Gospel' (chaps. i-vi) consists of two double cycles and eight healings; and in the fulfilment (chaps. ix-xvi) there are two double cycles and three healings. His numerical scheme is somewhat modified in his later work.[3]

R. H. Lightfoot attempted no such elaborate analysis, but his writings contain many suggestions for understanding the framework of the gospel. He shows, for example, that i. 1-13, and not merely the first eight verses, constitutes the introduction; chaps. iv and xiii are parallel teaching sections, the purpose of the former being to say that in spite of temporary hindrance the Kingdom of God will finally triumph; there are three significant points at which Jesus engages in prayer, and always at night and at times of tension; chap. xiii is linked to the Passion Narrative by at least five parallel passages; and, finally, one of Mark's principal aims is to show that Jesus' conduct, in spite of the great impression he made, was free

---

[1] E. Lohmeyer, *Das Evangelium des Markus* (Göttingen, 1951), *ad loc.*

[2] E. Lohmeyer, *Galiläa und Jerusalem* (Göttingen, 1936); cf. R. H. Lightfoot, *Locality and Doctrine in the Gospels* (London, 1938).

[3] A. M. Farrer, *The Glass of Vision* (London, 1948); *A Study in St. Mark* (London and New York, 1951); *St. Matthew and St. Mark* (London, 1953).

from any attempt to arouse public attention, and gave no basis for a charge of seditious messianic activity.[1]

The ingenious hypothesis of Archbishop Carrington, that the gospel was designed for liturgical reading, and that its sections correspond to a Christian calendar based on that of the synagogue, has not had wide acceptance, yet it should be taken into account because Christians must surely have used the gospels in worship.[2]

More recent work on Mark's structure stems from the ground-breaking study of Willi Marxsen, one of the pioneers of redaction criticism. He holds that the gospel is, so to speak, 'composed backwards', that is, that the earlier parts of the books are controlled by a theme that will be developed only later, and that the purpose of the evangelist is theological throughout, to proclaim the *kerygma* of the Son of Man, who should not be 'historicised' as though he existed only in the past.[3]

Redaction criticism, with its emphasis on the theological purpose of each of the four evangelists, is necessary as a supplement to the earlier form criticism which concentrated on the separate units of the gospel tradition. It has, however, produced many theories about the composition of Mark that conflict with one another, and one cannot say that there is yet a consensus. Yet by concentrating on the unity of the gospel, this method deals with the objection that Dr. Helen Gardner made towards studies such as those of Farrer, that one is left with a series of patterns and *disjecta membra*.[4] Many issues are still debated, for example: (1) Is the principal theme the Kingdom of God in all parts of the gospel or only in its first half? (2) Does the section vii. 24–ix. 29 prefigure the Church's mission to the Gentiles? (3) is Mark's portrayal of the blindness of the Twelve a criticism of the leaders of the Church in his own day? The outline given below implies that the geography of Mark and the mission to the Gentiles are significant factors.

[1] R. H. Lightfoot, *GM*, pp. 9, 23, 37-39, 49.
[2] Philip Carrington, *The Primitive Christian Calendar* (Cambridge, 1952); cf. W. D. Davies in *The Background of the NT and Its Eschatology*, pp. 124-152.
[3] Marxsen, *op. cit.*, pp. 18 f.
[4] Helen Gardner, *The Business of Criticism* (Oxford, 1959), pp. 118 f.: 'this method does nothing to illuminate, and indeed evaporates, St. Mark's sense of what we mean by historical reality . . . I find it hard . . . to believe that the first readers of St. Mark could have been as ingenious in picking up symbolic references as is suggested.'

One must, however, acknowledge that careful attention to the structure of Mark reveals a number of interconnexions between the various parts. The evangelist (or his tradition) sometimes strings sayings together by verbal links, as in ix. 48-50 and xi. 22-25. It may not be fanciful to see in iv. 35-v. 20 the motif of storm followed by calm, or in viii. 22-ix. 8 that of blindness replaced by sight. Reminiscences of the Exodus story can be seen here and there, 'not however in order'. There are at least three transition sections (ii. 1-12; viii. 22-26; x. 46-52), where Mark leads from one topic to another. Chapter x seems to involve a catechetical scheme designed for various groups in the Church. It is characteristic of the evangelist that he follows a revelation or teaching with a private explanation to the disciples; see, e.g., iv. 10-20; vii. 17-19; viii. 16-21; ix. 9-13, 28-29; x. 10-12, 42-45; xiii. 3-37. Above all, it is his custom to anticipate his main subjects of teaching by brief notices earlier in the gospel: i. 16-20; ii. 14, call of the first disciples, preparing for the call of the Twelve; ii. 10, 28, the Son of Man; i. 21-22, Jesus as teacher; i. 15, the Kingdom of God; iii. 22-30, speaking in figures; iii. 6, rejection; vi. 14-16, the opinions of men.

Only further study on the part of many scholars will bring agreement as to which alleged patterns are real and significant, but surely it is clear that the earliest gospel is not a naïve and fortuitous collection of incidents but the result of a long tradition of preaching and teaching. One may contrast the rhetorical method of Mark with that of Hellenistic and Roman writers by saying that it is oriental; in fact the gospel can be likened to an oriental rug in which many patterns cross one another. They are not made up with mathematical exactitude but developed spontaneously as the author writes. The result is a colourful piece of folk art, sometimes symmetrical, rich and full of endless fascination, and exhibiting the vitality of early Christianity.

With the above warnings in mind, an outline of the gospel is here offered:

I. The Beginning of the Good News, i. 1-15

   A. Keynote, i. 1

   B. Three manifestations of the Spirit, i. 2-13

GOSPEL ACCORDING TO ST. MARK

1. Prophecy: the Baptism of John, i. 2-8
2. Epiphany: Baptism and Temptation, i. 9-13
C. Proclamation of the Kingdom, i. 14-15

II. The Early Ministry in Galilee, i. 16–iii. 12
  A. Power: response to the News, i. 16-45
    1. Call of the first four disciples, i. 16-20
    2. Teaching with power, i. 21-22
    3. Healings with power, i. 23-45
  B. Controversies begin, ii. 1–iii. 6
    1. Transition: power to forgive, ii. 1-12
    2. Four defences of Jesus' action, ii. 13–iii. 6
  C. Summary: the crowds and the demons, iii. 7-12

III. Jesus Prepares the Disciples (Part I), iii. 13–vii. 23
  A. Appointment of the Twelve, iii. 13-19
  B. Controversy and confusion, iii. 20-35
    1. The charge of madness, iii. 20-21
    2. The Beelzebul controversy, iii. 22-27
    3. Blasphemy against the Holy Spirit, iii. 28-30
    4. Jesus' true family, iii. 31-35
  C. The secret of the Kingdom of God, iv. 1-34
  D. Epiphany: the storm at sea, iv. 35-41
  E. Other manifestations of power, v. 1-43
  F. The rejection of Jesus and John, vi. 1-30
    1. Rejection in the home village, vi. 1-6
    2. The Twelve begin their ministry, vi. 7-30
      a. Mission discourse; success, vi. 7-13
      b. Herod's suspicion of Jesus; death of John, vi. 14-29
      c. The disciples return, vi. 30
  G. Two epiphanies, vi. 31-56
    1. The crowds, vi. 31-33
    2. Feeding of the Five Thousand, vi. 34-44
    3. Jesus prays on the mountain, vi. 45-46
    4. The walking on the water, vi. 47-52
    5. Return to Gennesaret; summary, vi. 53-56
  H. Controversy: Clean and Unclean, vii. 1-23

24

VI. The Passion Narrative, xiv. 1-xv. 47

VII. The Empty Tomb, xvi. 1-8

VIII. THE SOURCES

Theories as to the sources of Mark are extremely various and can be classified as follows: (1) the gospel is almost entirely composed of oral tradition; (2) it is the abbreviation of a longer 'original gospel'; (3) it has gone through more than one stage, so that a shorter *Ur-Markus* or Proto-Mark lies behind it; (4) it is made up of several sources, partly written and partly oral.

(1) Goodspeed, for example, holds that practically the entire gospel is derived directly from oral tradition, that 'almost everything in Mark might have been obtained from Peter', so that we have to do with 'an original source, unrevised', though the little Apocalypse 'comes nearest to being a written source'.[1]

(2) Rudolf Otto believed that a *Stammschrift*, or parent document, which lies behind our synoptic gospels, was abbreviated by Mark.[2] In this he was the successor of a long line of scholars, beginning with St. Augustine,[3] who noted that Matt. iii and Luke iii contain a fuller account of the beginning of the Good News. A recent variant of this theory has been developed by Pierson Parker, who postulates a common source of Mark and Matthew (known as K, for *koine*), which includes most of Matthew's special material.[4] Parker's K is not altogether convincing, for its contents are too miscellaneous and some of them appear to come from a late, not an early stratum of tradition. The hypothesis would, however, explain Mark's apparent 'abbreviations' in chap. i.

(3) *Ur-Markus* theories have taken various forms, but in most cases proceed from the assumption that a Palestinian gospel, relatively simple and primitive in its theology, has been expanded and rewritten for the Gentile world. Wendling and

[1] E. J. Goodspeed, *An Introduction to the NT* (Chicago, 1937), pp. 129-135, 149. [2] R. Otto, *KGSM* (London, 1943), pp. 82-86.
[3] Augustine, *The Harmony of the Gospels*, i. 2. 4, *Marcus Matthaei tanquam breviator et pedisequus.*
[4] Pierson Parker, *The Gospel before Mark* (Chicago, 1953). For other theories of this type, cf. McNeile-Williams, p. 64.

Cadoux distinguish three stages in the production of Mark,[1] and Bacon, Crum and Guy two stages.[2] The 'reconstructed' documents are often plausible, but there is no satisfactory criterion for preferring one solution to another, and it is not necessary to suppose that the development to be observed in the tradition behind Mark was embodied at each point in written documents.

In another type of *Ur-Markus* theory, it is supposed that Matthew and Luke, in writing their gospels, made use of a form of Mark which differs from the one preserved to us; for example, Luke omits a large section of Mark because he worked from a mutilated scroll, or Matthew had an edition of Mark, more complete than ours, which contained the account of an appearance of the risen Lord in Galilee. Most scholars have, however, preferred to explain the phenomena in other ways.[3]

(4) The most satisfactory solution seems to be that the evangelist used several short written sources along with oral tradition. Eduard Meyer sought to distinguish one source in which the Twelve were prominent, while in another Jesus' companions were merely called 'disciples'.[4] W. L. Knox held that nine independent units of material lay behind the gospel.[5] Grant divides the source material into the reminiscences of Peter, sections derived from Q, the Passion Narrative, the Little Apocalypse, a series of controversy stories, a collection of miracles (iv. 35–v. 43), the parables of the Kingdom in chap. iv, and miscellaneous elements from the gospel tradition, principally oral.[6]

---

[1] E. Wendling, *Die Entstehung des Marcusevangeliums* (Tübingen, 1908), summarised by J. Moffatt, *An Intro. to the Literature of the NT* (New York, 1911), pp. 227 f.; cf. the criticism of N. P. Williams in *OSSP*, pp. 389–424; A. T. Cadoux, *The Sources of the Second Gospel* (London, 1935); J. Jeremias, *ZNW*, xxxv (1936), 280–282.
[2] B. W. Bacon, *The Beginnings of Gospel Story* (New Haven, 1909), postulating a redactor; J. M. C. Crum, *St. Mark's Gospel: Two Stages of Its Making* (Cambridge, 1936); H. A. Guy, *The Origin of the Gospel of Mark* (New York, 1955).
[3] Cf. McNeile-Williams, pp. 75 f.; Johnson, *IB*, vii., pp. 236 f.
[4] E. Meyer, *Ursprung und Anfänge des Christentums* (Stuttgart, 1921–1923), i. 133–147. [5] Knox. *Sources*, i.
[6] Grant, *Gospels*, pp. 114 f.; S. J. Case (ed.), *Studies in Early Christianity* (London, 1928), pp. 85–101. For a more recent study, see H. W. Kuhn, *Ältere Sammlungen im Markusevangelium* (Göttingen, 1971).

The influence of Dibelius, Bultmann and other form critics has led NT scholars to emphasise the importance of the oral stage of the gospel tradition, with the result that they are less inclined than formerly to seek for lost written sources. Mark may, for example, have used Q,[1] but that document may have had more than one form, and Mark's parallels to Q are often variant forms of the traditions in Matthew and Luke. One therefore wonders if the evangelist had heard Q read and quoted it from memory. It is very likely that he used a 'Little Apocalypse' (represented by xiii. 5-8, 14-19, 24-27). The supposed 'Twelve-source' has attractive features, for it is only occasionally that the evangelist refers to the Twelve, and in these instances his own theological ideas do not appear. Such a source, or cycle of tradition, may have included iii. 13-19; vi. 7-13; ix. 33-37; x. 32; xi. 11; and it would seem to overlap the Passion Narrative in xiv. 1-2, 10-11, 17-25, 43-46.[2] The attempt to isolate a source in which our Lord's followers are called μαθηταί is not as convincing; this is Mark's own favourite designation for them, and the material is more heterogeneous. It seems likely that the two stories of the miraculous feeding, and the other doublets in the central section, belong to two separate sources. The Passion Narrative may have been a written document (cf. general note, pp. 220-22), for it is straightforward and rather well unified. The controversy stories in chaps. ii and iii are linked to those in chap. xii by the mention of the Pharisees and the Herodians; they do not form a perfect unity, but perhaps this should not be expected. It may be asked whether one strand of Mark's tradition dealt with the Kingdom of God; the idea is prominent in chaps. iv and x but the phrase occurs only sporadically elsewhere. It is also possible to suppose that the traditions of Jesus' activity in Jerusalem come from a source distinct from the Galilean tradition. Several of the sections in chaps. xi and xii present Jesus as a prophetic-rabbinical teacher, and one must ask whether or not they are related to certain elements in the account of his Galilean

[1] Cf. A. Meyer in *Festgabe für Adolf Jülicher* (Tübingen, 1927), pp. 35-60; B. H. Throckmorton, *JBL*, lxvii (1948), 319-329.
[2] Knox's analysis includes most of these passages and also iii. 7-11; vi. 30-32; ix. 38-39; x. 33-45; xiv. 27-31.

ministry. Finally, it is altogether likely that for some parts of his gospel Mark drew on his memories of Peter's teaching (perhaps in i. 16-20, 23-26, 29-31, 35-39; ii. 3-9; xiv. 27-31, 66-72; and parts of viii. 27-33).

IX. THE TEXT

The history of the text of Mark is linked to that of the other canonical gospels, for all four were generally copied together. Thus, in a given MS., such as Vaticanus (B), the four gospels tend to conform to the same type of text, in this case the Alexandrian (or, as Hort called it, 'neutral'). But there are exceptions, as in the case of Cod. W, where the text-type varies from gospel to gospel and even within the separate gospels. Furthermore, no MS. represents perfectly the ancestral form from which the text or family was descended but is partly mixed. As all modern editors have recognised, the textual form of the original autographs can be approximated only by constructing an eclectic text. In practice this means that the editor bases his text on B, S,[1] 33, and other MSS. of the Alexandrian text-type, but adopts readings from the 'western' (i.e. Cod. D and the Old Latin), the Old Syriac, the Caesarean text (Θ, fam. 1, fam. 13, Origen, etc.) and elsewhere.

Any attempt to establish the text of Mark must take into account the strong tendency to harmonise Mark's readings with those of the better-known gospels, Matthew and Luke. J. P. Brown has recently argued, with much plausibility, that the text of Mark used by the later evangelists had been slightly revised, and that our MS. tradition of Mark contains readings from both the revised and unrevised recensions. In such cases the reading that disagrees with Matthew and Luke is often to be preferred.[2] Another canon to be borne in mind is that the

---

[1] The symbol S is used in this book for the codex Sinaiticus. The other symbols correspond to those in Nestle's *Novum Testamentum Graece* (22nd edition, edited by K. Aland, Stuttgart, 1956).

[2] J. P. Brown, *JBL*, lxxviii (1959), 215-227. This study, by the way, tends to destroy one of the arguments against the priority of Mark; the minor agreements of Matthew and Luke against the earlier gospel thus become illusory. Cf. also T. F. Glasson, *Expository Times*, lv (1943/1944), 189-94; *JBL*, lxxxv (1966), 213-33.

reading which is in accordance with Mark's style and ideas has a superior claim to authenticity.

In recent years a unique MS., Cod. 2427, containing only the Gospel of Mark, has come to the attention of textual scholars. Since it obviously belongs to the Alexandrian type, and even appears to represent it more purely than do Vaticanus and Sinaiticus, as well as containing a few unique readings, it is of great interest. Its authenticity has not, however, been established.[1]

[1] E. C. Colwell, *Emory University Quarterly*, i (1945), 65-75; H. R. Willoughby in *Munera Studiosa*, ed. M. H. Shepherd, Jr., and S. E. Johnson (Cambridge, Mass., 1946), pp. 127-144; R. P. Casey, *Journal of Religion*, xxvii (1947), 148 f.

THE GOSPEL ACCORDING
TO ST. MARK

CHAPTER I

i. 1. KEYNOTE

Beginning of the Good News of Jesus Christ, the Son of 1
God.

Beginning suggests Gen. i. 1, 'In the beginning'; cf. John 1
i. 1. The nearest literary parallel may be Hos. i. 2, 'The beginning of the word of the Lord by Hosea'. The first verse thus
serves as a keynote for the book, not necessarily a title. In the
earliest Church the beginning of the new action of God was
considered to be the preaching of John (Acts x. 37), but it seems
far-fetched to translate verses 1-4 as 'the beginning of the Good
News . . . was John who baptized'. **Good News,** i.e. 'gospel',
denotes the story of God's activity through Jesus, which is a
'power of God for salvation' (Rom. i. 16). Here it does not refer
to the book which Mark writes or primarily to Jesus' own
preaching, but to the news about him. The message was originally oral and took many forms; outlines of it are given in Acts
ii. 14-36; iii. 12-26; xiii. 16-41; and especially x. 34-43. The
word is not applied to the gospels, so far as we know, until the
time of Justin Martyr, c. A.D. 150. It is a favourite word of
St. Paul, who uses it at least 46 times; of the evangelists only
Mark (seven times) and Matthew (four times) employ it. Luke
calls his work a διήγησις. In Homer εὐαγγέλιον means 'a reward for good news', but it comes later to mean the news itself,
and a famous inscription from Priene of 9 B.C. speaks of the
birthday of the god (the emperor Augustus) as the beginning of
good news for the world; cf. A. Deissmann, *Light from the
Ancient East* (London, 1927), pp. 345, 366. In the NT the word

31

carries with it the associations of the Heb. *besôrâh*, which means 'news' and generally 'good news', and is used in Isa. xl. 9; cf. lxi. 1, to refer to God's new deliverance. Cf. *TWNT*, ii, 705-735; J. W. Bowman in A. J. B. Higgins (ed.), *NT Essays* (Manchester, 1959), pp. 54-67. *TG*, pp. 102-15.

The combined name and title **Jesus Christ** is common in the Pauline letters but not much used in the gospels except in such places as this where a formal statement of Christian faith is made; cf. Matt. i. 1; John i. 17. The name Jesus represents the Heb. *Yehôshua*', Joshua, and the later Jewish *Yeshua*', which was probably the given name of our Lord; cf. A. Deissmann in G. K. A. Bell and A. Deissmann (eds.), *Mysterium Christi* (London, 1930). On Christ, i.e. Messiah, cf. on viii. 29. Some important MSS. and fathers omit **the Son of God,** but the phrase is probably original, since it fits with Mark's style and ideas. The term is used in the OT and Jewish literature to describe angels or divine beings (Gen. vi. 2; Job. xxxviii. 7), the Israelite nation (Hos. xi. 1), and once an anointed king (Ps. ii. 7). In the OT it usually has a moral force; God loves Israel, and Israel in turn should love and obey his Father (Deut. xxxii. 6). Only two of the late apocalyptic books seem to use it of the Messiah (Enoch cv. 2; 2 Esd. vii. 28-29; xiii. 32, 37, 52), but it is so employed in Mark xiv. 61. The Graeco-Roman world knew of gods and heroes, usually saviours and healers, who were called sons of God; cf. L. Bieler, θεῖος ἀνήρ (Vienna, 1935–1936); Bultmann, *Theol. of NT*, p. 130. For Mark's earliest Gentile readers the title would have something of this flavour. It is understandable that the centurion at the foot of the Cross remarks, 'Certainly this man was a son of God' (xv. 39) and that the demons address Jesus as Son of God (iii. 11; the possessed man in v. 7 may have been a Gentile). Otherwise Mark uses the title only at high points in his narrative, such as the Baptism and Transfiguration (i. 11; ix. 7; cf. xii. 6; xiii. 32). Nevertheless it may be for him the most complete and satisfactory designation of Jesus. It is the title by which God himself addresses him; it includes the ideas of the Son of Man, which dominates so much of the gospel (cf. on ii. 10), the Servant of the Lord who must suffer, and the Messiah, though Mark rejects the Jewish doctrine of messiahship (xiv. 61; xii. 35-37); and it suggests the

filial relationship of Jesus, who is obedient even to the point of
dying on the Cross (xii. 1-11; xiv. 36).

i. 2-3. PROPHECIES

As it is written in Isaiah the prophet: 2
 'See, I send my messenger before you,
 Who shall prepare your way';
 'A voice of one crying, "In the wilderness prepare the 3
way of the Lord, make his paths straight".'

The Good News is preceded by a forerunner who announces 2
its coming, but he in turn was believed to be predicted by
scripture. The quotations are from Mal. iii. 1 and Isa. xl. 3. The
former originally referred to the 'messenger of the covenant'
who by his judgement will prepare for that of God himself; the
latter calls for a straight way in the desert in preparation for
God's saving act. The best MSS. generally read **Isaiah the
prophet,** not 'the prophets' (AV); thus the text seems to ascribe
both citations to Isaiah. Either (1) Mark quotes from a book of
testimonies in which the Malachi quotation has already been
attached to one from Isaiah; or, more probably, (2) Mal. iii. 1
was added to the text after it left the evangelist's hand; only the
Isaiah quotation is found in the parallels in Matt. and Luke.

Early Christians probably collected from various OT books
the passages which were thought to foreshadow the coming of
the Lord and the events of his ministry, and these have affected
the content and form of the gospels; cf. p. 4. The Essenes of
Qumran, who wrote the Dead Sea Scrolls, also had 'testimonies'
which they thought referred to events of their own history; see,
e.g., J. A. Fitzmyer, *Theological Studies*, xvii (1957), 513-537.

Mark illustrates a trait common to Essenes and early Christians, that of making a slight change in the quoted text; in the
Malachi citation 'my way' is changed to 'your way' so that the
prophecy now refers to the Messiah. The change in Greek is only
from μου to σου; it may be due to conflation of the quotation
with Exod. xxiii. 20. The same passage from Isaiah is used in 3

the Manual of Discipline (1QS viii. 12-15; cf. ix. 19-20) to indicate that in the desert the Essenes are by their practices preparing the Lord's way; in fact, just as in the LXX and the gospels the phrase 'in the wilderness' is construed with 'prepare'. Such ingenious uses of the OT are familiar in rabbinic literature but are especially prominent in Essene and Christian writings; see, e.g., S. E. Johnson, *ZAW*, lxi (1954), 113.

Thus Mark identifies John the Baptist, not the Essene community or the exilic prophet, as the one who calls for a way to be prepared for the Lord, and for him Jesus is that Lord. The prophecies are part of a sentence that continues through verse 4.

i. 4-8. THE MANIFESTATION OF THE SPIRIT

4 **John the Baptiser appeared in the wilderness proclaiming**
5 **a baptism of repentance for remission of sins. And all the Judaean country and all the people of Jerusalem used to go out to him and be baptised by him in the Jordan river,**
6 **confessing their sins. John was clad in camels' hair and wore a leather belt about his waist, and he used to eat**
7 **locusts and wild honey. And he preached, saying, 'One stronger than I comes after me, the thong of whose**
8 **sandals I am not worthy to stoop and loosen. I baptise you with water, but he will baptise you with Holy Spirit.'**

No one can say whether Mark knew any traditions of Jesus' birth and infancy; to him at any rate they were not part of the essential matter of the gospel. He begins at approximately the same point as John, Marcion's Luke, and the kerygmatic speech Acts x. 34-43, namely the opening of our Lord's public ministry. Marcion, however, begins with the sermon in Capharnaum, while the others regard John's activity as the introduction to the gospel. Mark's narrative overlaps that of Q at this point, and Matthew and Luke have fuller accounts of John's preaching and the temptation of Jesus; note that the Isaiah quotation in its Christianised form occurs also in a Q passage, Matt. xi. 10 =Luke vii. 27. The most probable view is (1) that Mark and Q

drew common material from the oral tradition; but it is possible
(2) that Mark had some slight acquaintance with Q or (3) that
at this point the three evangelists do not use Q but another
written source; cf. Introduction, p. 26.

The section divides naturally into three parts: the preaching
of John (verses 4-8), the baptism of Jesus (verses 9-11) and the
temptations in the wilderness (verses 12-13). These are bound
together by the theme of the Holy Spirit, for John promises that
his successor will baptise with the Spirit, the Spirit descends
into Jesus at his baptism, and the Spirit drives him into the
desert. This is significant, for Mark mentions the Spirit elsewhere only in iii. 29; xii. 36; and xiii. 11. Having once laid down
the principle that Jesus possesses the Holy Spirit, he finds it
unnecessary to make the point again except in iii. 29 where it is
part of the traditional saying and essential to the story. Mark,
unlike Luke, does not elaborate the theology of the Spirit, yet
the Spirit is the decisive factor in this new event.

As prophesied in Isaiah, **John the Baptiser appeared in the 4
wilderness.** Christian literature gives the impression that John
was only a forerunner of Jesus, but he was an important religious figure in his own right. For some time his disciples
maintained their identity as a separate group; cf. M. Goguel, *Au
seuil de l'Évangile: Jean-Baptiste* (Paris, 1928); J. Thomas, *Le
Mouvement baptiste en Palestine et Syrie* (Gembloux, 1935); C. R.
Bowen, *Studies in the NT* (Chicago, 1936), pp. 30-76; C. H.
Kraeling, *John the Baptist* (London, 1951); M. Dibelius, *Die
urchristliche Überlieferung von Johannes dem Täufer* (Göttingen,
1911). There is little reason to accept Marxsen's contention
(pp. 20-22) that the 'wilderness' is a purely theological concept;
cf. R. W. Funk, *JBL*, lxxviii (1959), 205-214. The traditional
place of John's baptisms **in the Jordan river** is a little north-
east of Jericho near the *Hajleh* ford. One gains the impression
that he lived and worked in various parts of the region, which
is mainly desert. Here were to be found the Essenes of Qumran,
the hermit Bannus mentioned by Josephus (*Vita* ii), and perhaps other groups and individuals that sought more rigorous
forms of piety than the prevailing Pharisaism demanded. John
resembled the Essenes in his asceticism, his apocalyptic beliefs,
his rejection of the conventional religion of the time, and in the

fact that both he and they performed ablutions. But to consider him an Essene, or to suppose that he had been trained by them, is to force the evidence. He attracted disciples or followers, but he was a prophet and hermit, not a founder of a community. What has been preserved of his teaching centres in ethical conduct and the coming judgement, not ritual purity. The Essene ablutions do not appear to have been a baptism with the decisive character of that of John; one entered the Qumran community by taking vows and renewing the covenant; while the central fact remembered about John was that he proclaimed a **baptism of repentance for remission of sins.** The phrase must mean a baptism denoting repentance or accompanied by it. Josephus, using the rationalistic language of Hellenism, explains that it was for purification of the body, the soul having been previously purified by righteousness (*Ant.* xviii. 5. 2); but John probably demanded repentance as a condition and administered baptism as an effective sign that God was now making the people pure. Thus, as Lohmeyer says (*ad loc.*), both the repentance and the baptism were at the same time the act of man and of God. Passages such as Ezek. xxxvi. 25; ix. 4 suggest such an act of divine purification; cf. Isa. i. 16-18. This seems more natural than the theory that John modelled his baptism on that of proselytes to Judaism, as though the whole people had apostatised and it was necessary to enter afresh into the holy com-
5 munity. The fuller account in Matthew and Luke, and the statement that **all the Judaean country,** etc., went out to him, show that John was trying to reach the entire nation with a message of the utmost urgency. Repentance, μετάνοια, etymologically means a change of mind; the corresponding word in Hebrew is *teshubhah*, the complete 'turning' away from sin which demands not only sorrow for misdeeds but restitution, a changed life, and the resolve to sin no more.

Baptised by him: the middle ἐβαπτίζοντο may mean that they immersed themselves under John's direction rather than that he personally baptised them. This is likely, in view of the mode of proselyte baptism, and because of the crowds that must have come; cf. B. S. Easton, *AJT*, xxiv (1920), 313-318; H. G. Marsh, *The Origin and Significance of the NT Baptism* (Manchester, 1941), chap. ii.

John may have been dressed in rough garments of **camels'** 6 **hair,** less likely in skins; cf. F. C. Grant, *ATR*, xx (1938), 103-119. His mode of life suggests the prophet Elijah (2 Kings i. 8; cf. Zech. xiii. 4). Several species of **locusts** were eaten by Jews, as by Arabs today (Lev. xi. 22; Strabo, xvi. 4. 2; Pliny the Elder, *Hist. nat.* vi. 35). Some commentators, however, understand ἀκρίδες as carob beans or vegetables.

He probably did not describe further the **stronger than I.** It 7 might refer to God himself coming to judgement. Other passages suggest a 'coming one' (Matt. xi. 3 =Luke vii. 19) who is a man, but, at least early in his ministry, John did not identify him with Jesus. That he **comes after** John is to the evangelists ironic; Jesus appeared, but only appeared, to be a disciple of John. Such a figure must be the Messiah or the Son of Man, God's agent in judgement and establishment of the new and final order. The Talmud states that a disciple will perform every service for his rabbi that a slave might do for his master except to **stoop and loosen** his **sandals,** but John does not consider himself **worthy** to do even this for the Stronger One.

I baptise you; the aorist may be a semitism (Klostermann) 8 or a dramatic aorist. **He shall baptise you with Holy Spirit.** Matthew and Luke add 'with fire'; i.e. while some are to receive the fullness of divine gifts, others will be consumed in the fire of judgement. It has been conjectured that John originally said: 'I have baptised you with water, but he will baptise you with fire'. If so, the reference to Holy Spirit was added in the pre-Marcan tradition, for the evangelist usually employs the article. The prophecy of an outpouring of God's Spirit was well known (Joel ii. 28).

i. 9-11. THE SPIRIT AT JESUS' BAPTISM

And it happened in those days that Jesus came from 9 **Nazareth of Galilee and was baptised into the Jordan by John. And just as he was coming up out of the water he** 10 **saw the heavens parting and the Spirit as a dove coming down into him; and a voice came from the heavens, 'You are my Son, the Beloved; in you I delight'.**

The baptism of Jesus is linked to the sections before and after by the theme of the Spirit, and to the Transfiguration by the fact that both are epiphanies in which God sets his seal on Jesus (John vi. 27) by designating him as his Son, the Beloved. It also has a counterpart in the feeding of the Five Thousand (vi. 34-44), an epiphany climaxing the Galilean ministry. The two stories may thus be connected with the two great sacraments; cf. B. W. Bacon, *Story*, p. 147 f.; cf. p. 196. Like Jesus, the Christian believer will receive the Spirit at his baptism. It is not certain whether the story belongs to the Son of Man tradition, or, as Bacon thinks, to the incarnate Wisdom Christology of Q (*ibid.* pp. 249-253). The Jewish tradition that the Messiah is unknown, even to himself, until Elijah comes to anoint him, is found in Justin, *Dial.* viii. 4.

9. **Nazareth,** mentioned in a Hebrew inscription found in Caesarea, is to be identified with the Christian Arab town en-Naṣira. Mark either does not know, or has no interest in, the story of Jesus' birth in Bethlehem (Matt. ii. 1; Luke ii. 4-6), and to him descent from David is irrelevant (xii. 35-37). He probably thinks of Nazareth as the place where he was reared, since he calls Jesus Ναζαρηνός (i. 24), though he does not mention the village in vi. 1-6, and Capharnaum is his headquarters in the early chapters. **Galilee** means 'circle', and its full name was 'Galilee of the Gentiles' (Isa. ix. 1). Only gradually did it become Jewish. In Jesus' time the larger cities such as Sepphoris and Tiberias were predominantly pagan, and not all the Jews of the region followed the Pharisees, but in the second century A.D. it came to be an important rabbinical centre; cf. S. E. Johnson, *JOT*, pp. 18-23; W. Bauer in *Festgabe für Adolf Jülicher* (Tübingen, 1927), pp. 16-34; L. E. Elliott-Binns, *Galilean Christianity* (London, 1956).

Why should Jesus be **baptised** if John's baptism was for the remission of sins? Matthew's answer is that 'it is fitting to perform every righteous act' (Matt. iii. 15); i.e. this is what any right-minded person would do in this situation, even though he may not be conscious of personal sin. Israel as a whole needs to repent and Jesus does not disclaim membership in the nation; cf. Ignatius, *Smyrn.* i. 2. This is more logical than the clumsy tradition in the Gospel according to the Nazarenes: 'In what

38

have I sinned, that I should go and be baptised by him? Unless perhaps this very word that I have just spoken is an ignorance.' These later additions to the tradition illustrate the difficulties felt by early Christians. Mark, however, does not speculate; for him the important part is what happened immediately after the baptism.

Just (εὐθύς, immediately, one of Mark's characteristic words) 10 **as he was coming up out of the water he saw the heavens parting.** Violent storms are characteristic of the Jordan valley (Bishop, p. 55), but this is more than an atmospheric phenomenon; it is an apocalyptic event, to be understood from *Testament of Levi* xviii. 5-12: 'The heavens shall be opened . . . the Father's voice . . . sin shall come to an end . . . And Beliar shall be bound by him.' The **Spirit** descended **as a dove;** in Jewish tradition the dove is a symbol for Israel, for the Spirit (Chag. 15a), and sometimes for the Spirit of the Messiah (Gen. Rabba 2; Yalkut on Gen. i. 2; cf. Targum on Cant. ii. 8). Philo compares Wisdom or the divine Logos to a dove (*Quis rer. div. heres* xxv. 48). Mark says only that Jesus saw the event, but like Matthew and Luke he probably thought of it as visible to others. The Spirit descended **into him;** most translators refuse to render this literally and prefer 'upon him'; cf. Matt. iii. 16; Luke iii. 22; John i. 33. The expression may be naïve; Mark stands near the beginning of Christological speculation and it is doubtful that he consciously held an adoptionist Christology.

The opening of the heavens means that revelation has been 11 resumed, and God speaks directly in **a voice from the heavens.** There are many rabbinic traditions of a *bath qol* or voice of God (literally 'daughter [i.e. echo] of the voice'). It often, though not always, speaks words of scripture (cf. Midrash Eccl. vii. 9; Talmud Berachoth 3a), and is not always taken as final authority. Here the voice is connected with an epiphany. The words are evidently a quotation from Ps. ii. 7, conflated with Isa. xlii. 1, the latter from an independent translation, not the LXX. The **Son** is called the **Beloved,** which may be a messianic title (Eph. i. 6), particularly if this is the same as the Elect One of Enoch, who in turn is identified with the Son of Man; there are, however, good reasons for translating ὁ υἱός μου ὁ ἀγαπητός as 'my only Son'; cf. C. H. Turner, *JTS,* xxvii (1926), 113-129; A. Souter, *ibid.* xxviii (1927), 59 f. cf. also *MR*, p. 16 f. The latter part of the quotation clearly refers to the Servant of Second Isaiah, who represents Israel. That ηὐδόκησα should be translated as a present tense is shown by its use in the LXX of 2 Sam. xxii. 20; Isa. lxii. 4; Mal. ii. 17; Ps. xliv. 3. Thus in Mark's mind Jesus is uniquely God's Son; and he may be at the same time the Son of Man or Elect One and the Servant who suffers on behalf of all nations. We cannot be certain that the evangelist made all these connexions as he wrote, for the quotation may have come to him from tradition.

There is no way to determine exactly what Jesus experienced on this occasion. It has been argued that he alone recognised the descent of the Spirit and recounted the event to his disciples; it does in any case seem likely that the Baptism marks the sudden beginning of his ministry and in some sense his call to undertake it. Mark is content to set down the tradition and allows it to speak for itself; he seems not to speculate on our Lord's 'messianic consciousness' or to try to interpret his thoughts.

i. 12-13. JESUS IS DRIVEN BY THE SPIRIT

12 **And immediately the Spirit drove him out into the desert.**
13 **He was in the desert forty days being put to the test by Satan, and he was with the wild animals, and the angels were serving him.**

12   John had promised a baptism in Holy Spirit; the Spirit descended at Jesus' baptism; and now **the Spirit drove him out into the desert.** Ezekiel tells of being carried away into far places by the Spirit, not for temptation but for revelation (Ezek. iii. 14-15; viii. 3; xi. 24), and Philip figures in a similar story (Acts viii. 39-40). With this abrupt and forceful language Mark indicates that God is powerfully at work in the life of Jesus. The first event is a tremendous struggle and overthrow of Satan, by whom he is tempted or **put to the test.** Except for the narrow Jordan valley, the oasis of Jericho, and a few other places such as 'Ain Feshkha near Qumran, the whole surrounding country was a rocky wilderness. Such places were thought of as the home of

demons (Matt. xii. 43 = Luke xi. 24), and the scapegoat was driven
into the desert (Lev. xvi. 22). Jesus thus seems to invade the
domain of **Satan** (Heb. 'the adversary', 'enemy'), who was
thought of in the OT as the evil spirit who seduces men towards
evil and then accuses them before God. In the gospels he is the
supreme demon whose kingdom is now coming to an end
(iii. 26).

In other religions there are stories of how their founders or
prophets are put to the test, often at the beginning of their ministry; cf. S. Eitrem and A. Fridrichsen, *Die Versuchung Christi*
(Kristiania, 1924); E. Fascher, *Jesus und der Satan* (Halle, 1949);
H. P. Houghton, *ATR*, xxvi (1944), 166-175; Mary E. Andrews,
ibid. xxiv (1942), 229-244. The Marcan narrative is briefer than
the highly stylised account in Matthew and Luke, which records
subtle temptations, such as the demand for a sign, that may have
occurred more than once in Jesus' ministry.

Moses was **forty days** and nights in the mount (Exod. xxiv. 13
18; xxxiv. 28; Deut. ix. 9; x. 10) and Elijah made a journey of the
same duration to Horeb (1 Kings xix. 8). This is the language of
revelation and intimate fellowship with God; in the midst of
temptation **the angels were serving him** (Ps. xci. 11). The
reference to **the wild animals** is no doubt drawn from verse 13
of the same psalm, though jackals, hyenas and even lions have
been seen in the Jordan valley.

i. 14-15. ANNOUNCEMENT OF THE KINGDOM OF GOD

**And after John was arrested Jesus came into Galilee pro- 14
claiming God's Good News: 'The time is fully come and 15
the Kingdom of God has drawn near; repent and believe
in the Good News'.**

According to Mark, it was only **after John was arrested** 14
(the same verb is used to denote Jesus' betrayal in ix. 31; xiv. 10,
etc.) that Jesus preached the **Good News**. This seems more
probable than the statement of John iii. 22-24; cf. Matt. xi. 2-6
= Luke vii. 18-23.

15 The struggle against Satan and his kingdom has not ended; it continues later in Jesus' expulsion of demons and in the history of the Church as reflected in other parts of the NT; cf. Robinson, *Problem*, p. 30. But Jesus' victory on this occasion, and his endowment of the Spirit, prepare him for the message that **the time** is fully come. The concept of the καιρός, the moment, the decisive time for God's action, is found elsewhere in the NT, e.g. Matt. xiii. 30; John vii. 6, 8; Rom. xiii. 11, but the word is not often used in a technical theological sense and the idea can be expressed otherwise (τὸ πλήρωμα τοῦ χρόνου, Gal. iv. 4).

Here the moment that has arrived is the near approach of **the Kingdom of God.** The Kingdom (more precisely, the Reign or Sovereignty of God) is perhaps the central message of Jesus' teaching, though it does not occur in all strands of the tradition. The basic idea, which cannot be understood apart from the OT and Judaism, is that God is king of all the earth (Ps. xlvii. 7); the universe is the Lord's, and everything in it (Ps. xxiv. 1). Yet the believer is faced with a paradox: *de jure*, God is king, but *de facto* he is not, for his will is ignored and resisted and Satan appears to have a temporary realm of his own. According to Jewish thought, God's Law had been offered to all nations, but only Israel accepted it, and even Israel was disobedient so that only a remnant remained and the lordship of the world passed to the heathen. But wherever men take upon them the yoke of the Kingdom of God by professing true faith (formally by reciting the *Shema*‘, Deut. vi. 4-9; xi. 13-21; Num. xv. 37-41) and doing acts of obedience, to that extent God's Reign is effective; thus 'thy Kingdom come' means 'thy will be done' (Matt. vi. 10). The question is, when will the reign of God be complete and all disobedience come to an end? This triumph of God was for Jews and early Christians the *eschaton*, the final event of history. The earliest synagogue prayers, the Eighteen Benedictions and the Kaddish, contain petitions that God's Reign may be revealed. Later rabbinic thought, like later Christian theology, transferred this to the indefinite future, but the present passage and Jesus' parables of the Kingdom indicate that he expected it very soon. There are two difficult problems: (1) Did he definitely prophesy it within a generation, as ix. 1 seems to indicate? (2) Did he teach that it was already present?

(1) In answer to the first question, one must acknowledge the overwhelming NT evidence that the earliest Christians expected an early advent of the Kingdom, and the numerous sayings of Jesus that point towards this. At the same time, he seems to have warned against calculating when this should be, and indicated that many would be disappointed by the delay (xiii. 33-34; Luke xvii. 20-22).

(2) Certainly the so-called 'present Kingdom' sayings, such as Matt. xii. 28 =Luke xi. 20; Matt. xi. 12-13 =Luke xvi. 16, cannot mean that the Kingdom has been completely established throughout the world. One might say that in Jesus and his disciples the nucleus of the Kingdom is thought of as present; at least God has manifested his sovereignty in a new and powerful fashion, and the new age, radically different from the old, has dawned. The hope and joy evoked by this dawn, combined with the stern moral demands laid upon those who would enter the Kingdom, the mingled urgency and expectation, impart a unique tone to the NT literature. Mark emphasises the future fulfilment, but his whole gospel is a record of the stupendous acts which God has already accomplished. See also *TG*, pp. 102-28.

The command **Repent** shows the continuity of Jesus' work with that of John the Baptist. Judaism glorifies repentance— indeed there is a famous saying of R. Aḥa (*c*. A.D. 320), 'If the Israelites would repent for one day, the Messiah Son of David would come immediately'—and teaches that repentance unfailingly brings divine forgiveness. Jesus not only accepts this teaching and sets it forth in unforgettable parables but goes further by emphasising God's seeking and saving the lost. What is new here is not repentance as such but the call to believe **the Good News.** Mark does not include parables illustrating this invitation to sinners (Luke xv; Matt. xx. 1-15; Matt. xxii. 2-5, 8-10 =Luke xiv. 16-21); instead he illustrates the News dramatically with his stories of healings (particularly ii. 1-12 with its antecedent forgiveness), casting out of demons and association with sinners.

16 **And as he passed alongside the sea of Galilee he saw**
Simon and Andrew, Simon's brother, casting a circular
17 **net in the sea; for they were fishermen. And Jesus said to**
them, 'Come after me, and I will make you into fishers of
18 **men'. And immediately leaving their nets behind they**
19 **followed him. Having gone a little farther, he saw James,**
Zebedee's son, and John his brother, who were in the boat
20 **mending their nets. He immediately called them, and**
leaving their father Zebedee in the boat with the hired
men they came away after him.

16   The divine initiative is next shown in the call of four disciples who, so far as one can tell from the story, have not previously been associated with Jesus. Suddenly he is **alongside the**
sea of Galilee. The fragmentary and episodic character of
Mark's source material is evident. In itself this narrative is
similar to that of any prophet or rabbi enlisting his followers.
By placing it here the evangelist gives it particularly dramatic
force. For the proper names, cf. on iii. 13-19. The **circular net**
for casting (ἀμφίβληστρον), weighted with stones at the circum-
ference and with a draw rope around it so that it 'encloses' the
fish as in a purse (Luke v. 6), has been used in modern times on
the lake. Lohmeyer objects that fishing takes place at night
(Luke v. 5; John xxi. 3), while the men would be **mending**
their nets in the daytime; but some fishing no doubt went on
during the day. The nets being repaired may have been of the
type just described, or σαγῆναι, drag-nets, and the **boat** the
large craft with a sail (*shakhtûra*) still used today; cf. E. W. H.
Masterman, *Studies in Galilee* (Chicago, 1909), chap. ii; G.
Dalman, *Arbeit und Sitte in Palästina*, vi (Gütersloh, 1939), pp.
347-370. If verses 16-39 are from Peter's reminiscences, the
passage must include the events of more than one day, for the
disciples are called on a working day, and verses 21-31 consist
of stories of a Sabbath.

17   **Come after me** is an invitation to become disciples of Jesus.
Lohmeyer remarks that the evangelist gives this in the form of

a curt military order which suggests the divine initiative. An ancient rabbi might so invite a student, or the man might apply to him. The disciple literally followed in his master's footsteps and often lived in his house. Here the purpose is not the detailed study of the legal tradition but to make the four **into fishers of men**. This phrase, in rabbinical and Greek literature, usually has an evil sense, as in Jer. xvi. 16; the late writer Aristaenetus (*Ep*. iii. 23) speaks of catching virgins. Here the thought may be that they fish for men in order to save them, but C. W. F. Smith, *HTR*, lii (1959), 187-203, comparing 1QH v. 7-8 and Matt. xiii. 47-50, argues that it is a gathering of the people for judgement.

Elijah, after his forty-day journey to Horeb, returned to find 18 Elisha and cast his mantle on him (1 Kings xix. 19-21); cf. Farrer, *A Study in St. Mark*, p. 62 f. The successor was given time to bid his parents farewell, but these men followed Jesus immediately (contrast the examples in Luke ix. 57-62). The narrative is strictly compressed; yet the sudden turning to follow a prophet is more natural in an ancient oriental culture than in our own.

i. 21-28. AUTHORITY IN TEACHING AND EXORCISM

They entered Capharnaum; and on the Sabbath he went 21 right into the synagogue and began to teach. And they 22 were astonished at what he taught, for he was teaching them as one possessing authority, and not as the scholars. Just then a man with an unclean spirit was in their syna- 23 gogue, and he shrieked out: 'What have you to do with 24 us, Jesus, man of Nazareth? You have come to destroy us. I know who you are, the Holy One of God.' And Jesus 25 rebuked him: 'Be quiet and come out of him'. The un- 26 clean spirit, convulsing him and shrieking loudly, came out of him. And all of them were astonished, so that they 27 argued with one another, saying, 'What is this? A new teaching, authoritative! And he commands even the unclean spirits, and they heed him!' And this report of him 28

went out at once everywhere into the whole country round about in Galilee.

Jesus had manifested authority in calling four disciples; now Mark adds that he teaches and casts out demons with the same
21 authority. The scene is laid in **Capharnaum**. This is identified with the site Tell Ḥum on the north-west shore of the Sea of Galilee. Lying on the border of Herod Antipas' tetrarchy, it was an important toll station. The main road from Ptolemais (Acre) to Damascus passed through here and there were connexions with the cities of the Decapolis. The name means 'village of Nahum' or 'village of consolation'; the form 'Capernaum' is a Syriac corruption; cf. F. C. Burkitt, *The Syriac Forms of the NT Proper Names* (London, 1912), pp. 27 f.

As in the canonical Luke and in Marcion's gospel, Jesus' first public appearance is in **the synagogue** of Capharnaum. The term συναγωγή, 'congregation', 'assembly', is used in Greek for the local congregation and for the building in which it met (the older word προσευχή is also used for the latter, Acts xvi. 13). The formation of synagogues may have begun during the exile when Jews gathered on the Sabbath to hear the scripture read and to offer prayer. In the first century its primary purpose was education, as it is today, but after the destruction of the Temple worship assumed a more prominent part in it. The service consisted of prayers, blessings, the reading of scripture (Luke iv. 16; Acts xiii. 15) and its free translation into Aramaic; and ordinarily preaching or teaching. The synagogue was a lay institution not only in the sense that it needed no *kohen* or priest, but it did not even require a rabbi; any man who was competent might expound the scriptures. It was therefore natural for Jesus to occupy the teacher's chair. Worship was led by a 'ruler of the synagogue' (ἀρχισυνάγωγος, v. 22, Heb. *rosh ha-keneseth*); in large congregations there might be several such persons (Acts xiii. 15). A *ḥazan* (the ὑπηρέτης of Luke iv. 20) acted as caretaker, meted out punishments and sometimes taught the children. At Tell Ḥum there are ruins of a fine synagogue of the second century A.D. The one existing in Jesus' time (cf. Luke vii. 5) has not been found, and indeed no first-century synagogues are known in Galilee; they were probably small and unpretentious.

Jesus now teaches **as one possessing authority** (ἐξουσία), 22 not only the right given by God but with it the inner power to accomplish mighty deeds. Mark's statement here is noteworthy because elsewhere he always uses the word to denote his power to work miracles. The OT prophets did not teach in quite this way but as they were bidden by God, and sometimes reluctantly. There is no record that Jesus ever said 'thus saith the Lord'. He expected his teaching to be accepted either because its truth was self-evident or because of his word. It was characteristic of the **scholars** (γραμματεῖς, 'scribes') or rabbis that whenever possible they rested their teaching on tradition. In theory the oral Law was given by Moses along with the written Law and passed down to the prophets, the men of the 'Great Synagogue', and the famous pairs of rabbis (Mishnah Aboth i. 1-12). This dependence on tradition can be exaggerated, for Hillel, Jesus' contemporary, often appealed to exegesis of scripture instead of tradition. On the other hand, the gospels contain examples of Jesus' argument from the OT. Luke has a tradition of what Jesus taught in Capharnaum (Luke iv, 21-27; cf. John vi. 24-59), but Mark's interest is the in fact *that he taught* in this authoritative fashion. The theory of D. Daube, *The NT and Rabbinic Judaism* (London, 1956), pp. 212-16, is that these 'scribes' are village teachers, not great rabbis.

The next story is told in popular form and contains expres- 23 sions that may be Semitisms (Lohmeyer). Here, if anywhere, we may have an example of the stories told by Peter to the church in Rome. The combat with the demonic world is now carried on aggressively, and the **unclean spirit** fights back. Belief in demons and the delusion of being possessed by them, though well attested in modern Syria and elsewhere, was at a high point in the first century. Jewish demonology had developed, perhaps under Persian influence—the Jewish Pseudepigrapha and rabbinic sources contain abundant references—and the unsettled conditions of Palestinian life probably produced many nervous disorders. The rabbis of the first century often ascribed illness to sin (e.g. John ix. 2), but alongside this there was the concept of a hostile and alien power which invaded men and for which they were therefore not responsible. The two ideas are not, however, absolutely opposed, for the demons might seduce men into sins for which they would then be punished. It is not impossible that in the earliest stage of the gospel tradition all sickness was ascribed to demons (Acts x. 38; Luke xiii. 11).

That Jesus was able to heal possessed people and exercised this power to an unusual degree, is well attested by the gospels. Even his contemporary opponents did not deny the fact (iii. 22; cf. the charge in Sanh. 107a that he practised magic). Unlike the early Christians and Jewish and pagan healers, he did not use formulae of exorcism but cast out demons by his simple word of command; cf. S. V. McCasland, *By the Finger of God* (New York, 1951), pp. 110-115. On demon possession in antiquity, cf. E. R. Dodds, *The Greeks and the Irrational* (Berkeley, Calif., 1951), p. 72. R. M. Grant, *Miracle and Natural Law* (Amsterdam, 1952).

The evil spirits are probably **unclean** by nature and may
24 render their victims unclean. This one **shrieked out** words reminiscent of those addressed to Elijah by the fearful widow (1 Kings xvii. 18). Only a divine or demonic power can say, **I know who you are. The Holy One** in the OT is usually God, though occasionally a priest or prophet (Deut. xxxiii. 8; Ps. lxxxix. 19); in the NT it is Christ (e.g. Acts iii. 14). The demon is trying to get control by a kind of exorcism in reverse, shout-
26 ing out Jesus' name. **Be quiet,** φιμώθητι, etymologically 'be muzzled'. The **convulsing** is characteristic of the exorcised demon; cf. on ix. 17.

27 Mark often speaks of the people being **astonished;** cf. vi. 2; vii. 37; x. 26; xi. 18. Verse 27 appears to resume verses 21-22 and the second mention of astonishment is curious; the evangelist may have combined two pieces of tradition. The subject of the **new teaching** is not demons or the way to cast them out, though Mark's readers might understand this as 'a new, power-
28 ful religion' (διδαχή) which gives control over demons. Verse 28 is one of the evangelist's usual editorial summaries.

i. 29-31. PETER'S MOTHER-IN-LAW

29 **They went right out of the synagogue and into Simon's and Andrew's house, accompanied by James and John.**
30 **Simon's mother-in-law was lying there suffering from a**

**fever, and they immediately told him about her. He came 31
forward, took her by the hand, and raised her up; and the
fever left her, and she waited on them.**

This may be another story told by Peter, for the language may 29
easily be turned into the first person: 'We went . . .' (Zahn,
J. Weiss, C. H. Turner). There is no motive for the naming of
the four disciples; perhaps their presence was simply recalled.
The story contains traits of Mark's style, with εὐθύς used twice
and the pleonastic ἐξελθόντες ἦλθον. **Simon's mother-in-** 30
law evidently lived in his and **Andrew's house** and was probably a widow. We are no doubt to think of a one-room dwelling
with an earth floor. The **fever** cannot be identified; such ailments, which come and go quickly, are common in the Near
East. Malaria is a possibility.

He . . . took her by the hand, and raised her up. This 31
gesture of healing has parallels in Hellenistic miracle stories; in
the Talmud 'to cause to rise' is an expression meaning 'to
heal'. It is the suddenness of the cure and the fact that at once
she waited on them, that mark this as a miracle. The rabbis
generally disapproved of a woman's serving at table (SB, i, 480),
but in villages women have always had more freedom, and the
Pharisees still had little influence in Galilee.

i. 32-34. SUMMARY OF HEALINGS

**At evening, when the sun had set, they were carrying to 32
him all the sick people and those possessed by demons,
and the entire city was gathered at the door. He healed 33, 34
many who had various ailments and cast out many
demons, but he did not permit the demons to speak because they recognised him.**

This is partly Mark's editorial summary, for the κακῶς ἔχον-
τας καὶ τοὺς δαιμονιζομένους appears to be his style (cf. v.
15, 16, 18; vi. 55), but the curious double note of time at the
beginning suggests the use of tradition. Mark may know of
several stories but generalises them here.

32 **At evening,** ὀψία, a word not used by the Atticistic stylists,
probably the·twilight after sunset. The Sabbath has ended and
34 it was lawful to carry to him **all the sick.** Mark's theory is that
the demons, being spiritual beings, **recognised him.** Matthew
always omits such remarks as this, and Paul and John say nothing
of Jesus' work of casting out demons, although exorcism was an
important feature of the work of early Christians. Since part of
the usual technique of exorcism was to force the demon to speak
(cf. on ix. 17), it is significant that **he did not permit** them to
do so. On the other hand, Mark regards Jesus as no ordinary
wonder-worker who must follow the prescribed procedure; and
Jesus' nature must not be disclosed until he is ready to reveal it.

i. 35-39. WITHDRAWAL; SUMMARY

35 **Early in the morning while it was still very dark, he got
up and went out and away into a deserted place, where**
36 **he began to pray. Simon and his companions hunted him**
37 **down, found him, and said to him, 'Everyone is looking**
38 **for you'. He said to them, 'Let us go elsewhere to the
neighbouring towns so that I may announce the News**
39 **there also; this is why I came out'. And all through Galilee he went into their synagogues preaching and casting
out demons.**

35   The double note of time at the beginning (cf. verse 32), and
the linguistic peculiarities, suggest that verses 35-38 are a piece
of tradition, with verse 39 added as a summary.
    Jesus seeks **a deserted place** in order **to pray** fully and alone
(cf. vi. 31; xiv. 32); Lightfoot, *GM*, p. 23, remarks that on the
three occasions when this gospel tells of our Lord praying, it is
always at night and at times of tension. Mark may think of him
37 as praying aloud. **Everyone** (presumably all the people of Capharnaum) **is looking for** him but he wishes to go **to the neigh-**
38 **bouring towns.** A κωμόπολις is one that may be of some size
but has only the governmental status of a village; cf. Sherwin-
White, pp. 127-32. Jesus' main purpose is to **announce the**

News; healing is not excluded but is incidental to the purpose. The emphasis is on the words **there also;** it was his task to preach in many places. **I came out,** presumably from Capharnaum, though Mark's thought may be of his coming from the wilderness, from his previous life, or from God.

He went into their synagogues preaching; in place of 39 ἦλθεν some important authorities read ἦν, which may be original.

i. 40-45. HEALING OF A LEPER

A leper came to him begging him and saying to him, 'If 40, **you are willing you can cleanse me'. Moved with compassion, he stretched out his hand, touched him, and said, 'I am willing; be clean'. The leprosy at once left him and** 42 **he was cleansed. He then gave him a stern warning and** 43 **sent him away, saying to him, 'Be sure not to say anything** 44 **to anyone, but go show yourself to the priest and for a witness to them offer for your cleansing what Moses prescribed'. But the man went out and began to proclaim it** 45 **a great deal and spread the news, so that Jesus was no longer able to go into a city openly, but stayed outside in lonely places; and they kept coming to him from everywhere.**

This story and the one following (ii. 1-12) can be considered as connected with the first manifestations of power or with the controversy sections that follow, since this one implicitly raises a question about the Mosaic Law; cf. Lightfoot, *GM*, pp. 25 f. The two narratives form a kind of transition section. Mark may place the story of the Leper here because in the tradition the miracle stories were already grouped together; it is, however, a climax to the healings, since the rabbis remarked that the healing of a leper was as difficult as raising the dead.

The difficulties in the account suggest that it is a piece of old 40 tradition. One is a textual problem. In place of **Moved with compassion** (σπλαγχνισθείς), D and some OL. MSS. read ὀργισθείς, 'moved with anger'. The usual reading may be correct because Jesus expresses and shows his willingness; yet the mention of **a stern warning** is in favour of the other. Some commentators have also supposed that the anger is not directed at the man but at the demonic powers causing the leprosy.

Another question concerns the reason for Jesus' injunction of silence. Perhaps in the original story, as in Luke xvii. 12-19 (cf. 2 Kings v), he tested the man's faith by sending him to the priest, and the cleansing took place on the way. In this case he was to be silent until he was cured, and verse 42 anticipates the healing.

The term leprosy today is usually confined to Hansen's disease. In the Bible, however, it refers to a number of skin ailments, such as perhaps contagious ringworm, psoriasis, leucoderma and vitiligo, though Hansen's disease may have been known also. It also includes conditions due to fungus observed in clothing or on the walls of buildings (Lev. xiii. 47; xiv. 34). As the rules for purification show, it was believed to be sometimes curable. For the biblical law, see Lev. xiii-xiv; Deut. xxiv. 8. The rabbis ordinarily regarded it as a direct punishment for sin; the tractate Negaim of the Mishnah contains some of the earlier rabbinical traditions.

41 The leper's remark, **'If you are willing'**, implies no necessary doubt of Jesus' desire to heal but may be intended as a compliment; cf. Epictetus, iii. 10. 14 f., 'Why then do you flatter the physician? Why do you say, "If you are willing, sir, I will get well"?' **Jesus stretched out his hand** not in repulse but as a gesture of healing (2 Kings v. 11; Mark viii. 22-23). When he **touched him** he risked ceremonial defilement, for a leper was unclean (Lev. xiii. 45-46; Mishnah Negaim iii. 1). If a leper entered a house, he polluted everything within it (Mishnah Kelim i. 1, 4). Jesus' act is, to say the least, a remarkable indication of his compassion. Perhaps it also reveals his attitude to his own vocation. The Good News comes not only in words but in action; it breaks through fears and scruples, even the fear of separation from one's own people; and its power to cleanse is greater than the power of defilement.

42 **The leprosy at once left him;** this heightens the miracle (cf. Exod. iv. 6-7; Num. xii. 9-14) and does not fit with the verse following.

He then gave him a stern warning. The word ἐμβριμάομαι 43 originally means to snort or groan, and is used in the Greek Bible to express indignation, disapproval and other strong emotions; cf. xiv. 5; John xi. 33, 38; Matt. ix. 30; Dan. xi. 30 LXX; Lam. ii. 6. Bishop remarks (p. 242) that there is a corresponding word in modern Arabic. The verb is also used to denote the sound made by an exorcist when expelling a demon; and if so, **sent him away** (ἐξέβαλεν) may mean 'he drove the demon out'.

The command **not to say anything to anyone,** as suggested above, can be explained by the fact that the cure was not yet complete; but in any case Jesus does not wish to be regarded as an ordinary wonder-worker.

It was necessary for the man **to show** himself **to the priest,** i.e. one on duty in the Temple, in order to be pronounced clean and resume a normal life. The ceremony involved an offering of **what Moses prescribed** (Lev. xiv. 1-7), namely two clean living birds, one of which was killed and the other dipped in its blood and released. The blood of the slain bird was sprinkled over the healed man, and this completed the ritual purification.

Why **for a witness to them?** One might expect 'to him', i.e. the priest. Mark perhaps has the crowds in mind, in spite of the previous command of silence; or he may consider that the healing is a testimony to the power of God now available to believers.

The summary verse contains two ideas: Jesus preferred to 45 stay not in **a city but . . . in lonely places** and to work not **openly** but secretly. This was only a temporary freedom from the crowds; cf. ii. 1-2.

CHAPTER II

---

ii. 1-12. THE PARALYTIC; POWER TO FORGIVE

1 **When he came back to Capharnaum after several days,**
2 **people heard that he was at home. And many people col-**
lected, so that there was no room even in front of the door,
3 **as he spoke the Word to them. Some men came bringing**
4 **a paralytic toward him. He was carried by four men; and**
since they could not get him to Jesus because of the
crowd, they removed the roof over him by digging
through and lowered the mat on which the paralytic was
5 **lying. Jesus, when he saw their faith, said to the paralytic,**
6 **'Child, your sins are forgiven'. Some of the scholars were**
7 **sitting there and were saying to themselves, 'Why does**
this man say such a thing? He is blaspheming! Who can
8 **forgive sins except God, the One?' Jesus at once perceiv-**
ing with spiritual insight that they were thinking in this
9 **way, said to them: 'Why do you think these things? Which**
is easier, to say to this paralytic, "Your sins are forgiven",
10 **or to say "Get up, pick up your mat and walk"? But so**
that you may know that the Son of Man has authority to
forgive sins on earth'—he now speaks to the paralytic:—
1, 12 **'I tell you, get up, pick up your mat, and go home'. And**
he got up and at once picked up the mat and went out in
everyone's presence. As a result all were astonished and
glorified God, saying, 'We never saw such a thing!'

The early Church attached great importance to Jesus' de-
claration of the forgiveness of sins. It was implicit in the Good
News as proclaimed by him, and the Church made it explicit
by teaching that baptism marked the annulment of past sins and
the beginning of new life. At least in the churches founded by
St. Paul, penitents were reconciled and post-baptismal sins ab-
solved (2 Cor. ii. 5-11). Matthew significantly interprets this

54

story as meaning that God has now given men the authority to forgive on his behalf (Matt. ix. 8).

The pericope is thus the climax of Jesus' first manifestations of power. However important and striking his authoritative teaching, expulsion of demons and healing of the leper, the supreme miracle is the preaching of Good News to the poor (Matt. xi. 5 = Luke vii. 22): through Jesus, God has taken the first step without even waiting for an expression of repentance. At the same time this marks the beginning of controversy. Healing and teaching with authority would not necessarily arouse hostility, although they caused astonishment; but the aggressive word of forgiveness was regarded by the rabbis as the invasion of God's prerogatives. Certain parables in the other synoptics show that the Good News actually met with bitter opposition (cf., e.g., Matt. xx. 1-15; Luke xv. 25-32; Matt. xxii. 8-9 = Luke xiv. 21; cf. also Matt. xi. 18-19 = Luke vii. 33-35).

Mark either does not know these parables or prefers to make his point through the medium of a healing story. The evangelist may have taken a simple healing narrative (verses 3-5a, 11-12), and inserted the controversy into it, although the two do not fit together well. Whether or not this is so, the result is dramatic and forceful; the healing becomes secondary and the interest centres in the controversy caused by Jesus' word of forgiveness. Dibelius rightly sees this as a paradigm or pronouncement story enshrining the saying of verse 10.

The scene shifts back to **Capharnaum** and Jesus is **at home,** 1 presumably in Simon's house (cf. i. 29). The house is full and 2 there is **no room even in front of the door** when he speaks the Word, i.e. the Good News. This one-room dwelling probably has an outside stairway to the roof, and the **four men** who carry the sick man take him above. The illness of the **paralytic** 3 is not described, for the purpose of the story is not that of the miracle tales. F. Fenner, *Das Krankheit im NT* (Leipzig, 1930), pp. 55-57, argues, however, that the disease was functional and actually healed through the word of forgiveness. Many of the gospel healings may have had to do with nervous or mental ailments, and there is every reason to believe that both Jesus, and the Jewish and pagan healers, often accomplished cures. What is remarkable is the testimony of the gospels to the extent of

Jesus' healing work and the authority with which he carried it
on, even though the Pauline epistles are silent regarding this.

4   The paralytic's friends **removed the roof . . . by digging
through;** in Palestine many houses were built of stone or mud-
brick with poles or beams placed over the top of the walls. Over
these were placed branches of trees, reeds, or sticks, then a
matted layer of thorns, and lastly a covering of clay. At the
beginning of the rainy season the roofs were resurfaced and
rolled. It was thus possible for grass to grow on top of the house
(Ps. cxxix. 6). The man was lying on a **mat,** a pallet or rug
(κράβαττον is a non-literary word denoting a poor man's bed),

5 and he was **lowered** into the room. This eagerness of the four
men to help was seen as an example of **their faith.** Sometimes
(as in v. 34, 36) faith is mentioned in connexion with Jesus'
healings, though frequently not (e.g. v. 1-20; vii. 32-37; viii.
22-26). In general the NT view is that God's gifts come as a
result of prevenient grace; God's power is always available to
heal and save and he wishes to exercise it, and faith is the means
whereby the individual (or the group) lays hold of it. Here the
man's own faith is not excluded, but that of his helpers is
emphasised.

Child; τέκνον could also be translated 'Son' (cf. Matt. xxi.
28; Luke ii. 48; xv. 31). In x. 24, but apparently not elsewhere,
Jesus is quoted as using the word in affectionate address to his
disciples. **Your sins are forgiven,** i.e. by God; the passive
form is used to avoid mentioning the divine name. Jesus speaks
of forgiveness of sins in the Lord's Prayer (Matt. vi. 12 =Luke
xi. 4; cf. Mark xi. 25) and elsewhere, both with reference to
God's forgiveness and that of humans towards one another. In
one other instance (Luke vii. 47-48) he is represented as saying
that the sins of a particular person have been forgiven; cf. also
John viii. 11, where this is implied.

The loftiness of the rabbinic doctrine of forgiveness must not
be minimised. Forgiveness depends, according to Judaism, on
true repentance—sorrow for sin, open acknowledgement of it,
and resolute turning away from it, together with such restitution
as may be possible. Where these conditions are present, God
forgives sin unfailingly without the need of any human media-
tion or absolution. The sinner can know that his repentance,

and therefore his forgiveness, is complete when he is put in the same temptation as before and successfully resists it. The sin-offering and trespass-offering of the OT were held to atone for certain sins, usually unwitting or ritual ones (Lev. iv-vii), and the ritual of the Day of Atonement covered the miscellaneous sins of the holy people (Lev. xvi), but in general the rabbis held that repentance was the only remedy for a sin in what we would call the ethical realm; cf. Moore, *Judaism*, i, 117, 500-520; ii, 58. What is different here is that Jesus pronounces the actual forgiveness of a person, independent of the carefully prescribed conditions of the sin-offering or the Day of Atonement, or any evidence of his repentance.

Some of the scholars wonder how he can **say such a thing. 6** No one **can forgive sins except God, the One** (Exod. xxxiv. 6-7; Isa. xliii. 25-26; xliv. 22)—or perhaps 'except one, namely God'; but 'the One' may be a title for God, as in Islam (Bishop, p. 96). According to the rabbis, even Messiah could not forgive. Jesus would no doubt have agreed with this principle; but in that case he claims to know what only God can know. He **per- 8 ceives** the questions of the rabbis **with spiritual insight,** literally 'in' or 'by his spirit'; in the gospels he is often pictured as knowing what is in the minds of others (cf. xiv. 18; Luke iv. 23; vii. 39-42; John i. 45-49). The rabbis consider that **He is 7 blaspheming;** the Greek verb and the corresponding noun refer to railing or abusive speech, but in the Bible they often denote wrong speech towards or concerning God. Later rabbinic teaching restricted the blasphemy punishable by death to the cursing of God by name (Mishnah Sanhedrin vii. 5); in the gospels Jesus' opponents nevertheless regard him as worthy of death because of his messianic claims (xiv. 63-64).

The scribes think that it is **easier** for him to say **Your sins 9 are forgiven** than to heal the man, for no one but God can tell whether the pronouncement is correct. Jesus answers the un-spoken question by asking a question in turn, as elsewhere in the gospels (e.g. xi. 27-33); this is also common in rabbinical debate.

He goes on, however, to say that **the Son of Man has 10 authority to forgive sins on earth.** The problem centres in the meaning of 'Son of Man'. There is no doubt about Mark's understanding of the term. The celestial Son of Man, who comes with the clouds of heaven to exercise judgement, is now on earth with the full authority of God to acquit or condemn. In Dan. vii. 13-28, which contains the idea of the authority of the Son of Man on earth, this figure is simply the symbol for the coming rule of the 'saints of the Most High', which will be humane in contrast to the beast-kingdoms that have preceded it, while in the so-called Similitudes of Enoch (Enoch xxxvii-lxxi) he is personified into an angelic figure who holds the final judgement on behalf of God and establishes the new age. Iranian speculation regarding the Primal Man may have had a part in developing the concept. St. Paul, who never uses the term Son of Man, nevertheless equates Christ with the Second Adam (or Man), who is the prototype of the new humanity and reverses the process by which mankind fell (1 Cor. xv. 20-28; Phil. ii. 5-11; Col. i. 12-20; Rom. v. 12-21). In the four gospels the term Son of Man usually refers to the coming judge, but there are a few passages, particularly in the Q material, where it has no necessarily eschatological reference and means simply 'I, a man' (e.g. Matt. viii. 20 = Luke ix. 58). This is natural, since in Semitic idiom the words ordinarily denote 'a human being', as in Ezek. ii. 1, 3, 6, 8, etc., where the prophet is so addressed. 'Son of Man' in the gospels is always a self-designation of Jesus and it is found elsewhere in the NT only in Acts vii. 56; Rev. i. 13; it is therefore likely that our Lord himself is responsible for its currency in the gospel tradition and sometimes meant by it 'I, a human being'. It is also possible that he used it in an eschatological sense, but did he do so in the present instance? In the Gospel of Mark it occurs before the Caesarea Philippi story only here and in ii. 28, and in both cases it can mean 'man'. But he would have been unlikely to say that 'man on earth has power to forgive sins', i.e. sins against God, except in the sense of a man like himself specially sent by God to proclaim the Good News. So Matthew may have understood it (Matt. ix. 8), and this may have been the meaning of the tradition behind Mark, but the evangelist himself must have given the phrase the eschatological signification. In viii. 38, Mark practically identifies Jesus with the exalted Son of Man who will come in glory (cf. xiii. 26) and in xiv. 62 the Son of Man is equated with the

Son of God (cf. xiii. 32). Mark's other instances of the term, all
of which occur after Peter's confession at Caesarea Philippi,
teach that the Son of Man must suffer, be rejected, die and rise
again (viii. 31; ix. 31; x. 33, 45; xiv. 21, 41).

Other problems remain. The phrase is not found in all parts
of Jesus' recorded teaching, and is conspicuously lacking in the
parables, except where editorial work can be distinguished, e.g.
Matt. xxv. 31, which may originally have referred to King
Messiah. Nor is the phrase closely associated with Jesus' teaching about the Kingdom of God. On the other hand, in the gospels it is always found in words attributed to Jesus himself.
There is little difficulty in accepting as genuine the passages in
Q where it is used to mean 'I myself' or 'a man', or the other
Q passages where it refers to the coming judge but where Jesus
does not explicitly identify himself with this figure (e.g. Luke
xvii. 22-24; xviii. 8). It seems possible that Jesus gave teaching
about the coming of the Son of Man. Although his words were
enigmatic, perhaps because of his humility, his hearers drew the
conclusion that Jesus was to be the future judge. Mark then
belongs to a stage of tradition later than that of Q, in which the
sayings were made more explicit. Cf. *BC*, i. 368-384; *TG*, pp.
152-63 and literature cited there. N. Perrin, *A Modern Pil-
grimage in NT Christology* (Philadelphia, 1974), pp. 1-40, 58-84,
denies authenticity of the Son of Man sayings; but see B.
Lindars, *NTS*, xxii (1975), 52-72. J. M. Ford, *JBL*, lxxxvii
(1968), 257-266, holds that 'Son of Man' is a periphrasis for
'Son of God'.

The phrase **he now speaks to the paralytic** is the evangelist's aside to his readers, as in xiii. 14.

And he . . . picked up the mat; a similar conclusion to a 12
healing miracle is recounted by Lucian, *Philops*. xi.

ii. 13-17. THE CALL OF LEVI; A CONTROVERSY

**He went out again along the lake, and as the crowd kept 13
coming to him he would teach them. As he passed by he 14
saw Levi, the son of Alphaeus, sitting at the tax office, and**

he said to him, 'Follow me'. And he arose and followed
him.

15 It happened that he was having a meal in his house,
and many tax collectors and sinners were eating with
Jesus and his disciples—there were many who followed
16 him. When the scholars who belonged to the Pharisees
saw that he was eating with sinners and tax collectors,
they said to his disciples, 'Why is he eating with tax col-
17 lectors and sinners?' Jesus, hearing this, said to them,
'Healthy people have no need of a doctor, only those who
are ill. I did not come to call right-living people but
sinners.'

Controversy had begun with the healing of the paralytic,
though the thought was only in the minds of Jesus' opponents,
not expressed. He is now criticised in the presence of his disciples for associating with disreputable people (verses 15-17),
the disciples are reproached for not fasting (verse 18) and for
violating the Sabbath laws (verse 24); then the Pharisees and
Herodians are represented as plotting to destroy Jesus (iii. 6);
and, finally, he is charged with being mad and with casting out
demons through Beelzebul (iii. 21-22). Mark, or an earlier collector, has evidently gathered into one place controversies that
took place at different times. Controversy resumes in chap. vii,
and there is another group of such stories in xi. 27-xii. 27,
35-40.

14 Mark inserted the call of Levi into this group; it is not necessary for the action of verses 15-17. The scene is set **along the
lake,** as in i. 16-20. The four disciples mentioned in the earlier
call are included in the list of the Twelve (iii. 14-19), but **Levi,
the son of Alphaeus,** who is summoned in a similar manner,
is not in this list and therefore appears to be a thirteenth disciple. Elsewhere Levi is mentioned only in the *Gospel of Peter*
(xiv. 60). The evangelist Matthew sought to solve the apparent
problem by identifying this disciple with Matthew, one of the
Twelve (Matt. ix. 9). It would be curious, however, for a Jew
to have two Jewish given names, Matthew and Levi, unless he
was 'Matthew the Levite'. Origen's solution (*Contra Celsum*
i. 62) was that Levi was a follower of Jesus but not an apostle.

D, Θ, some OL codices and Tatian read at this point 'James
the son of Alphaeus'; cf. iii. 18. It must, however, be remembered that in the OT there are thirteen tribes, Levi plus the
twelve, since the two Joseph tribes of Ephraim and Manasseh
are always separately enumerated. This disciple corresponds to
the priestly tribe of Levi, which has a special prominence in
Jewish thought; cf. Farrer, *St. Matthew and St. Mark*, pp. 36 f.
In this there is a certain irony, for Levi is a tax collector, called
as he is **sitting at the tax office.** The contrast between Jesus
and his Pharisaic opponents could not be suggested more vividly.

The scene shifts to **a meal in his house;** literally, 'he was 15
reclining at table'. This was the practice followed by Jewish
city dwellers at formal dinners, but although the verb is used
here the custom of reclining may not have been current in a
Galilean village. In the present context the house is Levi's, but
in the underlying tradition it is perhaps the house mentioned in
verse 1. The **tax collectors** are not the wealthy tax-farmers
(*publicani*) but their employees, who were generally drawn from
the local population. The gospels elsewhere couple them with
sinners, as in Matt. xi. 19 = Luke vii. 34; Luke xv. 1; Matt.
xviii. 17; xxi. 31; and cf. Matt. v. 46. Their position gave them
opportunities to extort money for themselves and in any event
the tax collector was not popular. In Galilee taxes and customs
revenues went to the government of Herod Antipas, while in
Judaea they were collected for the Roman administration.
Lucian (*Necyom.* xi) speaks of 'adulterers, brothel-keepers, tax
collectors, flatterers and informers'. The 'sinners' here mentioned may include those of evil life and also perhaps the *'amme
ha-aretz* or 'people of the land' (originally 'country folk') who
neglected the details of the Law, particularly as taught by the
Pharisees. R. Hillel said, 'No *'am ha-aretz* is religious'. The
hostility between this class and the Pharisees is illustrated by a
remark of R. Aḳiba (*c.* A.D. 132): 'When I was an *'am ha-aretz*
I used to say, "If I could get hold of one of the scholars I would
bite him like an ass." "You mean, like a dog," said his disciples. "No," said Aḳiba, "an ass's bite breaks bones."'

Here Mark for the first time mentions the **disciples** (μαθηταί), by which he usually means the Twelve, as distinct from
the **many ... who followed him.**

16 **The scholars who belonged to the Pharisees** is a precise statement. Not all rabbis or scribes were Pharisees, though the great scholars, whose work is known to us, belonged to this party. The origin of the term Pharisees, *perushim*, is unknown. It must mean 'separated'; perhaps separated from sin or defilement, or from sinners. The incident in which Peter drew away from the Gentiles (Gal. ii. 12) illustrates the idea. The Pharisees are first mentioned in connexion with events of the reign of John Hyrcanus (135–105 B.C.). Together with the Essenes, they probably developed out of the *hasidim* who in Maccabean times formed groups to keep the Law more strictly and resist the influence of paganism. They were opposed to John Hyrcanus, Aristobulus and Alexander Jannaeus because of the despotism of these kings and their preference for the Sadducees, who were more lax in their interpretation of the Law. The Pharisees first came into power under Queen Alexandra Salome (78–69 B.C.). They resisted Herod the Great and the Romans only when religious issues were at stake and were generally pacifists who tried to abstain from politics, though there was one fanatical group among them that believed in revolt against Rome and finally gained the upper hand at the time of the first Jewish revolt (A.D. 66–70). In the time of Jesus, as in later Judaism, they were the most influential religious party; cf. Josephus, *Vita* xxxviii; *Ant.* xviii. 1. 3; Moore, *Judaism*, i. 56-82; L. Finkelstein, *The Pharisees* (Philadelphia, 1938). They had some influence even on the early Christians; cf. Acts xi. 2-3; xxi. 20-21; xxiii. 6; Gal. ii. 4-5, 12; Matt. xxiii. 2-3. In general, however, the gospels see them in the light of hostility between Church and Synagogue, while modern Judaism (which derives from Pharisaism) tends to idealise them. It is only fair to acknowledge that the Pharisees were part of the main stream of the Jewish tradition stemming from the OT. Indeed, some of the later Psalms (e.g. cxix) represent the Pharisaic ideal very well. The great rabbis of the Tannaitic period were deeply concerned for the material and spiritual welfare of the people as well as zealous for the Law, and their influence was ordinarily thrown on the side of mercy and loving kindness. For example, they mitigated the harshness of the divorce law, by means of a legal fiction provided for a farmer to borrow when the nearness of the sabbatical year

made it almost impossible, protected the accused by the
cross-examination of witnesses, and carefully restricted the
application of the death penalty. They were at the same time
traditionalists and innovators; in theory all the Law came from
Moses on Sinai through the 'tradition of the elders' (cf. vii. 3),
and the oral law was equally binding with the written; yet this
oral law was continually being enlarged by decisions of the
rabbis, often on the basis of ingenious interpretation of scripture. Montefiore remarks on Jesus' 'greatness and originality',
as shown by this passage, and the fact that 'he opened a new
chapter in men's attitude toward sinners'. 'Nevertheless,' he
says, 'the Rabbis would not have condemned Jesus merely because he cared for the outcast, the poor and the sinners. They
too welcomed the *repentant* sinner. And they were eager to re-
lieve distress, to mitigate suffering. Any other description of
them is untrue. But the Law of God came first. God came
before themselves, and even before their neighbour' (*The
Synoptic Gospels, ad loc.*).

Thus when they asked, **Why is he eating with tax collectors and sinners?** the difference between Jesus and the
scribes turned on the nature of God's will, for Jesus also gave
the demands of God first place. The Pharisees believed that
God's all-loving will towards man was contained perfectly in the
Law as they understood it, even though 'the disciples of the
learned must not sit at table in company of the *'am ha-aretz'*
(Berachoth 43b). Jesus saw the supreme revelation of God's will
in his outreach through the Good News. This annuls defilement
and the fear of it.

The answer of Jesus is in the form of a poetic *mashal* or pro- 17
verb consisting of two parts, each containing a contrast. For the
form, cf. Prov. xiv. 21. A similar proverb is attributed to Diogenes in Stobaeus, *Eclog.* iii. 13. 43 (iii. 462. 14 ed. Hense).[1]
There is no reflection on the question whether, in the absolute
sense, there are any **healthy people.** Paul saw this problem
(Rom. iii. 12, 19-20), but Jesus did not hesitate to draw the usual

---

[1] 'When an Athenian criticised Diogenes on the ground that, although he
praised the Spartans most highly, he did not live among them, he remarked,
"A physician, in that he brings good health, does not spend his time among
the healthy".'

contrast between those who are on the whole **right-living** and those who are **sinners**. He came **to call** the latter to the Kingdom of God; Lohmeyer sees in this invitation, connected with table-fellowship, a reference to the coming Messianic Banquet (cf. vi. 30-44; also Matt. xxii. 1-4, 8-10 =Luke xiv. 16-21).

ii. 18-22. CONTROVERSY OVER FASTING

18 **John's disciples and the Pharisees were fasting, and people came and said to him, 'Why do John's disciples**
19 **and the Pharisees' disciples fast, and yours do not?' Jesus said to them, 'Can the men of the wedding party fast**
20 **while the bridegroom is still at the party? But days will come when the bridegroom will be taken away from them, and then they will fast—on that day!'**
21 **'No one sews a patch of raw new cloth on an old garment. If anyone does, what he put in pulls away, new**
22 **away from old, and there is a worse tear.' 'No one puts new wine in old skins. If anyone does, the wine bursts the skins, and the wine and the skins are gone.'**

18   The only obligatory **fasting** was on the Day of Atonement (*Yom kippur*). Special fast days were sometimes proclaimed in times of emergency, such as drought. In addition, individuals and groups sometimes fasted out of penitence, sorrow, or as a special act of devotion, and there is some evidence for fasting on Mondays and Thursdays (*Didache*, viii. 1). Since Jesus' disciples constituted an earnest religious brotherhood, it astonished many that they did not follow the example of **John's disciples and the Pharisees;** cf. Matt. xi. 18 =Luke vii. 33.

The present section gives two answers to the question **Why . . . yours do not:** (1) fasting is inappropriate; (2) later, after the Crucifixion, Jesus' disciples will fast. The first answer seems to be original and is reinforced by verses 21-22; the second probably reflects the later thought and custom of the Church.

19   The age inaugurated by the Good News is compared to the most joyful of all festivities, and Jesus' disciples are like **men of**

the wedding party, literally 'sons of the bridechamber', i.e. friends of the groom or other guests. For the figure of the wedding, cf. Matt. xxii. 2-3; xxv. 1-12; Luke xii. 36. That joy and feasting characterised Jesus' life is shown by Matt. xi. 19 =Luke vii. 34 and the parables of Matt. xiii. 44-46. The parable of the Great Supper connects this figure with that of the Messianic Banquet. In the ancient orient the **bridegroom,** rather than the bride, was the centre of the festivities, and the party ended when the groom took the bride to his home. Mark perhaps thought of Jesus as the heavenly bridegroom (cf. Eph. v. 22-32; Rev. xxi. 2; Hos. ii. 19), but the original saying was not allegorical; the point was that in a time of joy no one should fast. Klostermann cites an Indian proverb: 'Who eats gruel on Divali-day?' The phrase 'As long as the bridegroom is with them they cannot fast' should be omitted, with D 33, OL, etc.

Early Christians could not avoid thinking of the **days . . . 20 when the bridegroom will be taken away from them** (cf. John xvi. 20; ix. 4), and it is a natural contrast to the joy mentioned in verse 19. In this way Mark for the first time suggests the shadow of the Cross, which after Caesarea Philippi falls increasingly over the narrative. Rawlinson suggests that the words **and then they will fast—on that day!** already refer to the Friday fast in commemoration of the Crucifixion. At least by the time of the *Didache*, fasts were observed on Wednesday and Friday (*Did.* viii. 1).

Jesus may not have forbidden fasting—there is no evidence, for example, that he objected to the Day of Atonement—but according to the tradition he set forth conditions for a fast that would be genuine (Matt. vi. 16-18), quite in the spirit of the prophets (cf. Isa. lviii). Yet the tone of his ministry is that of wonder and thanksgiving for God's new order, rather than penitence and sorrow.

Mark inserts at this point two sayings that are among the most radical in the gospel tradition.

No one sews a patch of raw new (literally 'unfulled') cloth 21 on an old garment. The result of such foolish action would be that **what he put in** ($\tau\grave{o}$ $\pi\lambda\acute{\eta}\rho\omega\mu\alpha$, probably an Aramaism; the word is sometimes used technically to mean 'the fullness of .God', but here only 'that which fills up', i.e. the patch) shrinks

and **pulls away . . . and there is a worse tear.** The language
is curious and difficult grammatically. The point must be that
for the new age, as contrasted with the old, an entirely new set
of practices is appropriate. In this context the saying abolishes
fasting, but we do not know the original occasion or how far
Jesus might have carried the principle. There is evidence that
he was not opposed to the old Law as such (Matt. v. 23-24);
with him it is not so much a question of old and new as of what
is right in the new order.

22   The twin saying is to the same point: **No one puts new wine
into old skins;** cf. the similar proverb in Seneca, *Ep.* lxxxiii. 16.
(Just as new wine bursts the butt, so excessive drinking makes
a man reveal secrets.) Wine that has just begun to ferment
cannot be contained in skins at all; the reference is to wine that
is not fully aged, in which some fermentation still takes place.
Only elastic new skins can bear the pressure. Both logia seem
to teach the danger of the new to the old (Klostermann)—perhaps this is ironic playfulness on Jesus' part, or he adopts sayings
of his critics—at any rate, the hesitation of the early Church in
admitting Gentiles illustrates the fear felt by Jewish Christians,
even those who had known Jesus in the flesh. D and several OL
MSS. omit, no doubt correctly, 'But new wine [must be put] in
new skins'. This addition was probably made to early MSS. of
Mark used by the later evangelists; cf. J. P. Brown, *JBL*,
lxxviii (1959), 222.

ii. 23-28. CONTROVERSY OVER THE SABBATH

23 It happened that on the Sabbath he was passing through
     grain fields, and his disciples as they made their way
24 began to pluck the heads of grain. And the Pharisees said
     to him, 'Look! Why do they do something not permitted
25 on the Sabbath?' He said to them, 'Haven't you ever read
     what David did, when he was in need and he and his com-
26 panions were hungry?—how he entered God's house (it
     was in the time when Abiathar was high priest) and ate
     the loaves set before God, which only the priests are per-

**mitted to eat, and gave some also to his companions?'
And he said to them: 'The Sabbath was made for man's** 27
sake, not man for the Sabbath's sake. So then, the Son of 28
Man is master even of the Sabbath.'

The question of **the Sabbath** is for Judaism more important 23
than that of fasting. The holiness of the seventh day of the week
was believed to go back to the week of creation (Gen. ii. 2-3).
For **his disciples . . . to pluck the heads of grain** (American idiom; 'ears of corn' can refer to wheat in England, not
America) was harvesting and therefore a violation of the law forbidding thirty-nine acts of labour on the Sabbath (Exod. xxxiv.
21; Mishnah Shabbath vii. 2); indeed this applied to as small
an amount as two heads (Maimonides, *Hilchoth Shabbath* viii. 3;
cf. Philo, *Vita Mos.* ii. 22). Many rules were developed out of
Exod. xvi. 29, such as that of the Sabbath day's journey of
approximately a mile (Acts i. 12; Jerome, *Ep.* cxxi). Fasting was
forbidden on the Sabbath (Jubilees 1. 11; Judith viii. 6; cf. also
Jub. ii. 29; 1. 10). In a few cases other duties overrode the Sabbath law, such as temple offerings (Num. xxviii. 9-10; Matt.
xii. 5), and situations where a human life was in danger (Mishnah Erubin x. 13-14; Yoma viii. 6). At times the Jews even
abstained from military defence (Josephus, *Ant.* xii. 6. 2; xiv.
10. 12; 1 Macc. ii. 34-42).

The scene is laid in the spring when the wheat or barley is
still standing and ripe, or nearly so. The disciples **made their
way** through the fields (for a similar phrase cf. Judges xvii.
8 LXX), perhaps where there was no path. On other days of the
week there would have been no criticism; the law permitted
gleaning the corners of fields (Lev. xix. 9; xxiii. 22; Ruth ii) and
no one would object to a few handfuls of grain being taken by
wayfarers (cf. Mishnah Peah viii. 7). It is not even said that the
disciples were hungry, though probably verse 25 implies it;
whether they were or not, the only question has to do with the
Sabbath. Jesus answers by pointing to the example of **David,** 25
who committed an apparent breach of the Law but was not
condemned for it (1 Sam. xxi. 1-6). It is implied that what David
did could not be wrong, and that therefore the disciples were
justified in their trivial labour to obtain food. The text wrongly

26 dates the incident **in the time when Abiathar was high priest;** it was in that of his father Ahimelech. The phrase is omitted by D W it sy[s] and may possibly be a gloss. **God's house** was then at Nob, near Jerusalem. The **loaves set before God,** i.e. 'the shew-bread', were prescribed by Exod. xxv. 30; xxxv. 13; xxxix. 36. The bread was baked on Friday and laid on the holy table early on the Sabbath (Josephus, *Ant.* iii. 10. 7). On the following Sabbath, when it was replaced by the fresh bread, it could then be eaten by **the priests** (Mishnah Menahoth xi). The exceptional behaviour of David puzzled the rabbis, who advanced several theories; e.g. the bread may have been burned and therefore had not been offered to God at all. In the present case they would have ruled that no exception was permitted, since the lives of Jesus' disciples were not in danger.

The two Sabbath controversies (here and iii. 1-6) deal with concrete instances, as in so much rabbinic discussion. It is difficult to derive a general Sabbath principle from Jesus' teaching.

27 The phrase **And he said to them** may indicate that the following two sayings are from a different source or sources. The narrative ends in the fashion of a paradigm or pronouncement story, but it is curious that there are two sayings, not one.

Only Mark contains the logion of verse 27; the parallel passages in Matthew and Luke omit it. It has therefore been conjectured that it was not in the earliest MSS. of Mark which the later evangelists used. On the other hand, it fits well with the original point of the story and it has a Jewish parallel attributed to R. Simeon (*c.* A.D. 180), 'To you the Sabbath is given over, and you are not given over to the Sabbath'. The principle would therefore be that, since the Sabbath is meant for man's rest and enjoyment, the trivial plucking of grain does not violate it. The point of John vii. 22-23 is different: Christ, and therefore the Christian, is free from the Sabbath law.

The curious Cod. 2427, which is of doubtful genuineness, 28 includes verse 27 but not 28. But the second saying must surely have been written by Mark; it is in entire agreement with his ideas that **the Son of Man is master even of the Sabbath.** As a detached saying, the verse might mean 'Man is master even of the Sabbath'; thus it would have much the same point as verse 27 and its Jewish parallel. But to Mark it means immeasurably more. The celestial Son of Man, now present on earth, not only has the authority to forgive sins but is sovereign over the sabbath law itself. Perhaps he even thinks of the Son of Man as the Primal Man who was created just before or just after the Sabbath and thus has this unique authority. It is not surprising that Mark mentions the Son of Man twice in this chapter, even though the concept is not developed before Peter's confession at Caesarea Philippi; it is one of the partial unveilings of the secret of Jesus' nature, not yet understood even by the most intimate disciples.   Cf. F. W. Beare, *JBL*, lxxix (1960), 130-36.

The Son of Man theology in any event involves the deep insight that God himself is master of his own Law; his sovereign authority overshadows it, whether he exercises it directly, or through the Son of Man as the Man sent to proclaim the new order.

CHAPTER III

iii. 1-6. HEALING OF THE MAN WITH THE WITHERED HAND

1 Again, he went into a synagogue, and there was a man
2 there whose hand was withered. And they watched him
—Will he heal him on the Sabbath?—so they could accuse
3 him. He said to the man who had the withered hand,
4 'Stand up in front'. And he said to them, 'On the Sabbath
is one permitted to do good or bad, to save a life or kill?'
5 But they kept silent. And looking about him angrily,
grieved at the hard stupidity of their minds, he said to
the man, 'Stretch out your hand'. So he stretched it out
6 and the hand was restored; and the Pharisees went right
out and conspired against him with the Herodians, to see
how they might destroy him.

The many stories of Sabbath healings contained in the gospels
show that this theme was much used in early Christian apologetic. (1) In the story of the deformed woman, Luke xiii. 10-17,
Jesus argues that other Jews will untie and water an ox or an ass
on the Sabbath; therefore this woman, being not an animal but
a daughter of Abraham, should also be freed. (2) The account
of the dropsical man, Luke xiv. 1-6, contains (as in Mark iii. 4)
a question asked by Jesus: if your son or your ox falls into a well,
will you not pull him out on the Sabbath? Evidently this stood in
Q; it is partly represented in Matt. xii. 11. (3) The man at the
pool of Bethesda, John v. 1-18, is criticised because he carries
his bed on the Sabbath. The main part of this story is similar
in tone and content to the synoptic tradition, but Jesus' defence
is Johannine: 'My Father is working until now, and I am working'. (4) The man born blind, John ix. Here the Sabbath controversy is only one motif among several, and Jesus makes no
formal justification of his act of healing. Two points are, how-

ever, worthy of notice: (*a*) the man who is healed argues that if Jesus were a sinner and not from God he could not heal (cf. notes on ii. 23-28, above); (*b*) Jesus' judgement involves a blinding of the Pharisees (cf. Mark iii. 5). (5) Note finally that Mark i. 21-28 tells of a Sabbath exorcism in the synagogue. There is no mention of a controversy, only of astonishment, but to Mark the event is important as a witness to Jesus' person. The evangelist's view of the Sabbath controversies is theologically akin to that of John, although less developed, for Mark sees a Christological significance in them, while those in Luke (at least one of which may have been in Q), have more of the form of a debate within Judaism.

Again; the reference may be to the Sabbath incidents of i. 21 **1** and ii. 23, or the word may mean 'here is another example'. Nothing is said of the **man** except that his **hand was withered.** In controversy stories the centre of interest is not in the disease or the healing, and details are kept to a minimum. Cf. the healing attributed to an unnamed 'man of God' in 1 Kings xiii. 1-10; stories in the Elijah and Elisha cycles are often models for miracle stories in Mark. The emperor Vespasian is said to have healed a man with a diseased hand (*manum aeger*: Tacitus, *Hist.* iv. 81). The story in the *Gospel of the Nazarenes* probably had the usual form of a miracle tale, for the man said: 'I was a mason seeking a living with my hands; I beg you, Jesus, to restore my health to me, that I may not beg shamefully for my food'.

Will he heal him on the Sabbath? Here Mark's style, with **2** the future tense in direct discourse, is curiously colloquial. **Stand up in front** (εἰς τὸ μέσον), possibly 'in the midst', but **3** at any rate where the man could be seen; cf. Matt. xiv. 6; John viii. 3, 9.

Jesus' question, which appears to be an *argumentum ad* **4** *hominem*, reminds one of rabbinical debate. From the point of view of his opponents he does not deal directly with the issue but tries to put them on the horns of a dilemma. They would agree that on **the Sabbath** only an action in accordance with the Law is good; of course **to save a life** is **to do good** (cf. on ii. 23-28), but they do not see that this is the question. Jesus approaches the problem in a different way which they consider illegitimate. For him, to heal is to save a life; it is part of God's invasion of the world with the Good News. In the earlier part of the gospel the verb σώζειν is usually employed in its original non-technical sense of 'rescue', 'make well', 'make alive', but the evangelist may have begun to invest it with the reference to religious salvation. To neglect the opportunity to restore soundness and health, merely because it is the Sabbath, is **to . . . kill**. As Mark tells the story, it also contains a dramatic irony: the Pharisees are about to plot Jesus' downfall. Who therefore is in the right, the one who would heal or the one who would destroy the healer?

5   Mark elsewhere pictures Jesus as **looking about him,** cf. iii. 34; v. 32; x. 23; xi. 11; here it is **angrily,** because he is **grieved at the hard stupidity of their minds** (literally 'their hearts'; in Semitic speech 'heart' denotes the inner man, intellect as well as emotion). Their hostility keeps them from judging the issue on its merits. Farrer, *A Study in St. Mark,* p. 76, sees in this an echo of the hardening of Pharaoh's heart (Exod. ix. 34-35; x. 27-28) and the anger of Moses (Exod. xi. 8). The theme is further developed in iv. 11-12. D it sy[s] here read νεκρώσει, 'deadness', for πωρώσει, but πωρόω is a Marcan word (vi. 52; viii. 17). πώρωσις is used in the NT only here and in Rom. xi. 25; Eph. iv. 18; in the former passage it refers also to the rejection of the gospel by Israel.

6   It is surprising that the **Pharisees** should plan to **destroy** Jesus. We know from Jewish sources that they could be bitter in religious controversy, but the great rabbis appear to be warm-hearted, humanitarian, and often tolerant (cf. Acts v. 34-40). There were friendly contacts between Jesus and individual rabbis (xii. 28-34; Luke x. 25-28) and some early Christians were Pharisees (Acts xv. 5; xxiii. 6). It was the Sadducean high priest and his friends who, with Pilate, were responsible for the Crucifixion. On the other hand, the rabbinical sources distinguish between good and bad Pharisees, and these may have been fanatics. Here it is said that they **conspired with the Herodians.** This group is mentioned only here and in xii. 13 (= Matt. xxii. 16); it must refer to political circles close to Herod Antipas, not to a religious party. Josephus (*Ant.* xiv. 15. 10) mentions τοὺς τὰ Ἡρώδου φρονοῦντας. Such persons would have wished

to put down any movement which, like that of John the Baptist, might be a danger to the political order (cf. vi. 14-29). For the political unrest in Palestine in the first century, cf. Johnson, *JOT*, chap. vii.

iii. 7-12. SUMMARY OF HEALINGS AND EXORCISMS

Jesus with his disciples withdrew to the lake, and a great 7 crowd from Galilee followed him, and also from Judaea 8 and Jerusalem and Idumaea and Transjordan and the neighbourhood of Tyre and Sidon—a great crowd, which heard of all that he was doing, came to him. He told his 9 disciples to have a skiff wait for him because of the crowd so that they would not press him too hard; for he 10 had healed many people, so that as many as had diseases were falling all over him to touch him. The unclean 11 spirits, too, whenever they saw him, would fall on him and cry out, 'You are the Son of God!' He repeatedly 12 commanded them not to make him known.

These verses form a transition from the first set of controversies to the next important section, which deals with the appointment and training of the Twelve through word and example (iii. 13-v. 34).

He withdraws **to the lake,** for here he can teach and heal in 7 greater quiet, freed from the controversies in the synagogue, however necessary they are in the accomplishment of his task. The **great crowd** is more numerous than that which followed John the Baptist, for it includes not only people **from Judaea 8 and Jerusalem** (cf. i. 5), but also from all parts of Palestine inhabited by Jews. **Idumaea** is omitted by S* W Θ sy^s and some OL MSS., as by Luke. This region had been forcibly converted to Judaism by John Hyrcanus. Transjordan, πέραν τοῦ Ἰορδάνου, probably the region between the Jabbok and the Arnon. Mark omits Samaria; unlike Luke and John, he knows of no Samaritan mission.

Although this is an editorial section, largely in Marcan style,
9 it probably contains actual reminiscences. This is particularly
true of the order **to have a skiff wait for him.** There is no
reason, other than biographical interest, why this should be included, and Matthew and Luke omit it; cf. iv. 1, where he
10 teaches from the boat. In the LXX the word **diseases** ($\mu\acute{a}\sigma\tau\iota$-
$\gamma\alpha s$), literally 'scourges', denotes severe sufferings sent from
God; this usage is paralleled in Greek stories; cf. O. Wein-
11 reich, *Antike Heilungswunder* (Giessen, 1909), pp. 60 f. For the
cry of the **unclean spirits . . . 'You are the Son of God!'** and
the command of secrecy, cf. on i. 21-28, 32-34. The reading of
Cod. 2427, 'You are God', can scarcely be original.

iii. 13-19. APPOINTMENT OF THE TWELVE

13 **He went up into the mountain and called the ones whom**
he himself wished to have, and they came away to him.
14 **And he appointed twelve men, so that they could be with**
15 **him and so that he could send them out to announce the**
16 **News, and to have authority to cast out demons. He**
appointed these twelve men: on Simon he fastened the
17 **name Peter [Rock]; and James the son of Zebedee and**
John the brother of James—on them he fastened the name
18 **Boanerges, that is, 'sons of thunder'; and Andrew and**
Philip and Bartholomew and Matthew and Thomas and
19 **James the son of Alphaeus and Thaddaeus and Simon the**
Cananaean and Judas Iscarioth, the man who betrayed
him.

The training of the inner group of disciples occupies an important place in all four gospels. Matthew deals with it elabor-
ately, devoting a major section to it (viii. 1-xi. 1) and placing
it after the Sermon on the Mount, which he intends for all
Christians. Luke has a less formal arrangement; the Twelve are
chosen just before the Sermon on the Plain (vi. 13-16), but their
training continues after the Resurrection (xxiv. 25-53; Acts i.
1-11). John's gospel is throughout an education of the disciples

but the full secret of Christ's work and person is revealed in the Upper Room and on the Mount of Olives (xiii-xvii; xx. 19-29), with a final appearance at the Sea of Galilee (xxi. 15-22). It is a curious fact that the appointment of the Twelve is the only pericope that occupies a different place in all three synoptic gospels. Each of the evangelists wished to use it in accordance with his own literary plan, and its function in each gospel therefore varies slightly. Mark places the choice of the Twelve at this point but their training proceeds by stages, with a climax in chap. xiii, until at last they are bidden to go to Galilee to see him (xvi. 7).

Mark belongs to an early stage in the development of the concept of apostleship and apostolic authority. There are no signs that he is particularly concerned with church order; he regards the Twelve as the pattern of those disciples who proclaim the Good News and follow the Son of Man, who is also Son of God. Their weakness, even their denial of Jesus, is emphasised (e.g. x. 35-40; xiv. 37-42, 50, 66-72) but in spite of this they are not rejected. Just as John the Baptist (i. 2) and Jesus (ix. 37) were specially sent by God (cf. also xii. 2-6), so Jesus commissions the inner group of disciples to do the kind of work that he has already begun. Mark often calls them 'disciples', as in ii. 15-16, 18, 23; iv. 34; vi. 35, etc., but when he does so he does not clearly distinguish them from the larger group of adherents; otherwise he calls them the Twelve (vi. 7; ix. 35; x. 32; xi. 11; xiv. 10, 17, 20, 43). For the attempt to isolate a 'Twelve-source' cf. pp. 27 f. Originally an 'apostle' seems to have been anyone who, like St. Paul, had a commission from the risen Christ to proclaim the gospel and found churches (e.g. Rom. i. 1; xvi. 7; 1 Cor. ix. 5; Gal. i. 1, 19; Acts xiv. 14); thus the term could be used to include the Twelve but was not confined to them. The Hebrew word shāliaḥ corresponded to this. A shāliaḥ was one whom an individual or a court commissioned as legal agent, or who was entrusted with the offering of prayer. In later centuries the nāsî or Jewish patriarch often sent out such an apostle to collect funds or to root out heresy, and Paul's work, both before and after his conversion, had some similarity to this. It is the author of Luke-Acts who is responsible, more than any one person, for the equation of the Twelve with the apostles (e.g. Luke vi. 13; Acts i. 2, 26). When Matthew speaks of 'the twelve disciples' (e.g. x. 1) he thinks of them as the special students of a rabbi, but he also uses the term 'the twelve apostles' (x. 2). Mark, however, calls them 'apostles' only once (vi. 30), though he uses the verb ἀποστέλλω, 'to send with a commission', twice in connexion with their appointment and work (here and in vi. 7). This suggests that for him the words are not yet technical terms.

13   **He went up into the mountain.** The phrase εἰς τὸ ὄρος might mean simply 'into the hill country', but Mark perhaps thinks of a particular mountain or an ideal mountain as the place of revelation. Just as God called Moses and Israel to himself on Sinai (Exod. xix. 20) and as Elijah met God on Horeb (1 Kings xix. 8), so Jesus went into a mountain to pray (vi. 46) and in such a place he was transfigured (ix. 2). Cf. the parallel, Luke vi. 12, where Jesus spends the night in prayer before calling the Twelve. Matthew omits mentioning the mountain at this point (x. 1) but it is the scene of revelation for the Great Sermon (v. 1) and the final commission (xxviii. 16). Now Jesus summons out of the larger group of disciples **the ones whom he himself**
14 **wished to have** (cf. John xv. 16). They are **twelve;** that Mark has in mind the tribes of Israel has already been indicated by the choice of Levi (ii. 14) who as a thirteenth completes the number of twelve plus Levi. At an early stage of Christian theological thought these disciples were considered as constituting the rulers of Israel in the age to come (Matt. xix. 28 =Luke xxii. 28-30) and this apparently explains why a substitute had to be found for Judas Iscarioth (Acts i. 15-26) and also why a college of twelve was not maintained after the original disciples died. The idea may be paralleled in the Qumran Manual of Discipline (1QS viii. 1); 'In the council of the community there shall be twelve men and three priests, perfect in all that has been revealed from the whole Law'; cf. S. E. Johnson, *ZAW*, lxvi (1954) (=K. Stendahl [ed.], *The Scrolls and the NT*, 1958, p. 134). There is, however, no indication that Mark was acquainted with this theological development; cf. x. 35-45, where the intimate disciples are promised only a share in Jesus' cup and baptism.

It may have been a coincidence that the special disciples were

approximately twelve in number. Why should the personnel of
the group not have varied from time to time? Certainly there is
variation in the names. In place of Thaddaeus, D and some OL
MSS. read 'Lebbaeus', and the MSS. of Matt. x. 3 variously
read 'Lebbaeus', 'Thaddaeus', 'Lebbaeus surnamed Thaddaeus', and 'Thaddaeus surnamed Lebbaeus'. Luke vi. 14-16
and Acts i. 13 include no disciple with either name but in his
place, though in a different order, a 'Judas of James'. The
second century *Epistle of the Apostles* (chap. ii) has a very different list, in which James of Alphaeus, Thaddaeus and Simon
the Cananaean are replaced by Nathanael, Judas Zelotes and
Cephas. While John speaks of the Twelve he never lists them;
the disciples he mentions are Andrew, Simon Peter (i. 40),
Philip (i. 43), Nathanael (i. 45), Judas Iscariot (vi. 71). Judas not
Iscariot (xiv. 22), a disciple known to the high priest (xviii. 15-
16), a disciple whom Jesus loved (xix. 26), Joseph of Arimathaea
(xix. 38), and Thomas (xx. 24). Jewish tradition knows of a disciple of Jesus named Jacob of Kephar-Sekanya (Aboda Zara
16b-17a) and the Babylonian Talmud gives a list of five disciples: Mattai, Naqai, Netzer, Buni and Todah (Sanhedrin 43a).
Cf. also Lake, *BC*, v, 41-46.

Jesus **appointed** them (ἐποίησεν, 'made'); Lohmeyer translates *schuf*, i.e. created; this is a new creation or foundation. The
purpose is, first, to **be with him,** to share his life like the
disciples of a rabbi; second, to be sent **to announce the News;** 15
and third, **to have authority to cast out demons.** Matt. x. 1
includes this last but Luke vi. 13 does not; in its place Luke adds
'whom he also named apostles', a phrase that has crept into
many MSS. of Mark at this point. The sending of the Twelve
again specifies the authority to cast out demons (vi. 7 = Luke
ix. 1 = Matt. x. 1); but it is absent in the commission to the
Seventy (Luke x. 1-16), which may be the oldest form of the
tradition. Here the disciples discover to their surprise that they
have the power (Luke x. 17). But it is Mark's idea that the disciples, from the beginning, participate in the entire ministry of
their Lord.

Simon (Σίμων) is a good Greek name, but here it represents 16
Simeon, which was borne by one of the sons of Jacob (Gen.
xxix. 33); the Semitic form is found in Acts xv. 14; 2 Pet. i. 1.

The surname **Peter**, Πέτρος, was formed by giving πέτρα, 'rock', a masculine instead of a feminine ending; thus he is the 'Rock-Man'. In Aramaic the corresponding *Kepha* would not change its form. In the slightly Hellenised form Cephas (Κηφᾶς) this appears in John i. 42; 1 Cor. i. 12; iii. 22; ix. 5; xv. 5; Gal. i. 18; ii. 9, 11, 14. The nickname is so deeply imbedded in the tradition that it usually supersedes the proper name. Matt. xvi. 17-19 contains an account of its origin; whether or not it is historical, Jesus must have called Simon 'the Rock' to encourage him to be firm, so that the disciples could rally round him (Luke xxii. 31-32; cf. John xxi. 15-19). In Matt. xvi. 17 he is given the patronymic Βαριωνᾶ, Bar-jona or 'son of Jonah', but in John i. 42 and xxi. 15-17 he is 'Simon son of John'.

17   **James** is the usual English equivalent of Ἰάκωβος, Jacob, a common Hebrew name. **Zebedee**, Ζεβεδαῖος (cf. i. 19-20) is found in Aramaic tomb inscriptions in the form Zabdi. **John**, Yohanan or Yehohanan, 'God is gracious', is likewise a common name. The two are nicknamed Boanerges, perhaps Aram. *bânereges*, **'sons of thunder'**. Various attempts have been made to identify the Heb. or Aram. word, e.g. *reḡēz*, thunder; *reḡêsh*, restless noise or wrath; Jerome suggested *benê ra'am*. This name may have been derived from traits in their character (cf. ix. 38; Luke ix. 54). Peter, James and John appear to have a particularly close relation to Jesus; cf. ix. 2; x. 35. In xiii. 3 Andrew is included; he is apparently fourth in rank, as he is fourth in the lists of Mark and Acts. Matthew and Luke mention him after Simon, coupling him with his brother.

18   **Andrew and Philip** are Greek names; the proportion of Greek and Semitic names in the gospel is similar to that found on Jewish ossuaries and tomb inscriptions. **Philip** is always fifth in the lists, as Bartholomew is sixth, except in Acts. The name is evidently a patronymic, *bar talmai*, perhaps 'son of Ptolemaeus'; the given name is lost to us. **Matthew**, Mattai or Mattathiah, is seventh in Mark, Luke and Acts, but eighth in Matt. x. 3, where he is called 'the tax-collector'. In that gospel he replaces Levi the son of Alphaeus (Mark ii. 14 =Matt. ix. 9). **Thomas**, Aram. *teômâ*, is known to us only by his sobriquet 'the Twin'; in John (xi. 16; xx. 24; xxi. 2) this is translated into

Greek. The *Gospel of Thomas* (80: 11, p. 3) names him Didymos Judas Thomas. His position in the lists varies. **James the son of Alphaeus** (Aram. *ḥalpai*?) is always ninth; some MSS. of Mark substitute him for Levi in ii. 14. **Thaddaeus**, Aram. *taddai*, could stand for the Greek names Theodotus or Theudas. J. Klausner, *Jesus of Nazareth* (London, 1927), p. 284, argues, however, that this and 'Lebbaeus', found in some MSS. of Mark and Matthew, are Aramaic words of kindred sense, the first meaning 'breasts' and the second 'heart'. If so, both may be nicknames. As the eleventh disciple the lists of Luke and Acts have Judas the son of James (cf. John xiv. 22). **Simon the Cananaean:** the word cannot mean 'Canaanite' or 'of Cana' (cf. John ii. 1), but is evidently *qan'ana*, zealot, the sobriquet attached to him by Luke-Acts. Possibly he had been a member of the revolutionary party. H. Hirschberg, *JBL*, lxi (1942), 171-191, argues that Simon the Zealot and Simon Barjona were originally identical, interpreting *bariona* as 'violent'.

The synoptic lists agree that the twelfth is **Judas Iscarioth,** 19 'Ἰσκαριώθ as here or ὁ 'Ἰσκαριώτης, Matt. x. 4; xxvi. 14; Luke xxii. 3; John vi. 71. Jerome suggested that he came from the tribe of Issachar. This and the derivation *ish Kerioth*, 'man of Kerioth', i.e. from a village of this name, are unlikely. The most probable conjectures are that it is a corruption of *sicarius*, swordsman or assassin (the zealots were so called at the time of the First Revolt), or that it means 'liar' or 'false one', *shᵉqaryâ* or *ishqaryâ*; cf. C. C. Torrey, *HTR*, xxxvi (1943), 51-62. In the latter case it would mean almost the same as **the man who betrayed him;** for the superfluous καί see H. J. Cadbury in *Munera Studiosa*, ed. M. H. Shepherd and S. E. Johnson (1946), pp. 41-47.

iii. 20-21. THE CHARGE OF MADNESS

He went home; and again the crowd came, so that they 20 **could not even eat a loaf of bread. His associates, when** 21 **they heard about it, came out to seize him, for they said, 'His mind is disturbed'.**

Verses 20-35 correspond in structure to verses 7-12 (Loh-meyer). In the earlier section the motifs are: the sea of Galilee, the people of Israel, and the freeing of demoniacs with the demons hailing him as Son of God; in the latter the motifs are: the house in Capharnaum, the scribes, and the charge of demon possession. There may be a connexion between verses 20-21 and 31-35 with the controversy inserted to indicate the passage of time; cf. the combination of two miracles in v. 21-43, and the insertion of Peter's denial (xiv. 66-72) into the Passion story.

20 **He went home,** perhaps to the place mentioned in ii. 1, though the words may mean only 'into a house'. The **crowd**
21 is described in vivid terms recalling ii. 2. **His associates** is a deliberately ambiguous translation; the Greek can mean 'his family', near or remote (cf. Prov. xxix. 31 LXX; Susanna 33; 1 Macc. ix. 44), or 'his followers'. Verses 31-35 may resume this story, for according to one tradition the brothers of Jesus did not believe in him (John vii. 5), at least until after the Resur-rection (Gal. i. 19; 1 Cor. ix. 5); cf. also vi. 1-6. On the other hand, the disciples did not understand Jesus; but would they have gone so far as this? Lohmeyer notes the peculiar reading of D and the OL and conjectures that the original text read: 'When they heard about him (περὶ αὐτοῦ), the scribes and the others came out to seize him, for they said', etc. A similar sug-gestion was made independently by F. C. Grant, *ATR*, xx (1928), 111-115. It is only Jesus' opponents who would be likely to conclude that he was beside himself. On this theory, verses 20-21 are an introduction to the controversy that follows.

His mind is disturbed. The verb is used in ii. 12; v. 42; vi. 51, to denote the astonishment of the crowds or of the disciples, but here it must have the force of 2 Cor. v. 13, where it is con-trasted with σωφρονέω, to be of sound mind. It can denote a pathological excitement, whether it is thought of in the ordinary medical sense or as a religious frenzy induced by a god; cf. E. Rohde, *Psyche* (London, 1925), 290-293; F. C. Burkitt, *JTS*, xvii (1916), 11.

iii. 22-30. THE CHARGE OF POSSESSING BEELZEBUL

The scholars who had come down from Jerusalem were 22
saying, 'He has Beelzebul', and 'He is casting out demons with the help of the demons' ruler'. Summoning 23
them, he spoke to them in figures: 'How can Satan cast 24
out Satan? If a kingdom is divided against itself, that
kingdom cannot stand; and if a house is divided against 25
itself, that house will not be able to stand. And if Satan 26
has stood up against himself and has been divided, he
cannot stand but has reached his end. But no one can enter 27
the house of the Strong Man and plunder his goods, unless he first binds the Strong Man; then he will plunder
his house. I tell you truly: everything will be forgiven 28
mankind, their sins and whatever curses they speak; but 29
whoever curses the Holy Spirit has no forgiveness, not
ever, but is liable for an eternal sin.' This was because 30
they were saying, 'He has an evil spirit'.

A variant form of this story, which began by Jesus' expulsion
of a dumb demon, apparently stood in Q; it is represented more
purely in Luke xi. 14-26 than in Matt. xii. 22-32, where it is
conflated with the Marcan account.

The charge is made by **the scholars who had come down** 22
from Jerusalem; 'down' because the Sea of Galilee is at a
much lower elevation. This must be an historical reminiscence;
for in Jesus' time the Pharisees had not yet established their
control over the Jews of Galilee, while in the second century the
region was an important centre of Pharisaism. They were now,
apparently, actively engaged in propaganda. **He has Beelzebul,**,
i.e. he controls this demon and is using him, though the words
might conceivably be translated 'Beelzebul has him'. The name
must be the Aram. form of *Ba'al z*ᵉ*bhul,* 'lord of the [high]
house', i.e. the Temple. A god bearing this name may have been
worshipped in Syria from high antiquity, for in the Ras Shamra
texts, *c.* 1400 B.C., one of the titles of Aleyan Baal is 'Zebul,
baal of the earth'. Most English versions have adopted from the

Latin the form 'Beelzebub', which represents the OT *Ba'al zebub*, 'lord of flies', who was the god of Ekron; the Hebrews evidently corrupted the name in this fashion to show their contempt (2 Kings i. 2). As often in religious history, the foreign god is degraded to the status of a demon. The notion that he is the **demons' ruler** is not normal to rabbinic Judaism, which does not think of a Satanic kingdom opposed to the reign of God; but there is a stronger dualism in the Pseudepigrapha and the Qumran scrolls, and this type of demonology is not surprising in Galilee, which was on the border of pagan territory and indeed partly pagan.

23 **Summoning them,** as he would his disciples: the phrase suggests a monarch or a teacher of unquestioned authority. Perhaps in the tradition it was the disciples who were called to him. The verse has the traits of Mark's style.

Verses 24-26 contain the actual answer to this accusation. It is absurd to suppose that **Satan** will **cast out Satan,** for it is against his interests. Mark substitutes the Hebrew name of the tempter (cf. on i. 13), or perhaps there were variant forms of the story in which the different names were used. Matthew's form of the account uses two names and seems to combine two

24 stories. Granting, for the sake of argument, that Satan has a kingdom, the result will be **a kingdom . . . divided against itself** (perhaps a reminiscence of 1 Kings xii), one demon fighting another, and **that kingdom cannot stand.** The threefold 'cannot stand' suggests the statue of a pagan god (cf. Dan. ii). The Q story contains two other ideas (Matt. xii. 27-28 = Luke xi. 19-20): if Jesus casts out demons by Beelzebul, by whom do his opponents' sons, i.e. the Pharisees, cast them out? But if Jesus casts out demons by the finger (or the Spirit) of God, the Kingdom of God has come upon them. If Mark knows this tradition, he is content to make the single point, for he has already affirmed that Jesus has received the Spirit (i. 10), and he acts with a plenary authority that he need not explain.

27 Verse 27 is a detached saying which does not fit every well, but had probably been connected with the foregoing in the tradition. In itself it may be a secular proverb. Here it means that someone else (a 'stronger one', Luke xi. 22) must **enter the house of the Strong Man** and bind him. Cf. Test. Levi

xviii. 12, 'And Beliar shall be bound by him [i.e. the Messiah]
and he will give his children power to tread on the evil spirits;
cf. also Enoch x. 4-5; xxi. 1-2 and the Temptation story, Mark
i. 12-13. To **plunder his house** may mean to Mark the freeing
of those held captive by the Strong Man; the 'house' suggests
the name Beelzebul.

Did Jesus himself ascribe such importance to Satan and his
power? The later tradition, under the influence of Christian
eschatology, exaggerated this aspect of his teaching (cf. Luke iv.
6 with Matt. iv. 9, and note the 'Freer logion' inserted by W
after Mark xvi. 14). Of course, for purposes of debate, he may
have argued on the basis of his opponents' premises without
acknowledging their truth. On the other hand, he recognised
vividly the power and danger of evil in the world and did not
minimise it. His activity in proclaiming the Kingdom of God
was a fight against evil in which he saw God winning the final
victory.

I tell you truly: the solemn 'Amen' prefixed here is charac- 28
teristic of Jesus' sayings (cf. viii. 12; ix. 1, 41; x. 15; xii. 43; xiii.
30; xiv. 9, 18, 25, 30; and especially the Sermon on the Mount);
see F. A. Schilling, *ATR*, xxxviii (1956), 175-181. Here it is
probably an indication that verses 28-29 were originally an independent saying, perhaps contained in Q (in Luke xii. 10 the
context concerns confessing or denying Jesus). The Mishnah
(Sanh. x. 1) says, 'These have no share in the age to come: he
who says, "There is no resurrection of the dead"; he who says,
"the Torah is not from God", and the heretics' (cf. Mishnah
Aboth iii. 12). Branscomb regards the hard saying in the gospels
as not so much a threat of eternal punishment or a limiting of
divine grace, as a warning against presumption. To curse **the** 29
Holy Spirit is similar to the blasphemy of the name of God,
which the Pharisees considered a capital offence. In this context
(cf. verse 30) it means ascribing to Satan what is perhaps the
greatest gift of the Holy Spirit, that of rescuing those who are
in Satan's power. One who takes such an attitude overturns all
moral values and says, 'Evil, be thou my good'. So long as a
man is in this position he **has no forgiveness,** for he has shut
God out from his life. The word translated **eternal** shares the
ambiguity of the noun αἰών, which can mean 'world' or 'age';

therefore it might mean 'so long as this age lasts'. Rieu translates: 'a sin that outlasts time'. During Jesus' lifetime it was no
sin to reject him as Messiah; when Mark wrote, such rejection
30 denied the witness of the Holy Spirit. **This was because,** etc.:
Mark's explanation to his readers.

iii. 31-35. JESUS' TRUE FAMILY

31 **His mother and his brothers came, and standing outside,**
32 **they sent word to him that they were calling him. A**
crowd was sitting about him and they said to him, 'See,
your mother and your brothers are outside looking for
33 **you'. He answered, 'Who are my mother and my**
34 **brothers?' And looking around at those seated in a circle**
35 **about him, he said: 'See, here are my mother and my**
brothers; whoever does the will of God is my brother and
sister and mother'.

This little anecdote enshrines the sayings of verses 34-35. It
is not necessary to connect it with verses 20-21, as it was probably an independent piece of tradition which Mark has included
in his major section dealing with the education of the Twelve
(iii. 7-v. 43) because it ranks discipleship higher than family
ties. It has a counterpart in x. 28-30, in the midst of another
section on discipleship; it is a further working out of the themes
of i. 16-20, and it prepares for the rejection of Jesus in his home
village, vi. 1-6. Such passages as Matt. viii. 19-22 =Luke ix.
57-62; Matt. x. 34-38 =Luke xii. 51-53; xiv. 26-27 show that
this was important in the instruction of Christian converts.
The present passage appears to stand at an early stage in the
development of the tradition.

Behind this may lie the protest of some early Christians
against the claim of Jesus' earthly family to leadership over the
Church. A sort of caliphate might easily have developed; James
the brother of the Lord became head (traditionally the bishop)
of the Church in Jerusalem (cf. Acts xii. 17; xv. 13; xxi. 18; Gal.
ii. 9, 12; Eusebius, *H.E.* ii. 2. 2-5). According to Eusebius, other

members of the family later ruled the Palestinian Church (*H.E.* iii. 11-12, 19-20, 32). The statement of John vii. 5 may reflect another protest against this development; cf. also Luke xi. 27-28.

His mother and his brothers came; the story has no bio- 31 graphical interest as such, for the names are not given as they are in vi. 3; it is told only for the sake of the concluding sayings. Since they are **standing outside,** Mark may think of the house in Capharnaum (ii. 1), which for the time being is Jesus' home. 32 The **crowd,** usual in Mark's narrative style, is **sitting about him in a circle.** This is a natural Palestinian picture; cf. Bishop, p. 120. The remark of some members of the crowd gives Jesus occasion to ask the question; to begin with a query is normal in rabbinic anecdotes.

Elsewhere Mark pictures Jesus as **looking around;** cf. on 34 iii. 5. There are two sayings. The first simply designates the disciples and hearers, who need him most, as his **mother and . . . brothers.** Here is his primary relationship and responsi- bility, bound up with the work of the Good News. The second 35 saying is on a moral basis: **whoever does the will of God,** a variant of the Jewish idea that he who does God's will is a Jew (cf. Rom. ii. 28-29), though the relationship is now put on a new basis, that of fellowship with Jesus, not membership in a nation. Cf. the parallel in Luke xi. 27-28 which comes after the controversy over Beelzebul and other sayings that Luke has connected with it. **Sister:** some MSS. add 'and your sisters' in verse 32 after 'brothers'. Women may have been present at this scene.

CHAPTER IV

iv. 1-9. PARABLE OF THE SOWER

1 Again, he began to teach alongside the lake, and a very great crowd gathered to him so that he got into a boat and was seated in the lake, and all the crowd was on the 2 land facing the lake. And he was teaching them many things in figures, and in the course of his teaching he said 3, 4 to them: 'Listen. See, a Sower went out to sow. And it happened as he was sowing that some seed fell along the 5 path, and the birds came and ate it up. Other seed fell on rocky soil where it did not have much earth, and it sprang 6 up at once because it did not have depth of earth, and when the sun came up it was scorched and because it 7 had no root it withered away. Other seed fell among the thorns, and the thorns grew up and choked it, and it pro- 8 duced no crop. And other seed fell into the good earth and produced a crop, growing up and increasing, and it bore thirty, sixty, and one hundred times the sowing.' 9 And he said, 'Whoever has ears for hearing, let him hear'.

Mark's great section on the training and empowering of the disciples began with a transition passage (iii. 7-12) and the choice of the Twelve (iii. 13-19). The next parts (iii. 20-35) were mainly controversial. Now follows an important teaching section (iv. 1-34), which leads in turn to the story of the storm at sea (iv. 35-41) with its motifs of the fear of the disciples and their stupidity, the section being concluded by the three miracles of chap. v.

The evangelist's purpose in chap. iv is to show Jesus as teaching publicly and privately, with the message ostensibly open but really concealed, and not understood even by the disciples to whom it is explained. Mark has previously told how Jesus pro-

86

claimed the message in Galilee (i. 14-15) and has emphasised the authoritative character of his words (i. 21-22). In ii. 13 he pictured him as teaching beside the sea; now this scene is duplicated (verse 1) and the message of the Kingdom of God is resumed. The teaching is in figures or parables, as in the controversy over Beelzebul; cf. Robinson, *Problem*, p. 50. Jesus' original purpose in using parables was to make the message clear, not to conceal it, but the evangelist was faced by two puzzling facts: the parables, as they came to him in tradition, were difficult to understand, for much of the original context was lost; and the Jewish people, with a few notable exceptions, still rejected the Teacher who had spoken to them with authority. Therefore, like St. Paul (in Rom. ix-xi) he reasoned that God must have willed or permitted the hardening of their minds, and the teaching of Jesus had come in parables to conceal its meaning except for the initiates (verses 11-13, 22, 33-34).

Much of this material may have been contained in a written source available to Mark. If so, the three parables (verses 3-8, 26-32) were the nucleus; the interpretation of the parable of the Sower was added in the second stage; and finally Mark brought together the other material and added interpretations of his own. The section overlaps Q, which contains also the parable of the yeast (Matt. xiii. 33 =Luke xiii. 20-21); and Bacon, *Story*, pp. 211-213, conjectured that the Seed Growing Secretly (verses 26-29) was also part of Q. Mark's section contains other reminiscences of Q material, e.g. verses 21-25 are paralleled in Matt. v. 15 =Luke xi. 33; Matt. x. 26 =Luke xii. 2; Matt. vii. 2 =Luke vi. 38; Matt. xxv. 29 =Luke xix. 26; but it is almost as though Mark has heard the sayings from oral tradition and presents them in a garbled form.

The three Marcan parables can be considered as teaching encouragement in different ways: do not worry about the seed that is lost, look at that which succeeds (the Sower); do not worry about the seed once it is sown, the result is in God's hands (the Seed Growing Secretly); do not worry about the smallness of the seed, look at the result (the Mustard Seed). The first two may be particularly addressed to the disciples as heralds of the Kingdom, but nowhere else in early Christian literature is 'sowing of the word' a metaphor for missionary preaching.

1 **Again, he began to teach alongside the lake;** cf. ii. 13 for
this touch and also for the **crowd.** The scene is more vivid than
in chap. ii, for Jesus is actually in **a boat and . . . seated in the**
2 **lake;** perhaps an actual memory. On Jesus' teaching in **figures**
or parables, cf. B. T. D. Smith, *The Parables of the Synoptic
Gospels* (Cambridge, 1937), pp. 16-29. The term is applied to
several types of stories and figures found in Jesus' teaching,
including: (*a*) stories drawn from life, or lifelike but fictitious
stories, which illustrate one and only one point, the other details
usually being without significance; e.g. the Sower; and Matt. xx.
1-16; Luke xvi. 1-8a; etc. These represent the authentic parable
(*mashal*) type and are characteristic of both Jesus and the rabbis.
(*b*) Example stories, such as Luke x. 29-37. (*c*) Brief metaphors
or similes, e.g. Matt. vii. 16. (*d*) Allegories, perhaps Mark xii.
1-12, though these are infrequent in the synoptic tradition.
3 The introduction **Listen** suggests the *shema*ʿ or 'Hear, O
Israel' of Deut. vi. 4. In Mark's mind it may indicate that here
is a mystery to which one must attend in order to understand.
The *Gospel of Thomas* (82:3-13, p. 7) has a simplified form of the
parable which begins: 'Whoever has ears to hear, let him hear'.
A Sower went out to sow. The picture is that of a peasant
with a leather bag tied to his waist, who broadcasts wheat or barley
seed. In Palestine the seed is often sown first and then ploughed
in with a wooden plough which does not cut deeply; cf. A. M.
Rihbany, *The Syrian Christ* (Boston, 1916), pp. 286 f.; G. Dalman, *Arbeit und Sitte in Palästina* ii (Gütersloh, 1932), pp. 130-
4 218, especially 194 f. **Some seed fell along the path,** either the
road on the edge of the field or the way through it; Dalman
illustrates such a path and the various soils (*ibid.* pp. 14-28,
5 figs. 59-63). The **rocky soil** may refer to rocks scattered
through the soil, as is often the case in Palestine; but that **it did
not have depth of earth** suggests a limestone ledge a few
6 inches underground. The rock became warm and the seed
sprang up at once . . . and because it had no root it with-
7 **ered away.** Various kinds of **thorns** are common in Palestine;
8 cf. Jer. iv. 3. But although much of the seed is lost through such
accidents there is **good earth.** The plain of Gennesaret, near
Capharnaum, was proverbially rich, and Josephus speaks of it
as 'the ambition of nature' (*B.J.* iii. 10. 8), praising both the soil

and climate, and yields of **one hundred times the sowing**
are perfectly possibly there; by contrast, the average yield of
wheat for the United States is 15 to 20 bushels to the acre, or
twenty to thirty times the sowing. B. T. D. Smith conjectures
that the original reading in verse 8 is not εἰς ... ἐν ... ἐν (B)
but ἐν ... ἐν ... ἐν (A D), representing the Aram. ḥad of Dan.
iii. 19; cf. *Parables*, p. 124, n. 3.

Whoever has ears for hearing, let him hear. Goodspeed, 9
taking ἀκούειν as a translation of the Semitic infinitive absolute,
which has an intensive force, translates: 'Let him who has ears
be sure to listen!' The LXX, however, usually renders this construction by a participle. The origin of this little saying is not
known. Jesus perhaps uttered it to emphasise the importance of
heeding the message; to Mark it suggests that only certain
persons were capable of hearing and understanding.

iv. 10-12. THE FUNCTION OF THE PARABLES

When he was alone, his companions along with the 10
Twelve questioned him about the figures. And he said to 11
them, 'To you is given the secret of the Kingdom of God,
but to those who are outside everything comes in figures, 12
in order that
   "they may look and look and not see,
    and hear and hear and not understand,
     lest they should turn and be forgiven " ' .

When he was alone: Mark forgets at this point that Jesus 10
is seated in the boat, for apparently he is still there in verse 35
when they cross to the other side; or perhaps he thinks of the
explanation as taking place on another occasion. The framework
is clearly artificial. The phrase **his companions along with**
the Twelve is curious; possibly two readings have been
conflated.

The concept of a Christian **secret** or mystery (μυστήριον) 11
is a favourite idea of Paul, who speaks of a 'wisdom of God in
a mystery' which has been disclosed to the τέλειοι, another
word that suggests the mystery religions. This was hidden in the

past from the rulers of this world but has now been revealed through the Spirit (1 Cor. i. 26-ii. 16). Although the word is not used, the idea is prominent in another passage, 2 Cor. iii. 4-iv. 6. The secret is now open to anyone willing to receive it, and it is Paul's purpose to present everyone τέλειος in Christ (Col. i. 26; cf. Eph. iii. 3-7). Although the language is reminiscent of the mystery cults, Paul does not regard the gospel as esoteric; it is rejected only by those who are unwilling to hear, and this is shown by the way in which in Rom. ix-xi he deals with the problem of Israel's rejection. Mark actually seems more pessimistic than Paul about men's possibilities to respond to the Good News.

The secret, for Mark, even includes **the Kingdom of God.** Only the inner group was originally intended to understand it; **to those who are outside everything comes in figures** or dark sayings. Here παραβολή, which usually corresponds to the Heb. *mashal*, 'parable' or 'comparison', is assimilated in meaning to *ḥidah*, 'riddle' or 'enigma'; cf. Smith, *Parables*, p. 13.

12   The quotation **in order that they may look and look and not see,** etc., is from Isa. vi. 10, just after the account of the prophet's call. The words may originally have been ironical; Isaiah hoped to shock his hearers into obedience, not to state that it was God's purpose for them to disobey. Mark, however, seems to take the saying literally as expressing Jesus' purpose in giving the parables (cf. John xii. 37-41). If Jesus spoke the words at all, he may have meant only that this was the observed result of much of his preaching, and Torrey may be right in understanding ἵνα as rendering the Aram. *dī*, which in this case could serve as a relative pronoun; cf. also *KGSM*, p. 91. The saying behind verse 21 certainly is in contradiction to Mark's idea; the purpose of a lamp is to be put on a lamp stand and to give light.

iv. 13-20. INTERPRETATION OF THE SOWER

13 **And he said to them, 'You do not know this figure? Then**
14 **how will you understand all the figures? The Sower sows**
15 **the message. These are the ones along the path where the**

message is sown: when they hear, Satan comes at once
and takes out the message that is sown in them. Just so, 16
these are the ones sown on the rocky soil: when they hear
the message they at once receive it with joy, and they 17
have no root in them but are fickle, then when pressure
or persecution comes because of the message, they fall
down at once. As for the ones sown among thorns: these 18
are those who hear the message, and the worries of this 19
age and delight in riches come in and choke the message and it becomes fruitless. And those who are sown on 20
the good earth are the sort who hear the word and accept
it and produce thirty and sixty and one hundred times
the sowing.'

The interpretation is a kind of allegory, although unlike many
allegories it deals with a specific historical situation instead of
dissolving the story into a series of eternal truths, as in Seneca,
Ep. lxxiii. 15 f. cf. *Problem*, p. 50. Thus it resembles many NT
interpretations of OT passages. There is no antecedent reason
why Jesus should not have followed such a method; the difficulty is that verses 14-20 obviously refer to times after the
Resurrection, when the Christian message was proclaimed to the
second and later generations and the earlier zeal began to flag.
Instead of concentrating on the good earth and its produce,
which is of course mentioned (verse 20), the writer is interested
in the different kinds of soils and makes them the point of the
parable.

And he said to them: such a phrase often introduces a 13
change of source; cf. verses 21, 24. The saying contains a double
contrast: between **this** and **all the figures,** and between knowing by insight (οἴδατε) and by understanding (γνώσεσθε), i.e.
knowledge gained from others (Lohmeyer).

The Sower sows the message: λόγος often means the 14
Word of God (e.g. vii. 13) or the word of Jesus (ii. 2), but here
it particularly suggests the Christian message (cf. Luke i. 2;
Acts iv. 4; 1 Cor. i. 18, etc.).

Satan is often pictured as a serpent (Rev. xii. 9) or as a dragon 15
(Rev. xii. 3); the connexion of him with the voracious birds of
verse 4 is a vivid touch.

The allegory becomes confused in verse 16, for **the ones** 16
sown on the rocky soil should be the seeds of the message,
17 but they are now the hearers. **Pressure** or distress translates a
word that most often refers to external circumstances, as in
2 Cor. i. 4; Mark xiii. 19 uses it of the events that precede the
end. Here, coupled with **persecution,** as in Rom. viii. 35, it
calls attention to pressure from non-Christians **because of the
message,** which makes them **fall down at once.** A σκίνδαλον
was originally a stick placed in a trap or snare which when
touched by the animal sprung the trap. In biblical Greek the verb
means 'to cause to stumble' (and so to fall from the right path),
'to lead into sin or false teaching', and 'to offend'; the English
word 'scandal' is derived from the noun; cf. Matt. xiii. 41.

19   Jesus was fully conscious of **the worries** that distract men's
attention from what is most important (Matt. vi. 25-34 =Luke
xii. 22-31; cf. Luke x. 41); the allegorist, by mentioning **this
age,** implies that his readers should look towards the age to
come. The word translated **delight** came to have this meaning
in late Greek; originally it meant 'deceit', 'seduction'. Both
meanings are applicable here. Codices D W Θ and some others
omit **and desires for other things.**

iv. 21-25. SAYINGS: THE LAMP, MEASURE

21 **He said to them: 'The lamp is not here, is it, to be put
under a measuring jar or under the bed? Isn't it to be put
22 on a lamp stand? For there is nothing hidden except to be
made plain, nor anything secret, except to come out into
23 the open. If anyone has ears for hearing, let him hear.'
24 And he said to them: 'Take care what you hear. With the
kind of measure you use what you get will be measured
25 —and you will receive still more. For whoever has will
have something given to him, but whoever does not have
will have taken away from him even what he has.'**

Here Mark inserts two sayings which have parallels in the
Sermon on the Mount (verse 21 =Matt. v. 15; verse 24b =Matt.
vii. 2b), and in both cases adds his own interpretation.

21   **The lamp is not here,** literally 'does not come'; perhaps a

Semitism, but in Mark's mind 'coming' may have an eschatological significance (Lohmeyer). Every Galilean home would
have had at least one flat clay lamp in which olive oil was
burned. The **measuring jar** is a dry measure containing about
8·75 litres, almost exactly a peck. The **bed** was no more than
a mattress rolled up in the daytime, and the **lamp stand** a ledge
coming out of the wall. Jesus may have used the lamp to symbolise the Law (Ps. cxix. 105), which the rabbis have hidden
under an elaborate tradition (cf. Matt. xxiii. 13 =Luke xi. 52),
but which ought to shine out for the good of mankind. Mark of 22
course thinks of Jesus' revelations in the parables; they are
temporarily **hidden** and **secret** but must ultimately **be made
plain** and **come into the open.** Substantially the same saying
is found in Matt. x. 26-27 =Luke xii. 2-3, but there the thought
is that the disciples must proclaim on the house-tops what has
necessarily been told to only a small group. R. Otto compares
the idea with that of the parable of the yeast (Matt. xiii. 33
=Luke xiii. 20-21; cf. *KGSM*, pp. 147 ff.).

Take care what you hear, i.e. be alert to it, observe it; cf. 24
Luke viii. 18, 'Take care *how* you hear'. Verse 24b, as spoken
by Jesus, should mean: 'You cannot expect to be judged by a
more generous standard than that which you use in judging
others' (Matt. vii. 2) or 'if you give generously you will receive
generously' (Luke vi. 38; cf. 1 Clem. xiii. 2). The latter interpretation is more likely, for Mark transmits the words **and you
will receive still more,** an idea substantially found in Luke's
logion. Mark, of course, thinks of teaching: the disciple who
hears with understanding will receive even more insight.

But, says the evangelist, the converse is true: **whoever does** 25
**not have will have taken away from him even what he
has;** more and more he will lose insight into God's revelation.
It is hard to know what Jesus originally intended to convey; if
the context had to do with judging, he who has the forgiving
spirit will be forgiven even more abundantly, while he who does
not can expect greater condemnation. The saying can of course
apply to generosity in giving: he who does not give has little, and
at last even what he has is lost. Originally this may have been
a secular saying adapted by Jesus: 'the rich get richer and the
poor get poorer'.

93

iv. 26-29. PARABLE OF THE SEED GROWING SECRETLY

26 **And he said: 'The Kingdom of God is like this: as if a man**
27 **were to cast seed on the earth, and sleep at night and get**
up in the day, and the seed were to sprout and grow—he
28 **does not know how. Spontaneously the earth bears a crop:**
first the blade, then the head, then the full kernel in the
29 **head. When the crop allows it, at once "he sends the**
sickle, because the harvest is here".'

Cadbury remarks that this might well be called the Parable
of the Patient Farmer; the theme of patience with delay is
characteristic of Jesus' teaching; cf. Luke xii. 45; xvii. 22; xviii.
1-8; H. J. Cadbury, *Jesus: What Manner of Man* (New York,
1947), p. 40. Once the seed is sown, no one need worry; the
result is in God's hands, and the harvest will surely come. Mark
has edited this piece of old tradition only slightly, if at all.
Lohmeyer remarks several *koine* peculiarities and Latinisms in
it. The obscurity of the parable no doubt led the other evangelists to omit it, but Matthew seems to have modelled the Parable
of the Tares on it; at least he echoes four of its words.

26 The **man** is anyone who plants; the point applies equally to
27 Jesus or to any of his disciples. Man does not control the
growth of the seed and **he does not know how** it grows; the
28 coming of the Kingdom is God's secret. As **the earth,** not
the sower or the seed, produces a **crop,** so God is the author of
the marvellous growth. **Head** is American idiom for English
'ear'.

29 **He sends the sickle, because the harvest is here;** apparently a reminiscence of Joel iii. 13 (iv. 13, Heb.); cf. Rev. xiv. 15.
Jer. l. 16. The reference is apocalyptic, but the metaphor of
sowing and reaping in the OT is not always connected with
wrath. In. Hos. ii. 21-23 the future destiny of Israel is looked
upon as God's sowing; for the harvest of joy, cf. Ps. cxxvi, 5-6.
Jer. i. 16.

He said: 'How are we to compare the Kingdom of God? 30
Into what figure can we put it? It is like a grain of mustard 31
seed, which when it is sown on the earth is the smallest
of all seeds on earth, but when it is sown grows up and 32
becomes greater than all vegetables and makes great
branches, so that "under its shade the fowls of the sky"
can "roost".'

The third of the seed parables contrasts the insignificant beginnings of the Kingdom of God with the stupendous result.
Luke xiii. 18-19 contains a form of the parable somewhat different from that of Mark, while that of Matthew stands in a
middle position between the two; thus it is usually assumed that
Luke drew his version from Q, while Matthew combined the
two forms. In the old tradition it began with a double question,
which both Mark and Luke have preserved. Lohmeyer conjectures that still earlier there were two forms of the story which were
combined into the version underlying Mark and Luke. One began
with one question, the other with the other. The first form compared the Kingdom with the mustard seed which when it grows
puts out great branches; in the second the 'smallest of all seeds'
produces a plant greater than all vegetables. The *Gospel of Thomas*
knew the parable in Mark's combined form (84:26-33, p. 15).

The opening formula is like that in rabbinic parables: 'A 30
parable. To what is the matter like? It is like', etc. It is not
necessary to suppose that **the Kingdom of God** is equated with
the seed, which may represent the Good News; the introduction
affirms only that the story has to do with the Kingdom; cf. Matt.
xx. 1; xxii. 2, where the Kingdom cannot be identified with the
landowner or the king.

Jews sowed **mustard seed** in fields and the rabbis forbade 31
planting it in a garden (Mishnah Kilaim iii. 2); thus Matthew
preserves the Palestinian background better than Luke. The
smallness of its seed was proverbial, and it grows to be ten feet or 32
more tall. It was cultivated as a **vegetable** and also for its seed.

The point of comparison is difficult to determine precisely.

Like the two previous parables and that of the yeast (Matt. xiii. 33 =Luke xiii. 20-21) it is a figure of growth. But to early Christians it cannot have meant the gradual, slow, almost natural transformation of history by the presence of the Kingdom. The growth comes by the mysterious, direct action of God; cf. 1 Cor. iii. 6. Furthermore, as in the yeast parable, the emphasis is on the results which are out of all proportion to the seed or the yeast.

Certainly the concluding phrase, **so that "under its shade the fowls of the sky" can "roost"**, is apocalyptic. It is drawn from Dan. iv. 12, where Nebuchadnezzar's kingdom appears in his vision as a great tree whose top reaches to heaven. This tree is to be cut down with only a stump remaining (Dan. iv. 15). Thus there is an implied contrast with the Kingdom of God, which is permanent. If Jesus included the reminiscence of Daniel, it cannot be the main point of the parable, which contains no contrast between the transitory and the eternal; and it is possible that this touch was added by the early Church.

iv. 33-34. SUMMARY

33 **With many such figures he used to speak the message to**
34 **them as they were able to listen; and without a figure he did not speak to them; but privately he used to explain everything to his own disciples.**

33   Verse 33 appears to say that **figures** were Jesus' normal way of expressing **the message**; indeed he gave no teaching without providing an illustration. **As they were able to listen** may imply that he suited his teaching to the capabilities of the hearers, i.e. the parables were designed to explain, not to con-
34 ceal. If so, this belongs to the pre-Marcan tradition. Verse 34 expresses Mark's own viewpoint; cf. verses 10-12.

iv. 35-41. THE STORM AT SEA

35 **That day when evening had come he said to them, 'Let**
36 **us go over to the other shore'. And leaving the crowd be-**

hind they took him, just as he was, in the boat; and there
were other boats with him. And a great gust of wind arose, 37
and the waves were beating into the boat, so that the boat
was about to founder. He himself was in the stern sleep- 38
ing on the cushion, and they roused him and said to him,
'Teacher, don't you care that we are being lost?' And he 39
got up and gave a stern command to the wind and said
to the sea, 'Silence! Stop!' And the wind died down and
there was a great calm, and he said to them, 'Why are 40
you so cowardly? Why do you not have faith?' And they 41
were greatly afraid and said to each other, 'Now who is
this, that the wind and the sea obey him?'

This is the first of a group of miracle stories whose scene is
the neighbourhood of the Sea of Galilee. Mark does not indicate
on which side of the lake the teaching of chap. iv is supposed to
take place, but he may think of the incidents of iii. 20-35 as
occurring in Capharnaum, on the north-west shore. Jesus now 35
begins to cross **to the other shore**; apparently this crossing is
completed in v. 1 when he and the disciples arrive in the country
of the Gerasenes or Gergesenes.

It is no accident that the story of the demoniac follows this
narrative immediately. The howling, raging tempest which terri-
fies the disciples is stilled by Jesus' word of command and there
is a great calm; just so, after Jesus drives out the demon, the man
is left seated and in his right mind; cf. the sequence in viii. 22-
ix. 10. Hoskyns and Davey note that the story of the storm is
modelled on *Testament of Naphtali* vi; cf. *The Riddle of the NT*
(2nd ed., London, 1936), pp. 86-89. Naphtali and his brothers
are in a boat when a great whirlwind comes up and separates
them from their father Jacob, and the boat is smashed. The
patriarchs are scattered to the ends of the earth, but when Levi
puts on sackcloth and prays to the Lord, the storm ceases, the
boat is miraculously restored, and they make the land safely and
are reunited with Jacob. There may be connexions with OT
ideas: the Psalms use waters and storms to express the plight
of the righteous who are overwhelmed with woes (e.g. Pss. lxix.
1-2; cxxiv. 4-5); God stills the raging of the waves (lxv. 7) and
brings the mariner to the haven where he would be (cvii. 23-30).

Perhaps the passage also reflects the experience of the church in Rome. At the time of the first great persecution under Nero, and no doubt at other times, it seemed that the little community was about to suffer shipwreck, and Christians were tempted to ask whether their Lord cared that they were perishing. Yet they experienced the stilling of the storm and heard again the command of Jesus to have faith. The story, as Lohmeyer remarks, has two motifs, the calming of the storm and the relation of Jesus to his disciples, who still do not understand his nature but are protected despite their lack of faith. The account is richer in details than are the previous miracles and the style is almost poetic.

36   **Let us go over;** διέρχεσθαι usually describes a trip by land. Jesus went **just as he was,** presumably without other companions. It is therefore curious that the text should say that **there were other boats with him,** unless the thought is that the others who were left behind followed him.

37   The word translated **gust of wind** is found in poetry from Homer on, but also in classical prose and the LXX. Such sudden storms are frequent on the Sea of Galilee.

38   Jesus, like Jonah, **was . . . sleeping.** The despairing cry of the disciples, **don't you care that we are being lost,** reminds one of the captain's plea to Jonah (Jon. i. 5-6). The Babylonian Talmud (*Baba Meṣia* 59b) tells how Rabban Gamaliel (c. A.D. 90), encountering a similar danger, recalled that R. Eliezer ben Hyrcanus had put a curse on him; he appealed to God in prayer

39   and the sea was calmed. Jesus, however, does not pray on this occasion; he addresses **the wind** and **the sea, 'Silence! Stop!',** literally 'Be quiet, be muzzled!' These are words of exorcism; cf. Rohde, *Psyche*, p. 604. The story thus suggests the continuing conflict between Jesus and the demons.

40   **Why are you so cowardly? Why do you not have faith?**
41   Only here does Mark connect cowardice and lack of faith. The disciples still do not understand the mystery of Jesus' nature— **Now who is this?** This motif runs throughout the gospel, e.g. vi. 49-52; viii. 17-21; ix. 32; xiv. 37-42.

CHAPTER V

v. 1-20. THE DEMONIAC OF GERGESA

They came to the other shore of the lake, into the region 1
of the Gergesenes, and as he was coming out of the boat 2
a man from the tombs met him, one who had an unclean
spirit, whose home was in the tombs. No one was able to 3
bind him even with a chain, because many times he had 4
been bound with fetters and chains, and he had pulled the
chains off himself and broken the fetters, and no one
could subdue him. All night and all day long he was in 5
the tombs and the hills crying out and cutting himself
with stones. Seeing Jesus from a long way off, he ran and 6
did reverence to him, and cried with a loud voice, 'What 7
have you to do with me, Jesus, Son of God Most High? I con-
jure you by God, do not torture me'—because he had said
to him, 'Unclean spirit, come out of the man'. So he 8
asked him, 'What is your name?' and he said to him, 9
'Legion is my name, because we are many'. And he 10
begged and begged him not to send him out of the region.
Now there, near the hill, there was a large herd of pigs 11
pasturing, and they begged him, 'Send us among the pigs 12
so that we may get into them'. So he let them do it, and 13
the unclean spirits went out and entered the pigs and the
herd stampeded down the cliff into the lake, about two
thousand of them, and were drowned in the lake. The 14
men herding them ran away and told about it in the city
and the country and people came to see what had happened. And they came to Jesus, and saw the demon- 15
possessed man seated, clothed and sane, that man who
had had the Legion, and they were frightened. And those 16
who had seen it told them the story of how it had happened to the demon-possessed man, and about the pigs.
And they began to beg him [Jesus] to leave their territory. 17

18 **And when he had got into the boat the demon-possessed**
19 **man begged to be with him. He did not let him, but said**
to him, 'Go home to your own people, and report to them
how much the Lord has done for you and what mercy he
20 **has shown you'. And he went away and began to an-**
nounce in the Decapolis what Jesus had done for him,
and everyone was astonished.

The miracles of chapter v are closely connected with the
instruction of the inner group of disciples; it may be significant
that the latter fail to understand Jesus' unusual sensitivity (verse
31) and that the three most intimate followers go with Jesus into
the room where Jaïrus' daughter is lying (verse 37). Thus Mark
does not tell the healings merely to show Jesus' compassion but
uses them as examples of his nature and work.

1   **They came to the other shore of the lake.** The curious
Cod. 2427 omits 'to the other shore of the lake'. This may be
an intentional alteration because πέραν usually means the east
side, and the phrase is used in iv. 35 and again in v. 21. The
insane man must be a Gentile and his restoration takes place in
Gentile territory. In the pre-Marcan tradition the pericope cele-
brates the spread of the gospel to the heathen, but Mark does
not make this clear, for he thinks of Jesus' Gentile mission as
occurring later, in vii. 24-30 and perhaps viii. 1-10; viii. 27-ix. 1.
The style differs somewhat from that of other parts of Mark; the
sentences are longer and numerous participles are used. Thus
it is undoubtedly the evangelist who has brought the story into
this context.

Except that the scene is laid on the east shore of the lake, the
locality is not certain. (1) S* B D and the Latin and Sahidic
versions read 'Gerasenes'. Gerasa, the modern Jerash, was a
brilliant and flourishing Syro-Greek city of the Decapolis
league, but it lies many miles away to the east. If this well-
attested reading is correct, Gerasa would have had to control a
small area not contiguous with its other territory. (2) The same
objection applies to 'Gadarenes', the reading of A C G Σ, most
of the later minuscule MSS. and the Syriac Peshitta; Gadara
was nearer than Gerasa but still distant. There are, however,
many tombs there. Gadara is evidently the reading of Matt.

viii. 28. (3) 'Gergesenes' is read by L U Δ Θ, Cod. 1 and its allies, 33, the Sinaitic Syriac, Bohairic, Armenian, Ethiopic and Origen. It is thus a 'Caesarean' reading which may represent old MS. tradition or a conjecture on Origen's part. On the east shore of the lake, at el-Kursi, near the Wadi es-Samak, a monastery and church have been excavated, which were evidently believed to be the site of the miracle. Nearby there is a cliff which fits the story of the pigs. The name could have arisen from Gergesa. A passage in the Talmud states that the Girgashites of Deut. vii. 1 held the territory in this region. In any case, the east shore is the neighbourhood of the Decapolis (i.e. 'ten cities'). This was a league of Greek-speaking and generally pagan city-states, which had been hellenised under the Seleucid monarchy. Several of them were conquered by the Maccabees but restored to their independence by Pompey the Great after 63 B.C. The cities mentioned by Pliny (*Hist. Nat.* v. 18 [74]) as belonging to the league were east of the Jordan with the exception of Scythopolis (Bethshean). In addition to Gerasa, Gadara and Scythopolis the Decapolis included such places as Damascus, Pella, Philadelphia (Amman) and Hippos. The last-named was nearest to the locality of this story.

The **man** who **met** Jesus had his **home . . . in the tombs.** 2 Palestinian cemeteries were often located in caverns cut into the rock, and it would have been possible for the man to inhabit these. The rabbis believed that demons lived in such places. Verses 3-5 are said to give a vivid picture of the manic stage of a manic-depressive psychosis, which is 'characterised by great 4, 5 activity, combativeness and destructivity'; cf. S. V. McCasland, p. 39. The delusion of demon-possession is, however, also involved in the present story. McCasland, pp. 56-59, gives an instance of this from modern Syria. Some well-attested stories of demon-possession in China were published by J. G. Magee in the *District of Shanghai Newsletter*, xxii, 6 (June, 1936); xxii, 8 (Nov., 1936); and xxvi, 5 (June, 1940).

The insane man **did reverence;** in the NT προσκυνέω 6 usually refers to worship of a divinity (cf. Rev. xix. 10); and he addresses him as **Jesus, Son of God Most High.** Thus, as in 7 i. 24, the demons recognise Jesus' nature even when the disciples do not. 'God Most High' or 'the Most High God' seems to have been used by pagans to refer to the God of Israel; cf. Dan. iv. 2, 17. The epithet 'Most High' ($\H{v}\psi\iota\sigma\tau\sigma$) was applied to Zeus; cf. C. Roberts, T. C. Skeat and A. D. Nock, *HTR*, xxix (1936), 39-88; and syncretistic worship of a *Theos Hypsistos*, in which Judaism had some influence, existed in antiquity; cf. M. Nilsson, *Geschichte der griechischen Religion*, ii (Munich, 1950), pp. 636-638.

7 The demon which controls the man calls Jesus' name in order to attempt an exorcism in reverse. As in i. 24, he uses a phrase reminiscent of the OT in an effort to protect himself: **What have I to do with you?** and adds to it an exorcistic formula. Loisy remarks that this touch has *une assez piquante naïveté*. But the words **do not torture me** are not those of an exorcist but the despairing cry of a demon, and there are parallels to this in numerous early Christian stories; cf. McCasland, pp. 112 f.

8 Mark, perhaps as an afterthought, adds the words **Unclean spirit, come out of the man.** The tradition as he received it may not have contained the command; the presence of our Lord is enough to arouse the demon's fear. In any case it is significant
9 that Jesus uses no formula of exorcism. He does, however, ask the demon his name, as exorcists were accustomed to do; cf. Campbell Bonner, *HTR*, xxxvi (1943), 43 f. The answer **Legion is my name** may be a mischievous evasion (Wellhausen) or a boast (Bultmann); a Roman legion consisted of five
10 or six thousand men. Now the demon **begged and begged him** (the imperfect suggests repetition) **not to send him out of the region,** into the desert, which was thought to be the home of demons, or into Gehenna, but to let him remain among human beings where he could continue his activity. A rabbinic story tells of how R. Ḥanina ben Dosa (*c.* A.D. 70) forbade a female demon to prowl in inhabited territory, whereupon she said, 'I pray you, allow me some room!' The rabbi then gave her freedom on Wednesday and Sabbath nights (SB, iv, 514).

Much of the foregoing is psychologically understandable; the personality is split and the man believes that one of his char-
11 acters is demonic. But is the incident of the pigs part of the
12 original story, and would the insane man have said **Send us among the pigs so that we may get into them?** It has been
13 suggested that the noise and gestures of the insane man terrified

the animals so that **the herd stampeded,** and the bystanders
concluded that the demons must have **entered the pigs.** One
can imagine Jews telling with some amusement of the fate of the
unclean animals, and this popular theory of demonology would
agree with the story of R. Ḥanina. The round number, **about
two thousand,** corresponds to the name Legion.

The men herding them were of course Gentiles, and it was 14
natural that their neighbours should **beg Jesus to leave their** 17
territory, for valuable property had been destroyed; furthermore, their superstitious fear was aroused.

Mark ordinarily thinks of Jesus as requiring that healings be
kept secret (cf. i. 44; iii. 12; v. 43), but here he preserves a tradition that the man should **Go home to** his **own people, and** 19
report to them how much the Lord has done for him.
ἀπαγγέλλειν, 'report' or 'announce', is a word used in connexion with early Christian missionary propaganda; cf. Acts
xvii. 30; xxvi. 20; 1 Cor. xiv. 25; also Matt. xi. 4 =Luke vii. 22.
The message is to the Gentiles, and it is not primarily about
Jesus' deeds but those of **the Lord,** the God of Israel; just so
Naaman the Syrian was a witness to God (2 Kings v. 15-17).

v. 21-43. TWO MIRACLES

When Jesus had crossed in the boat once more to the 21
other shore, a great crowd gathered to him, and he was
beside the lake. And one of the synagogue presidents, 22
Jaïrus by name, came and seeing him fell at his feet, and 23
begged him repeatedly, saying, 'My little daughter is
about to die—please come and lay your hands on her so
that she may get well and live'. He went away with him, 24
and a great crowd followed and pressed upon him.

A woman who had had a haemorrhage for twelve years, 25
and had endured much at the hands of many doctors and 26
had spent everything she had, yet got no better but rather
worse, when she heard the news about Jesus came from 27
behind in the crowd and touched his outer garment, for 28
she said, 'If I can only touch his clothing, I can get well'.
At once the flow of her blood dried up, and she knew in 29

30 her body that she had been healed of the disease. Jesus, at
once realising inwardly that power had gone out of him,
turned about in the crowd and said, 'Who touched my
31 clothing?' His disciples said, 'You see the crowd pressing
upon you and yet you are saying, "Who touched me?"!'
32 And he looked around to see the woman who had done
33 this, and the woman, fearful and trembling, knowing what
had happened to her, came and fell down in front of him
34 and told him the whole truth. He said to her, 'Daughter,
your faith has made you well. Go in peace, and be healed
of your disease.'

35   While he was still speaking, people came from the
home of the synagogue president, saying, 'Your daughter
36 has died. Why keep on bothering the teacher?' But Jesus,
overhearing what was said, said to the synagogue presi-
37 dent, 'Do not be afraid, only keep believing'. And he did
not permit anyone to follow him but Peter and James and
38 John, James' brother. They came to the house of the
synagogue president, and he saw a commotion and
people crying and wailing a great deal, and he went in
39 and said to them, 'Why are you making a commotion
and crying? The child has not died but is sleeping.' They
40 laughed at him in contempt. But he put them all out and
took with him the father of the child and her mother and
his companions, and he went in where the child was.
41 And taking the child by the hand, he said to her, 'Talitha
42 kūm', which is translated, 'Girl, I tell you, get up'. And
the girl at once got up and walked; for she was twelve
43 years old. They were extremely amazed. And he gave
them strict orders that no one should know this, and he
said that she should be given something to eat.

Mark has artistically combined two stories, the healing of
Jaïrus' daughter (verses 21-24, 35-43) and that of the woman
with the haemorrhage (verses 25-34), suggesting in this way that
some time elapses between Jaïrus' plea to Jesus and the report
that the little girl is dead. The instantaneous healing of the
woman points up further the unbelief of those who came from
Jaïrus' house and Jesus' demand for faith. Differences in lan-

guage between the two stories tend to show that they were not connected in the tradition. The narrative of the woman is in standard though simple Hellenistic Greek, with periodic sentences and numerous participles, while the other story contains an Aramaic word, simpler syntax and such expressions as θυγάτριον and ἐσχάτως ἔχει (verse 23).

1. Jaïrus' Daughter: Scene I

The tradition of Jesus' healings includes two types of stories: in one faith is emphasised as the necessary condition for receiving the divine gift, as here and in ix. 14-29; in the other, this motif is absent, and physical means of healing are sometimes mentioned, e.g. i. 29-31; vii. 32-37; viii. 22-26. The stories of the second group tend to resemble pagan and Jewish healing narratives, and if the name of Jesus were absent it would be difficult to see in them anything Christian or monotheistic. It is possible that the religious element was originally present in certain stories but was later lost; note that in Luke's form of the story of the woman, faith is still emphasised, but more emphasis is placed on the power which goes out from Jesus (Luke viii. 46-48). On the other hand, Mark's story of the Syrophoenician woman (vii. 24-30) presupposes faith, but Matthew makes this explicit (Matt. xv. 28). Two opposite tendencies were at work in the tradition, but the appearance of the element of faith is significant. This distinguishes the healing stories of the gospels from those of non-Christian literature generally.

Elsewhere **the other shore** refers to the east side of the lake, 21 but that is where Jesus was in verses 1-20; cf. note on verse 1. Mark must think of the western (or why not northern?) shore, for in chap. vi Jesus goes from here to his home village.

An ancient Jewish synagogue usually had two officers: the 22 president or ruler (*rôsh ha-keneseth*) and the *hazzan* or attendant (ὑπηρέτης, Luke iv. 20). Mark speaks as though there were several **synagogue presidents,** and the plural is also used in Acts xiii. 15. In a few cases a synagogue may have had several such officers, who acted as a board or in rotation; or the plural may mean that there was more than one synagogue in the village.

Jaïrus is a Jewish name; cf. the *Yaʿîr* of 1 Chr. xx. 5 (Qerê) and the *Yaʾîr* of Num. xxxii. 41. For the latter, see Y. Yadin, *Masada* (New York, 1966), p. 201. He would have been appointed by the elders of the local sanhedrin and was a person of dignity and importance.

23   **My little daughter is about to die** (ἐσχάτως ἔχει), almost 'at her last gasp'. **Please** represents ἵνα with the subjunctive; either this is a substitute for the imperative infinitive or 'I beg you' is to be supplied. One of the Dead Sea Scrolls contains a striking parallel to the request to **lay your hands on her so that she may get well and live.** Pharaoh had been afflicted with a disease because he took Sarai into his house. He therefore sent to Abram 'to pray for the king and to lay my hands upon him that he might live'. Sarai was restored to her husband, 'and I laid my hand upon his head and the evil [spirit] was gone and he lived'; N. Avigad and Y. Yadin, *A Genesis Apocryphon* (Jerusalem, 1956), col. xx, lines 21 f. D. Flusser, *Israel Exploration Journal*, vii (1957), 107 f., remarks that neither the OT nor rabbinic literature knows of healing through the laying on of hands, but it is characteristic of Mark's stories of Jesus (cf. vi. 25; viii. 25), though often he heals through a simple command. The verb used in this Aramaic story is the same root (*samakh*) which rabbinical sources employ for the laying on of hands in ordination.

2. THE WOMAN WITH THE HAEMORRHAGE

24   Jesus now started for Jaïrus' house, **and a great crowd ... pressed upon him.** The verb is the one from which θλῦψις, 'pressure', 'tribulation' (iv. 17) is derived. Only one who has been in a crowd of excited Mediterranean or Near Eastern people is likely to appreciate this touch in the narrative. This prepares for the story of the woman.

25   It is common for healing stories, both ancient and modern, to mention the long duration of the illness, in this case **twelve years,** and to note that a cure has hitherto been impossible. The number occurs again in verse 42, where the little girl is twelve years old, but it is difficult to see what symbolic meaning this may have had for the evangelist. The sentence in verses 25-28

contains seven participles and is quite idiomatic. She **had en-** 26
dured much at the hands of many doctors. This is probably the thought, not merely that 'she had been a patient under
many doctors', for πάσχειν ὑπό τινος usually means that the
other person has caused the sufferings. Mark may share the
view of Mishnah Qiddushin iv. 14, 'the best among physicians
is worthy of Gehenna', in contrast to the praise of the profession
in Ecclus. xxxviii. 1-15. She **got no better but rather worse;**
cf. Tobit ii. 10, 'I went to physicians but they did not help me'.

The woman **came from behind,** perhaps in order not to be 27
observed, for her disease made her ceremonially unclean (Lev.
xv. 25-27). Because of the thick crowd, she could do no more 28
than touch his **outer garment;** it is probable that at this time
Jews wore the Greek chiton and himation (the latter word is
used here), not the Arab dress often portrayed in modern religious pictures; cf. W. F. Albright, *The Archaeology of Palestine*
(Harmondsworth, Pelican Books, 1949), p. 216.

At once ... she knew ... that she had been healed; the 29
perfect tense may indicate her conviction that the cure was
permanent (Swete). **Jesus, at once realising inwardly that** 30
power had gone out of him: to Mark this knowledge, like the
instant healing, is a sign of our Lord's divine attributes. A
spiritually sensitive person might well discern the presence of
someone in need, and at this point no one can say where human
qualities are to be distinguished from divine. **And he looked** 32
around: this is characteristic of the evangelist's narrative style
(iii. 5, 34; x. 23; xi. 11) but such a gesture may have been remembered in tradition, and here it is necessary to the story. The 33
woman was **fearful and trembling,** partly from awe in the
presence of the healer, but also because of the liberty that she,
an unclean person, had taken in her great need. Jesus' answer, 34
Daughter (cf. 'daughter of Abraham', Luke xiii. 16), is affectionate and reassuring; **your faith,** not contact with a healer,
has made you well. The words must not be pressed too far;
it was the divine power that accomplished the healing, and faith
had made it possible to receive the gift. If the story had been
told of a Hellenistic healer, 'faith' might mean no more than
trust in the wonder-worker. Mark thinks primarily of faith in
Jesus as Son of God (cf. ii. 5; iv. 40), but on Jesus' lips the word

must refer to faith in God. **Go in peace,** the Hebrew word of blessing (cf. Matt. x. 13 =Luke x. 5).

3. Jaïrus' Daughter: Scene II

35 The picture shifts suddenly—**while he was still speaking** —to those who **come from the house of the synagogue president.** It is too late to do anything for the girl; **Why keep on bothering the teacher?** A rabbi must be treated with respect and consideration. This is a touch of dramatic irony; they do not realise the depth of Jesus' compassion, which is that of God,
36 or his power to act even when everything seems lost (cf. John xi. 20-32). Jesus answers, **Do not be afraid;** such a phrase is used in the NT in connexion with divine revelations; cf. Matt. i. 20; Mark vi. 50; John xiv. 1, where it is also coupled with the command to **keep believing;** the present tense is iterative.
37 **Peter and James and John** are the three most intimate disciples who are permitted to see the Transfiguration (ix. 2).

4. Jaïrus' Daughter: Scene III

38 Among ancient Jews, as in the Near East today, death resulted in **a commotion and people crying and wailing a great deal,** often with the employment of professional mourners; 'even the poorest in Israel should hire not less than two flutes and one wailing woman' (Mishnah Ketuboth iv. 4; cf. Matt. xi. 17 =Luke vii. 32). An open display of sorrow may be a wholesome psychological relief, but here it points up the contrast between faith and unfaith.
39 The OT and classical literature use **sleeping** as a synonym for death (cf. Ps. xiii. 3); this passage, however, suggests the widespread Christian thought that death is only a temporary sleep in hope of the resurrection; cf. 1 Thess. iv. 13 f.; and John xi. 11-13, where Jesus' use of the word is misunderstood, as here.

5. Jaïrus' Daughter: Scene IV

In the stories of Elijah and Elisha, when children are raised 40
from the dead (1 Kings xvii. 19; 2 Kings iv. 33), and in the
raising of Tabitha by Peter (Acts ix. 40), the healer is alone;
here only the parents and the three disciples are permitted to
witness the miracle. Mark's view is that the revelation is as yet
for only a few and cannot be disclosed to profane eyes; cf.
verse 43.

The style of the narrative is similar to that of many ancient 41
wonder-stories. Jesus takes **the child by the hand** (cf. i. 31),
and physical contact is often mentioned in Hellenistic healings; cf. L. J. McGinley, *Form-Criticism of the Synoptic Healing
Narratives* (Woodstock, Md., 1944), p. 139 f. The words accompanying the gesture are given in Aramaic (as in vii. 34); M.
Dibelius, *FTG*, p. 84, gives instances of the use of foreign
words from both Greek and Jewish sources. The form critics,
particularly Dibelius and Bultmann, emphasise these parallels
and argue that the motives behind the stories are similar to those
reflected in pagan and rabbinic narratives. For a contrary view,
see McGinley, *op. cit.*, and B. S. Easton, *The Gospel before the
Gospels* (New York, 1928), chap. v. One must grant that the
gospel tradition would be likely to introduce incidental touches
characteristic of other well-known stories—indeed, the stories
of wondrous healings tend to take the same form the world over
—but through several of Jesus' miracles traits of his personality
shine out: his primary interest in the Good News, of which the
healings are only one expression; his demand for faith in God;
and his human compassion. When **he said that she should** 43
be given something to eat, this of course tends to confirm
the completeness of the healing, but Mark has already said
that **the girl got up and walked.** This command of Jesus 42
has no function in the narrative except to show that he had a
practical concern for the comfort and continued health of the
child.   41

Talitha represents the Aram. *taly^etha* or *t^elitha*, 'girl' or
'little girl'. **Kūm** may be the Mesopotamian form of the imperative; Codices A D and most late MSS. read κοῦμι, which

is the regular Palestinian form. Perhaps the feminine ending *i*
was no longer sounded. For the command **get up**, cf. Luke vii.
42 14; Acts ix. 40. The remark **for she was twelve years old**
seems intended to explain that the girl was not a baby, despite
the diminutive form κοράσιον.

vi. 1-6. REJECTION IN THE HOME TOWN

He left there and came into his home town, and his dis- 1
ciples followed him. When the Sabbath came he began 2
to teach in the synagogue; and most of the people when
they heard him were dumbfounded, saying, 'Where did
he get this? What is this wisdom that has been given him?
And such powerful things happen through his hands!
Isn't this the builder, the son of Mary and brother of 3
James and Joses and Judas and Simon? And aren't his
sisters here with us?' And they took offence at him. And 4
Jesus said to them, 'No prophet is without honour except
in his own neighbourhood and among his kin and in his
home'. He was not able to do any powerful deed there, 5
except that he put his hands on a few sick people and
healed them. And he was amazed at their unbelief.   6

A major section of the gospel begins here. As P.. H. Lightfoot
pointed out, *History and Interpretation in the Gospels* (London,
1935), pp. 182-205, the rejection of Jesus by his childhood
associates immediately follows the restoration of life to the girl,
and is part of the chain of events leading to his death. This is
exactly the pattern in the Fourth Gospel, where the raising of
Lazarus is the direct cause of the plot against Jesus (John xi.
45-50). In Matthew, the entire section xi. 2-xiv. 12 is dominated
by the theme of the rejection of Jesus and John the Baptist,
which is also the tragedy of the Jewish people, who through
their lack of faith lose the opportunity to be chosen. B. W.
Bacon suggested that the same theme occupied a major section
of the Q source; cf. *Studies in Matthew* (New York, 1930),
pp. 375-387.
The story is rounded off and complete in itself; its location
in the narrative is probably due to the evangelist. Luke places a

vivid variant of the incident at the very beginning of Jesus'
public ministry (iv. 16-30); as Lightfoot says (*op. cit.* pp. 196-
202), according to Luke the rejection is accomplished at the
start and the tragic element is lacking; the third evangelist's
purpose is to trace the spread of the gospel to Jerusalem and
from thence to the Gentile world.

The section vi. 1-16 is, as Lohmeyer notes, parallel to iii. 7-34.
In both instances a section on the Twelve (iii. 13-19; vi. 7-12)
is inserted between two pieces which have to do with the
response to Jesus' activity.

1   **He . . . came into his home town,** πατρίς, 'homeland' or
'fatherland'. Although Mark knows that Jesus was called 'the
Nazarene' (i. 24) this piece of tradition does not mention the
name. The word emphasises the paradox that 'he came to his
own land and his own people did not receive him' (John i. 11).

2   **When the Sabbath came he began to teach in the synagogue;** cf. on i. 21. Luke iv. 16-30 gives a good picture of the
synagogue worship. For the **dumbfounded** response of the
people, cf. i. 22. The **wisdom** and authority of his teaching and
the **powerful things** that **happen through his hands** are not
what they expected of their childhood neighbour, yet they are
unable or unwilling to recognise him as the bearer of divine
power. 'Wisdom' and 'power', which correspond to 'word'
and 'deed', are used of the future king in Isa. xi. 2, of the
Messiah in Ps. Sol. xvii. 24-25, and of God in Job xii. 13. In
1 Cor. i. 24, Christ is the power of God and the wisdom of God.

3   **The builder:** τέκτων can mean 'carpenter', 'woodworker',
as in Epictetus i. 15. 2, but also one who builds with stone; both
techniques would be necessary for building in the highlands of
Galilee and Judaea. Justin, *Dial.* lxxxviii. 7, says that he did
'carpenter's jobs' (τεκτονικὰ ἔργα), making yokes and ploughs;
it is not certain whether this is a tradition or merely a conjecture.
Elsewhere Jesus is not called a builder or carpenter.

It is curious that the text calls Jesus **the son of Mary.** At the
time when Mark wrote it was probably too early for slurs on
Jesus' parentage to arise, as they did in controversy with Jews
and pagans; this reading is probably influenced by the doctrine
of the Virgin Birth. But does it belong to the original text? A
variant is attested by P[45] 33 565 700 fam 13 it arm bo[codd] eth

Origen: 'Is not this the son of the builder and of Mary?' Luke
iv. 22 reads: 'Is not this the son of Joseph?' F. C. Grant, *ATR*,
xx (1938), 116, suggested that the true reading of Mark lies
behind that of Matthew: 'Is not this the son of the builder and
brother of James', etc.; cf., however, J. P. Brown, *JBL*, lxxviii
(1959), 222. The names of these four brothers are found here
only: Matthew substitutes 'Joseph' for **Joses**, a Jewish name
common in this period. **James** (i.e. Jacob) is evidently the
'brother of the Lord' who figures prominently in the later
history of the Church: cf. Gal. i. 19; ii. 9, 12; Acts xii. 17; xv. 13;
xxi. 18. No doubt it is the same man whom Paul claims (as a
witness of the resurrection (1 Cor. xv. 7), and the *Gospel according to the Hebrews* preserves a tradition of this (Jerome, *de vir.
illustr.* 2). Josephus gives an account of his martyrdom which
shows that he was held in high respect by the Jewish people
(*Ant.* xx. 9. 1). A more legendary story, in which James appears
as a Nazirite and ascetic, is quoted from Hegesippus by Eusebius, *H.E.* ii. 23. 4-18. Here, as in the *Gospel according to the
Hebrews*, he is called 'James the Just'. He is undoubtedly the
purported author of the Epistle of James (Jas. i. 1). Ecclesiastical
writers early identified him with James the son of Alphaeus
(iii. 18) and James the Less (xv. 40), but there seems to be no
basis for this. Paul knows of other 'brothers of the Lord' (1 Cor.
ix. 5). **Judas** also has a NT writing ascribed to him, the Epistle
of Jude. According to Hegesippus, his grandsons were brought
before the emperor Domitian and questioned. After their release
they 'ruled the church, since they were both martyrs and of the
Lord's family' (Eusebius, *H.E.* iii. 20). Mark's enumeration of
the four brothers may reflect the honour in which the Galilean
Church held Jesus' earthly family. Unless the reading 'the son
of Mary' is pressed very far, there is no reason to think that by
'brother' the evangelist meant 'cousin' or any other relationship.

And they took offence at him. It wounded their pride to
think that one who came from among them should speak and
act as Jesus did. 'Since we are only villagers, he cannot be very
important!'

No prophet is without honour except in his own neigh- 4
bourhood (πατρίς, translated 'home town' in verse 1). The
sixth of the Oxyrhynchus sayings and the *Gospel of Thomas*

(87:5-7, p. 21) contain this as a double proverb: 'Jesus says,
"There is nò prophet acceptable in his own neighbourhood,
nor does a physician do healings among those who know him"'.
Dibelius, *FTG*, p. 110, considers that because of the Semitic
parallelism this is nearer to the original form. In this case the
reference to the physician was changed into the remark of verse
5 that Jesus healed only a few people. But the apocryphal
saying could have developed out of Luke iv. 23-24, and its two
parts have no necessary connexion; they can be used together
but the points are not identical.

5 **He was not able to do any powerful deed there.** The
words should not be pressed too far, though they may reflect a
tradition that Jesus did not work in Nazareth. Mark believes
that he had the power, for he speaks of **a few sick people who
were healed.** As in v. 21-43, faith is a necessary condition,
while in other places the miracles occur independently of men's
6 belief. Only here and in xiv. 33 is Jesus **amazed** (cf. *Problem*,
p. 70); here he is in awe at the **unbelief** which shuts out the
grace of God.

vi. 6b-13. THE SENDING OF THE TWELVE

7 He made a circuit of the villages teaching. And he summoned the Twelve, and began to send them out by twos,
8 and gave them authority over unclean spirits, and directed them to take nothing on the journey except only a
staff, no loaf of bread, no knapsack, no money in their
9 belts, but that they should be shod with sandals, and not to
10 wear two undergarments. And he said to them, 'Wherever you enter a house, stay there until you leave that
11 place. And if any place does not receive you or listen to
you, as you go out of it shake off the dust from your feet as
12 a testimony to them.' And they went out and announced
13 that men should repent, and cast out many demons, and
anointed many sick people with oil and healed them.

The mission discourse is contained in the Synoptics in essentially two forms. Luke x. 1-16 (addressed to the Seventy, with a

sequel in verses 17-20) is the earliest form preserved, though
verses 13-15 may have been added to its original framework. It
is more Palestinian than Mark's account, because (a) it pro-
hibits sandals and salutations on the road (verse 4)—the journeys are to be brief; (b) the Semitic phrase 'son of peace' and the
idea that the *Shalôm* greeting rests on its hearers or returns to
the disciples (verse 6); (c) the message concerns the Kingdom of
God (verses 9, 11); and (d) it is only afterward that the disciples
discover their power over unclean spirits (verse 17). Indeed
Luke x. 16 with its plenary authority seems more appropriate
for the Twelve than for the Seventy.

Mark's version does not specify the message to be proclaimed,
but almost as an afterthought the evangelist speaks of repentance (verse 12); thus the disciples' preaching is modelled on that
of Jesus in i. 15. They are expressly given authority over unclean spirits (verse 7); they should wear sandals, as for a longer
journey (verse 9), and here only in the gospels is it said that they
anointed the sick (verse 13). Thus by Mark's time the discourse
has been adapted to a situation that may not be Palestinian. Its
composite nature is shown by the phrases **and directed them**
(verse 8), **And he said to them** (verse 10).

Luke ix. 1-6 is based on Mark, but the later evangelist omits
the mention of sandals, preaching of repentance, and anointing,
thus bringing the discourse into harmony with the address to
the Seventy. Matt. ix. 37-x. 40 is an elaborate construction
which weaves Mark's discourse and Luke x. 1-16 in with other
materials.

Behind the two forms of the mission charge may lie an early
tradition that Jesus sent the disciples out on short journeys to
herald the Kingdom of God. Like their teacher, they were to
travel in poverty and simplicity, and also in haste, because the
message must be spread as widely as possible. When they en-
countered barren ground they were to go to another place where
hearers might be more receptive (cf. iv. 3-8). Mark thinks of this
as more than a preaching mission. The Twelve, healing and
casting out unclean spirits, are initiated into the entire evangeli-
cal activity of their Lord.

He made a circuit of the villages, literally 'went about in 6b
a circle'. This was probably Jesus' actual method.

7 The **Twelve** were sent out by **twos;** cf. the activity of Peter and John (Acts iii. 1-10; viii. 14-25), Barnabas and Saul (Acts xi. 30; xii. 25; xiv. 28), and Paul and Silas (Acts xv. 40-xvii. 14).

8 They were to **take . . . only a staff,** perhaps as a protection against savage dogs, since Palestinian roads and paths are not usually difficult. But the parallels Matt. x. 10 and Luke ix. 3 forbid the staff, and the present text of Mark may be corrupt. The word rendered **knapsack** can refer to the beggar's bag which Cynic preachers carried; cf. P. Wendland, *Die hellenistisch-römische Kultur* (3rd ed., Tübingen, 1912), p. 84, but such a bag was carried also by shepherds; cf. Josephus, *Ant.* vi. 9. 4. Ancient Greeks, like the Arabs of Palestine today, kept **money in their belts,** i.e. girdles made of cloth; cf. Plutarch, *Moralia*, p. 665 B.

9 A long journey is implied by **sandals** and **two undergarments,** but one is permitted and the other not. Perhaps Mark thinks of an extended journey made in poverty, in which

10 the disciples depend on local hospitality. **Wherever you enter a house, stay there;** i.e. accept what is offered and do not seek something better; cf. the rules for travelling apostles and prophets in *Didache* xi. 3-xii. 5, whose purpose is to prevent the

11 visitor from self-seeking. To **shake off the dust from your feet** is a **testimony** that the disciples have done their duty in giving warning and are free from further responsibility from the fate of their hearers; cf. Luke x. 10 f.; Acts xiii. 51; Ezek. xxxiii. 1-9.

13 The use of **oil** in healing occurs only here in the gospels. Olive oil was regularly used as a remedy in the ancient world; cf. *Catalogus Codicum Astrologorum Graecorum*, vii, p. 178. It was used with wine in treating the wounds of the man who fell among bandits (Luke x. 34). In Jas. v. 14 the presbyters of the church are to pray over the sick man and anoint him. Mark may already think of this act as having a sacramental character.

vi. 14-16. HEROD HEARS OF JESUS

14 **King Herod heard about him, for his name had become well known, and he said, 'John the Baptist is raised from**

the dead, and that is why the powers are working in him'.
Others said, 'It is Elijah', and others said, 'He is a 15
prophet, like one of the prophets'. But when Herod heard 16
it he said, 'The one whom I beheaded—John—he has
been raised up'.

Here a section dealing with an estimate of Jesus follows a
pericope relating to the Twelve, as in iii. 20-30. The suggestions
anticipate those of viii. 28, which may be modelled on them.

King Herod is Herod Antipas, tetrarch of Galilee and 14
Peraea, son of Herod the Great and his wife Malthace, who was
born about 20 B.C. and ruled these territories from the death of
his father in 4 B.C. until A.D. 39. When Herod Agrippa I was
given the former tetrarchy of Philip (Luke iii. 1) with the title
of king, his sister Herodias, the wife of Antipas, became very
jealous and persuaded her husband to demand the royal title.
The emperor Caligula (A.D. 37–41) removed him from office and
exiled him. Antipas was a clever, and on the whole successful,
monarch who rebuilt Sepphoris and constructed forts there and
at Livias in Peraea. He also built Tiberias and named it in
honour of the emperor.

John the Baptist is raised from the dead. The statement
may reflect superstitious fear (cf. verse 20) or it may mean: 'It
is simply John all over again'. **Powers** usually means 'miracles';
hence Torrey, *The Four Gospels*, p. 293, conjectures that the
active verb **are working** is a mistranslation of the Aramaic.
Antipas may, however, have thought of demonic powers.

The coming of **Elijah** was expected to take place before or 15
during the Messianic era (Mal. iv. 5) and this belief was current even among Samaritans; cf. W. Bousset, *Die Religion des
Judentums im späthellenistischen Zeitalter* (3rd ed., Tübingen,
1926), pp. 232 f.

Jesus is significantly recognised as a **prophet**. His teaching
and healings suggested this; he was given the title by his disciples and the common people (Luke xxiv. 19; vii. 16) and may
have accepted it himself (Luke xiii. 33). Except for that of
Messiah, it was the highest rank for a human being which the
Jews could imagine. Cf. F. W. Young, *JBL*, lxviii (1949), 285-
299; F. Gils, *Jésus prophète* (Louvain, 1957).

17 **For Herod himself had sent to have John seized and con-**
fined him in prison on account of Herodias the wife of
18 **Philip his brother, whom he had married. For John had**
said to Herod, 'You are not permitted to have your
19 **brother's wife'. Herodias held this against him and**
20 **wished to kill him, but could not, for Herod was afraid of**
John, knowing him to be an upright and holy man; so he
protected him, and was greatly perplexed as he listened
21 **to him, but he used to listen to him with pleasure. An**
opportune time came when Herod on his birthday gave
a dinner for his grandees and high military officers and
22 **the aristocracy of Galilee, and Herodias' own daughter**
came in and danced, and it pleased Herod and the dinner
23 **guests. The king said to the girl, 'Ask me whatever you**
wish', and he swore to her, 'Whatever you ask I will give
24 **you, even as much as half my kingdom!' And she went**
out and said to her mother, 'What shall I ask?' And she
25 **said, 'the head of John the Baptizer'. At once she hastened**
in to the king and made her request: 'I want you to give
me, right away, on a platter, the head of John the Baptist'.
26 **The king, though very grief-stricken, because of his oaths**
and the dinner guests did not have the will to refuse her.
27 **So the king at once detailed an executioner with the com-**
28 **mand to bring his head. And he went and beheaded him**
in the prison and brought his head on a platter and gave
29 **it to the girl and the girl gave it to her mother. His dis-**
ciples, when they heard of it, came and removed his
corpse and laid it in a tomb.

The account of the death of John corresponds to that of
Jesus' rejection in verses 1-6. That this is its function in the
gospel is indicated by ix. 11-13. If it were not for this purpose
it would seem almost to be an intrusion.

Lohmeyer shows that the story itself is carefully constructed.
Its introduction consists of the imprisonment (verses 17-18),
Herodias' grudge (verse 19) and Herod's reluctance (verse 20).

The central part (verses 21-25) has three scenes, each marked
by a participle. The condemnation concludes the narrative, and
this again contains three participles.

The story is told with a curious objectivity. It has no religious character, and gives no judgement, favourable or otherwise, on any of the actors. It is such a tale as might have been
current in the bazaars of Palestine and was probably in Aramaic.
Antipas and Herodias are portrayed as oriental monarchs (cf.
Esther v. 3, 6; vii. 2), and the treatment of the girl suggests the
story in Herodotus ii. 121. 5, where the king puts his daughter
in a brothel. See also Plutarch, *Crassus* 33.

Josephus gives a divergent account of the Baptist's death. He
says nothing about the denunciation of Herod for his marriage;
Herod feared, according to Josephus, that John's great influence over the people might lead him to raise a rebellion (*Ant.*
xviii. 5. 2).

Herod . . . confined him in prison, according to Josephus 17
in the fortress of Machaerus on the east side of the Dead Sea.
This does not fit well with the story here told, for if Herod's
party took place in Machaerus it is curious that the chief men
of Galilee are there (verse 21). If, however, the scene is in
Galilee, John seems to be near by, for his execution takes place
at once (verses 27-28). The gospel tradition may therefore have
in mind *Qasr bint el-malik* on the hill overlooking Tiberias; cf.
Bishop, p. 141.

Herodias, according to Josephus, was not **the wife of
Philip his brother** but of another (half-) brother Herod. This
princess was a sister of Herod Agrippa I and grand-daughter of
Herod the Great and Mariamme. In order to marry her, Antipas
divorced his first wife, a daughter of the Nabataean king Aretas
IV. This monarch thereupon made war on the tetrarch. When
Antipas was subsequently defeated in A.D. 36, the Jewish people
regarded this as a divine punishment for the murder of John the
Baptist.

You are not permitted to have your brother's wife. This 18
was the Mosaic Law (Lev. xviii. 16; xx. 21).

Herod was afraid of John, almost superstitiously (cf. verse 20
14), and therefore **protected him** against Herodias' designs. In
Josephus' account, Herod is moved by political considerations

alone. The phrase, **and was greatly perplexed as he listened to him,** is textually uncertain. The Latin and Syriac versions, and most later MSS., read 'did many things' (ἐποίει) in place of 'was greatly perplexed' (ἠπόρει). Schmiedel conjectured that the phrase belongs in verse 16; cf. Luke ix. 7.

21   The **dinner** was attended by **grandees** or courtiers; **high military officers,** literally tribunes (commanding cohorts of about 600 men each), but it is not certain that his forces were organised on the Roman model and the tetrarch was not allowed to keep an army, only a police force; and the **aristocracy of**
22 **Galilee,** as distinguished from the courtiers. It seems strange that **Herodias' own daughter** should dance before a group of men who had probably been drinking heavily. If this is not just an imaginative tale, the manners of the court were corrupt and would have been shocking to religious Jews. Josephus gives the girl's name as Salome. Her father was Herodias' first husband Herod, and she must have been born about A.D. 10. At the time of the death of John she may already have been married to her uncle Philip, tetrarch of Ituraea and Trachonitis.

23   **Whatever you ask I will give you, even as much as half my kingdom!** Herodotus ix. 109 tells of a similarly rash promise made by Xerxes to a young woman with whom he had
24 fallen in love. It is almost like a fairy-tale or the *Thousand and One Nights* when the girl goes out and asks her mother what
25 request she should make. The **platter** is a gruesome touch
26 ascribed to the girl herself. The request put the tetrarch in an extremely difficult position; but, like Xerxes, **because of his**
27 **oaths** Antipas **did not have the will to refuse her.** The Latin loan-word σπεκουλάτωρ can mean 'spy', 'scout', 'courtier', but also **executioner;** cf. Sherwin-White, pp. 124, 136 f.

29   For the **disciples** of John, cf. on i. 4; ii. 18.

vi. 30-44. RETURN OF THE TWELVE; THE FEED-ING OF THE FIVE THOUSAND

30 **The emissaries gathered in Jesus' presence and reported**
31 **to him all their activities and teachings. And he said to**

them, 'You yourselves must come, all alone, into a deserted place and rest for a little'. For the people who were
coming and going were many, and they did not even have
an opportunity to eat. So they departed in the boat to a 32
deserted place, all by themselves. Many people saw them 33
leave and recognised them, so from all the towns they
converged, running there on foot, and got there ahead of
them. As he disembarked he saw a great crowd and felt 34
sorry for them because they were 'like sheep without a
shepherd', and he began to give them a great deal of
teaching.

By now the hour was late and his disciples approached 35
him and said, 'The place is deserted and it is already a
late hour. Send them away so that they can go into the 36
farms round about and the villages and buy themselves
something to eat.' He answered them, 'You yourselves 37
must give them something to eat'. They said to him,
'Should we go and buy two hundred denarii worth of
bread and give them something to eat?' He said to them, 38
'How many loaves have you? Go see.' And when they
found out, they said, 'Five; and two fish'. He directed 39
them to have them all sit down, group by group, on the
green grass. They got down, like so many garden plots, 40
in hundreds and fifties. And he took the five loaves and 41
two fish and, looking up to heaven, blessed and broke the
loaves and gave them to the disciples to set before them,
and the two fish he divided among all. All ate and were 42
satisfied, and they took up enough fragments to fill twelve 43
baskets and also some of the fish. And those who had 44
eaten the loaves were five thousand men.

Mark's gospel has been described by the word *chiaroscuro*.
After the deep shadows of the preceding sections, and before the
ominous controversy over the clean and the unclean (vii. 1-23),
come two epiphanies, the first of which is almost a pastoral inter-
lude. Although the disciples are not ready to appreciate the full
significance of the events, they are permitted glimpses of Jesus'
divine power over nature. Since the story of the Feeding inevitably suggests the Eucharist, it may look forward to the Trans-

figuration (ix. 2-8), the Last Supper (xiv. 17-26), and x. 38-40, where there is allusion to both sacraments.

Several motifs may be interconnected. Carrington, pp. 153-155, regards this section as the lesson for the first Sunday after the Pascha. The story exemplifies Toynbee's idea of 'withdrawal and return' (cf. i. 12-13, 35; iii. 7, 13; vii. 24), though this is of course subsidiary. The miracle of the manna (Exod. xvi) took place in the wilderness, and the Fourth Evangelist connects the miraculous feeding with both the manna and the Eucharist (John vi. 30-34, 48-51). It was a rabbinic belief that the manna, like other miraculous events of the Exodus, would be repeated in the Coming Age. This idea is found as early as 2 Baruch xxix. 8 and *Sibylline Oracles* frag. iii. 46-49. The form of the gospel stories (but especially that in John) is influenced by the miracle of Elisha in 2 Kings iv. 42-44; cf. also 1 Kings xvii. 9-16. There is the further question whether these narratives are related to the Messianic Banquet in the Kingdom of God, at which the sea-monster Leviathan was to be given to the people as food (Ps. lxxiv. 14; cf. SB, i, 684); the mention of fish in this passage suggests the possibility. The Banquet is evidently referred to in Matt. viii. 11 and may furnish the background for the parable of the Great Supper (Matt. xxii. 1-14 =Luke xiv. 16-24) and the prayers of *Didache* ix-x. The discipline fragment from Qumran published by D. Barthélemy and J. T. Milik, *Qumran Cave I* (Oxford, 1955), pp. 108-118, contemplates a common meal in which the Anointed (or lay Messiah) is to be present together with the priest. The priest takes precedence of the Messiah, for he first pronounces the blessing and 'stretches his hand out to the bread'. This is sometimes thought to be an 'eschatological sacrament' (to use Schweitzer's phrase) in anticipation of the Banquet in the age to come.

Certainly the metaphor of feeding is used frequently in the NT to refer to the reception of spiritual gifts (cf., e.g., John x. 9; 1 Cor. iii. 2; 1 Pet. ii. 2), and in this story Jesus' teaching is closely connected with the feeding (verse 34). Whether or not the Messianic Banquet is a motif of the story, Jesus is pictured as the father of a Jewish household who blesses the bread and distributes it to his family, and this family consists of his disciples (iii. 34-35). Indeed the miracle can be considered a dramatic illustration of the prayer 'Give us this day our daily bread' (Matt. vi. 11 =Luke xi. 3) and the teaching of Matt. vi. 26 =Luke xii. 24.

It is difficult to arrive at the nature of the original event. The modern suggestion, that everyone shared his food with his neighbour and therefore all had enough, is edifying, but misses the evangelist's point. It is no more satisfactory than the account in the docetic Acts of John xciii, according to which Jesus could satisfy people miraculously by giving each a tiny morsel. The evangelist thought of this as an actual multiplication of bread, and stories of marvellous plenty have been told in modern Syria. It is not fanciful, however, to suggest that at table Jesus was the father of the disciples and that all these meals had a religious character. T. W. Manson, *The Servant Messiah* (Cambridge, 1953), pp. 69-71, supposes that originally this was the story of Jesus' meeting with zealots, 'a maccabean host with no Judas Maccabaeus, a leaderless mob, a danger to themselves and to everyone else. He speaks to them at some length and later they share a meal, at which Jesus uses symbols which afterwards came to be associated with the suffering and death of Messiah.' Manson notes that according to John vi. 15 the men wished to take him by force and make him king. This theory fits well with the language of verse 34 and the 'hundreds and fifties' of verse 40.

The emissaries (ἀπόστολοι; here the word may be used 30 non-technically) . . . **reported** to Jesus, as in Luke x. 17. The story of John's death provides an interval of time during which the disciples are on their journey; cf. v. 25-34, where the same literary device is used.

The invitation to **rest for a little** (cf. Matt. xi. 28) suggests 31 the Sabbath rest for the people of God (Heb. iv. 9), but if it has typological meaning it is only for the evangelist; the interest of the tradition was in Jesus' compassion on the disciples, who have been travelling and **did not even have an opportunity to eat** (cf. iii. 20). 'Eating' and 'bread' recur as motifs in vi. 52; vii. 3, 27; viii. 14-21. Mark seems to think of Jesus as going **in the** 32 **boat** from the western or north-western shore **to a deserted place** on the eastern side of the lake. Knox, *Sources*, i. 45 f. regards the geography as confused.

Verses 33-34 serve as a second introduction to the narrative, in which the interest centres in the crowds rather than in the
33 disciples. The picture of the people going **on foot** around the edge of the lake is lifelike. They might have come from Capharnaum and Bethsaida, villages which probably had not more than
34 two or three thousand inhabitants apiece. **Like sheep without a shepherd** (Num. xxvii. 17; 1 Kings xxii. 17; Ezek. xxxiv. 5) suggests the divine compassion; initially they are fed with **teaching.**

37 Jesus' command, **You yourselves must give them something to eat,** which to the disciples seems so impractical, expresses the hospitality of the Man of God, who acts on behalf of God. Elisha gives such an order in 2 Kings iv. 42, and in the following verse his servant asks a question similar to that of Jesus' disciples. **Two hundred denarii worth of bread** might be required, a large amount, for a denarius was a day's wages for a labourer. The disciples' misunderstanding is a recurrent theme in this gospel and is further developed in John.

38 The **loaves** were perhaps the flat, pancake-like bread still eaten in Palestine. The **fish** served as relish for the bread and were probably pickled or smoked. Magdala (Taricheae) exported such delicacies to various parts of the empire. Bread and fish are used in early Christian art as symbols of the Eucharist, and the splendid mosaics of et-Ṭabgha on the Sea of Galilee are an example of this; cf. A. M. Schneider, *The Church of the Multiplying of the Loaves and Fishes* (London, 1937). It is here that tradition locates this miracle, but it is not a *deserted place* (verse 32). No symbolical meaning is to be seen in the numbers **five** and **two;** the disciples had come away with Jesus in the boat and had no more.

39 They sat down **group by group** (συμπόσια συμπόσια, literally 'banquets' or 'drinking parties'). On **the green grass**—which would have been green only in the spring—their appearance,
40 with their clothing of various colours—was **like so many garden plots** (πρασιαὶ πρασιαί). Lohmeyer quotes a Talmudic saying that pupils studying Torah 'arrange themselves in ranks like the vines in a vineyard'. The groupings by **hundreds and fifties** seems conventional in Jewish literature; cf. Exod. xviii. 21 and the Qumran War Scroll.

Looking up to heaven was a normal attitude of prayer, 41 particularly for the table blessing, and it has continued in Christian liturgical use. Jesus **blessed** ($εὐλόγησεν$) the food by giving thanks; this verb and $εὐχαριστέω$ are used interchangeably in viii. 6-7 and xiv. 22-23. The usual Jewish prayer at the beginning of a meal is: 'Blessed art thou, O Lord our God, king of the world, who hast brought forth bread from the earth'. A longer thanksgiving is customary after the dinner. He **broke the loaves** as the father of a family does at the time of the blessing.

The **disciples** acted almost as deacons at a Christian Euchar- 43 ist; they **set** the food **before them** and **took up . . . fragments** at the end. To collect the larger pieces of food afterward was good etiquette at Jewish banquets. The miracle, as Lohmeyer remarks, occurs quietly and is unnoticed except by the disciples and Jesus; thus what the story emphasises is that through the divine generosity **all ate and were satisfied.** This lavishness is like that of the wine miracle of John ii. 1-11. The **twelve baskets** were probably large ones; Juvenal (iii. 14; vi. 542) uses the same word to refer to food hampers carried by Jews so that they might observe the dietary laws. Their number may correspond to that of the disciples.

vi. 45-52. THE WALKING ON THE WATER

At once he made his disciples embark in the boat and 45 proceed to the other shore toward Bethsaida, while he dismissed the crowd. And when he had said good-bye to 46 them he departed into the hill country to pray. When 47 evening had come the boat was in the middle of the lake and he himself was alone on the land. And seeing them 48 desperately worn out by the rowing, for the wind was against them, about the fourth watch of the night he came to them walking on the lake; and he was on the point of passing by them. But when they saw him walking on the 49 lake they thought he was a ghost, and they cried out; for 50 all had seen him and were terrified. But he at once spoke with them and said 'Courage, here I AM! Do not be

51 **afraid.' He came up to them and got into the boat, and**
52 **the wind died down; and they were extremely bewildered, for they did not understand about the loaves, but
their minds were dulled.**

The second epiphany may be a double one, containing an
account of Jesus' walking on the water and the remnants of a
tale of the stilling of a storm (verses 48b, 51a). Two reasons are
given for Jesus leaving his disciples: to dismiss the crowd (verse
45) and to pray (verse 46). Note also that after the phrase **spoke
with them** the words **and said** are redundant, and that
Courage and **Do not be afraid** are doublets.

The location is carefully chosen; cf. iv. 35-41, which follows
the parables of the Kingdom, as this narrative follows the
Feeding. He who can feed (and teach) his people miraculously
is the Lord of space and time and the elements and can walk on
the water. This is suggested by verse 51 and also by John vi.
25-26; and in both gospels the disciples are too dull of mind
to see the connexion between the wonders. Lohmeyer suggests
further that, since the sea is often a symbol for death (Pss.
xviii. 15-17; lxix. 2-3; Od. Sol. xxxix). Jesus is shown to be the
Lord of life and overcomer of death (cf. Matt. xiv. 28-31 and
Ecclus. xxiv. 5, where Wisdom walks in the depths of the abyss).
Thus the passage vi. 30-viii. 26, where this teaching is given in
veiled form, corresponds to viii. 27-x. 45, with its themes of
suffering, death and resurrection.

45   The localities of the story are not certain. It has already been
noted that Mark seems to place the Feeding on the east side of
the lake. Because of the roughly oval contour of the Sea of
Galilee, a crossing from here to the neighbourhood of Bethsaida could be described as **the other shore.** This seems more
likely since the disciples arrive at Gennesaret or Gennesar
(verse 53), having been blown off their course. **Bethsaida** may
be the Bethsaida Julias, which lay on the east side of the Jordan
north of the point where it opens into the lake. This was rebuilt
by Philip and named in honour of Augustus' daughter. It is
possible, however, to identify Bethsaida with Khirbet el-'Araj,
on the lake; cf. Kraeling, *Atlas*, pp. 388 f.

46   Jesus went **into the hill country to pray;** cf. i. 35; iii 13.

From this point he could see them **desperately worn out by** 48 **the rowing** or 'straining at the oars'; the verb means 'to be tortured'. They would have been rowing with the **wind . . . against them** for about four miles. The **fourth watch of the night** was approximately from 3 a.m. to 6 a.m. This time division is Roman; the Jews divided the night into three watches. Rawlinson speaks of the encouragement which this story would have given to the church in Rome. 'Bereft of leaders and confronted by a hostile Government, it must have indeed appeared that the wind was contrary and progress difficult and slow . . . but the Living One, Master of winds and waves—will surely come quickly for their salvation, even though it be in the fourth watch of the night' (p. 88). The trip to Gennesaret by land was ten or eleven miles and would have required about three hours; cf. Bishop, p. 144.

Jesus **came to them walking on the lake.** It has often been noted that the shore is shallow because of silt brought down from Mount Hermon in the spring, thus Jesus could pass through shallow water and appear to be walking on its face. But such a rationalisation removes most of the point of the story; and, as Bishop says, this *sudd* seldom extends as far as Gennesaret.

He **was on the point of passing by them.** This translation of ἤθελεν, 'he was wishing', is a conjecture; cf. H. G. Meecham, *Exp. Times*, xlvii (March, 1936), 284 f. It is equally possible that the verb should be taken literally. If so, there are many conjectures as to Jesus' motive: to test their faith (Bartlet); to show himself to them as Lord of the water (H. J. Holtzmann); he walks across naturally as Lord of the elements, and it is only their danger that leads him to change his course (Klostermann); it shows the divine exaltation of the Son of Man, since Yahweh passed by Moses on Sinai and Elijah on Horeb (Lohmeyer). Goodspeed, following the Twentieth Century version, translates: 'and was going to join them'. This is a possible rendering of παρελθεῖν.

Courage, here I AM! ἐγώ εἰμί, the words of Yahweh in 50 Exod. iii. 14, are often used in the gospels to denote a real or pretended divine revelation; cf. xiii. 6; xiv. 62; Luke xxiv. 39; John vi. 35; viii. 12, etc.

52   The disciples' **minds were dulled.** The verb πωροῦσθαι, 'to be hardened', and cognate words, are used almost technically in the NT to describe the blindness of Israel in not accepting the Good News; cf. iii. 5; viii. 17; Rom. xi. 7, 25; 2 Cor. iii. 14; and John xii. 40 which quotes Isa. vi. 9, not however from the LXX, which does not use this verb.

vi. 53-56. SUMMARY: HEALINGS

53 **When they had crossed over to the land they came to**
54 **Gennesaret and moored there. As they were coming out**
55 **of the boat people at once recognised him and ran around**
through all that country and began to bring round to him
on their mattresses all who were sick, wherever they
56 **heard that he was, and wherever he entered villages or**
cities or farms, they laid the ill down on street corners,
and begged him that they might touch even the fringe of
his outer garment, and whoever touched him was healed.

53   The plain of **Gennesaret** ('the Gennesar' in Josephus, 'Ginnesar' in the Talmud) is known today as el-Ghuwēr. It lies on the north-west shore between Magdala and Khirbet Minyeh. Still further to the north-west is Tell Ḥum (Capharnaum). Because of the amazing fertility of the region, Josephus calls it 'the ambition of nature' (*B.J.* iii. 10. 8).

55   The account of healings resembles i. 32-34; iii. 7-12, except
56 that here there is no mention of demons. The vivid picture of verse 56 suggests that a traditional story underlies this. The **fringe of his outer garment** is perhaps the tassel or *ṣiṣith* which every Jew wore (Num. xv. 38-41; Deut. xxii. 12). Cf. the action of the woman in v. 27; also Acts v. 15.

vii. 1-23. CONTROVERSY OVER THE CLEAN
AND THE UNCLEAN

The Pharisees and some of the scholars who had come 1
from Jerusalem gathered to meet him. And when they 2
saw that some of his disciples ate loaves with 'profane',
that is, unwashed hands (for the Pharisees, indeed all the 3
Jews, do not eat unless they wash their hands up to the
wrist, thus observing the tradition of the elders; and when 4
they come from the market-place they do not eat unless
they purify; they observe many other rules handed down,
such as immersion of cups and jugs and copper vessels), 5
then the Pharisees and the scholars questioned him,
'Why do not your disciples behave according to the
tradition of the elders but eat bread with profane hands?'

He said to them, 'Isaiah prophesied splendidly about 6
you hypocrites, as it is written:
"This people honour me with their lips,
  But their heart is far away from me;
  In vain they worship me,
  Teaching commandments of men as their teachings". 7
You forsake God's commandment and observe the tradi- 8
tion of men.'

And he said to them, 'How splendidly you reject God's 9
commandment to keep your tradition! For Moses said, 10
"Honour your father and your mother", and "He who
curses father or mother must surely die". But as for you, 11
you say, if a man says to his father or mother, "The
benefit you might have had from me is Korban", that is,
"temple offering", you no longer permit him to do any- 12
thing for his father or mother. Thus you annul the word 13
of God by the tradition you transmit; and you do many
things like this.'

14 He summoned the crowd again and said to them,
15 'Listen to me, all of you, and understand. Nothing that
comes from outside a man and goes into him can make
him "profane", but the things that come out of the man
are what profane the man.'
17 When he entered a house away from the crowd, his
18 disciples questioned him about the figure, and he said to
them, 'Are you too as stupid as this? Do you not realise
that nothing from outside that enters into a man is able to
19 profane him, because it does not go into his mind but into
his belly, and it goes out into the latrine?' (Thus he made
20 all foods clean.) And he said, 'What comes out of a man,
21 that is what profanes the man. For it is from the inside,
out of men's minds, that evil plans proceed—fornication,
22 theft, murder, adultery, coveting, malicious acts, deceit,
wantonness, selfishness, foul speech, arrogance, foolish-
23 ness—all these evil things come from inside and profane
the man.'

Mark employs this controversy section as the climax of Jesus'
Galilean ministry. His opponents and his home village have
rejected him, and the minds of his disciples are still dulled. He
now denounces his enemies, and after this point he is only
momentarily on Galilean soil.

The section is composite and deals with three issues: (a)
verses 1-8, unwashed hands; (b) verses 9-13, the Korban vow;
(c) verses 14-15, 17-23, ritual uncleanness. Verses 1-13 are
directed to the Pharisees, verses 14-15 to the people and verses
17-23 to the disciples. A long tradition of controversy between
Gentile Christians and Jews lies behind the collection, although
it may contain some genuine sayings of Jesus. Matthew copies
this section, but rearranges and edits it. Luke ignores it altogether—it is the beginning of his 'great omission'—partly
because he regards its issues as already settled and not relevant
to the Gentile Church for which he writes. Mark, however,
represents a church in daily contact with the Jewish community
in Rome, and he feels the need of distinguishing Jesus' way
from that of the synagogue.

1   The scene is set by the appearance of the **Pharisees**, prob-

ably those who live in Galilee, and **some of the scholars who
had come from Jerusalem.** The Pharisees of the Holy City
had probably begun to extend their propaganda to the north;
in the next century Galilee was an important centre of rabbinic
Judaism.

Their criticism is that **some of his disciples ate loaves 2
with 'profane', that is, unwashed hands.** The use of this
adjective, literally 'common', in a technical sense, seems to be
Jewish; cf. 1 Macc. i. 47, 62; *Letter of Aristeas* 315; Acts x. 14;
Rom. xiv. 14; Rev. xxi. 27. The use of the word in Plutarch
(*Eroticus* iv, p. 751B), 'Love is good and proper, but pleasure
is common and slavish', points, however, in the direction of
this. The custom of washing before meals must have been
adopted only recently by the Pharisaic brotherhoods, and does
not seem to have been generally binding before A.D. 100.
Priests were required to make an ablution before partaking of
the sacrifices (Lev. xxii. 1-16) and the practice was extended to
laymen and to ordinary foods on the principle of a 'fence about
the Law' (Mishnah Aboth i. 1); i.e. if it is good for priests to
be holy, it is appropriate for all the Holy People. The tractate
Yadaim in the Mishnah contains many of the later regulations.

Verses 3 and 4 are a parenthesis supplied to explain the
situation to Gentile Christians; it is not included in Matt. xv. 3
1-2, but all MSS. of Mark except Cod. 2427 contain it. The
phrase **indeed all the Jews** would have been incorrect in
Jesus' time and even when Mark wrote; thus it and perhaps all
of the parenthesis is a later interpolation. **Up to the wrist** is a
conjectural translation of πυγμῇ, 'with the fist'; Yadaim ii. 3
says that water must be poured on the hands up to the wrist.
The variant reading πυκνά (S W vg syᵖ) indicates the difficulty
of the word. Torrey conjectures that the Aramaic read *ligmar la*
('unless they wash their hands they eat not at all') and the word
was misread as *ligmod*, 'fist'; but this is unnecessary. The parenthetic explanation would probably have arisen in a Greek-
speaking, not an Aramaic-speaking community. Rulings about
washings must immediately have become part of **the tradition
of the elders,** i.e. the Oral Law, which was first codified in the
Mishnah in the early third century. The Pharisees believed
that it was ultimately derived from Moses on Sinai, and they

put it on an equal footing with the Bible. The point of view is set forth in Aboth i. 1, 'Moses received the Torah from Sinai and transmitted it to the prophets, and the prophets transmitted it to the men of the Great Synagogue. They said three things: Be deliberate in judgement, raise up many disciples, and make a fence about the Law.' The passage goes on to enumerate the other teachers through whom the tradition was passed. It is altogether likely that Jesus rejected the Pharisees' claim of the authority of their tradition and that this was one of the most important issues between them. Indeed other Galileans resisted the Pharisaic programme; cf. *JOT*, chap. iii. The elders are the ordained and recognised scholars; cf. E. Lohse, *Die Ordination im Spätjudentum und im NT* (Göttingen, 1951), p. 51.

4   In **the market-place** they might come into contact with unclean persons or things so that they would have to **purify** or sprinkle themselves. The words may, however, refer to anything brought from the market. The **immersion of pots and jugs and copper vessels** is illustrated by the Mishnah tractate Kelim.

Verses 6-8 answer the question of verse 5 only by saying that
7 the Pharisaic rules are **commandments of men.** The quotation is apparently from the LXX of Isa. xxix. 13, though Mark's text is not identical with the latter. The answer probably cannot be derived from Jesus, for it depends on the Greek, not the
6 Hebrew. Here the Pharisees are called **hypocrites,** as in Matt. xxiii. 13, 15, 23, 25, 27, 29, because they pretend to follow God but follow men. The Greek word originally means a 'play actor', then a dissembler who pretends to be what he is not, as here. Elsewhere in the gospels it can mean a good-for-nothing fellow (Matt. xxiv. 51), perhaps the Aram. *han^e fa*, or one who is inconsistent in his piety (Matt. vii. 5; xxiii. 23, 25); cf. Cadbury, *Jesus: What Manner of Man*, p. 83. A second-century rabbi remarked: 'There are ten portions of hypocrisy in the world, and nine of them are in Jerusalem'.

8   The charge that they **forsake God's commandment** leads into the next section, dealing with oaths. Such phrases as
9, 11 **How splendidly** and **But as for you, you say,** are known in rabbinic controversies; cf. M. Smith, *Tannaitic Parallels to the Gospels* (Philadelphia, 1951), pp. 26-29. The appeal to the

biblical text (Deut. v. 16 =Exod. xx. 12; Exod. xxi. 15-17, both apparently from the LXX) might not at this time have been persuasive to Jews, for the law enforcing oaths was as much a part of the written Law as the Decalogue. If the Pharisees enforced a law which caused cruel hardship they were following what was believed to be God's commandment. The argument attributed to Jesus would convince them only if certain provisions in the Law are basic and others are subsidiary to them, an assumption that lies behind x. 5-8.

Korban originally means 'gift', i.e. **temple offering;** cf. 11 J. A. Fitzmyer, *JBL*, lxxviii (1959), 60-65; it came to be used as a formula for a vow or oath. It is not clear whether in the hypothetical case a man has vowed to God the property which might have **helped his father or mother,** or whether he has merely sworn (perhaps by the gift in the Temple, Matt. xxiii. 18) not to support them. Whatever may have been the 12 case in Jesus' time, later Pharisaism was more liberal and humane; by A.D. 100, the rabbis ruled that a vow taken to the detriment of father or mother could be abrogated (Mishnah Nedarim ix. 1), and it came to be a general rule of Jewish Law that Exod. xx. 12 took precedence over a number of other provisions, such as the Sabbath law. A legal tradition cannot operate without some means of resolving the conflict of laws. How early Pharisaism developed such a doctrine we do not know, but Jesus at any rate drew a clear distinction between the 'weightier' and more trivial matters of the Law (Matt. xxiii. 23; cf. Luke xi. 42). In doing this he seems to have appealed to common-sense standards of right and wrong. For his opposition to oaths, cf. Matt. v. 33-37; xxiii. 16-22. Thus verses 10-13 may ultimately be based on his teaching. On the Korban and related vows, cf. S. Lieberman, *Greek in Jewish Palestine* (New York, 1942), pp. 115-143; S. Belkin, *JBL*, lv (1936), 227-234.

The next teaching, which is much more radical, purports to 14 be addressed to **the crowd,** and is spoken with supreme authority (cf. 'Hear, O Israel', Deut. v. 1). It evidently comes from a 15 separate source. **Nothing that comes from outside a man and goes into him can make him 'profane'.** A simpler form of the saying is found in the *Gospel of Thomas* (83:24-27, p. 11). Such a principle sweeps away not only hundreds of traditions embodied in the Talmud but many parts of the OT Law. Christians were slow to accept it. St. Paul had difficulty in maintaining table-fellowship between Gentile and Jewish Christians because of the Law (Gal. ii. 11-13) and finally had to conclude that Christ had made the Law obsolete (Gal. iii. 19-29) since one must keep the whole Law if one is bound to it at all (Gal. v. 3; cf. Jas. ii. 10). The Book of Acts pictures Peter as needing a divine revelation before he can associate with a Gentile (x. 1-29). If the saying in verse 15 had been known and accepted by all followers of Jesus, the controversies of the early Church could scarcely have arisen. On the other hand, the activity of Jesus in reaching out to sinners, his un-hesitating help to the leper (i. 40-45) and his occasional con-tact with Gentiles (vii. 24-30) led logically to the position taken by the Hellenists and St. Paul. Furthermore, the tradition con-tains a saying about the outside and the inside of the cup (Matt. xxiii. 25-26 =Luke xi. 39-41) which makes the same point as Mark vii. 15. Bacon indeed thinks that Mark vii. 1-23 is built up out of this Q saying, which was just metaphorical enough that its full significance might not have been immediately per-ceived. It perhaps required time and the actual experience of the Christian mission for the implications of Jesus' teaching to be drawn out. To this extent there is truth in Mark's theory that the disciples' minds were dulled.

The last part of the section, of course, plays on this theme. 17 The teaching, like the interpretation of the parables (iv. 10), is given in private, and this is a sign that it is not part of the well- 19 known tradition. Verse 19, by using the rough word rendered **latrine,** in a vivid and literal way reinforces the idea that food has nothing to do with man's **mind** but with his bodily func-tions; thus there can be defilement only in the moral realm. Cf. 1 Sam. xxiv. 13, 'Out of the wicked comes wickedness'. **Thus he made all foods clean:** the participle καθαρίζων cannot be taken with ἐκπορεύεται and something must be sup- 21-23 plied, such as τοῦτο ἔλεγεν. The clause may be an early gloss. Catalogues of vices (verses 21-23) have often been thought to be characteristic of Hellenistic, not Jewish, teaching; but parallels are found in the Manual of Discipline (1QS iv. 9-11) as well as in Rom. i. 29-31; Gal. v. 19-23. The list is not in

completely logical order, but in general it proceeds from overt
acts to foul speech and from this to attitudes of mind.

vii. 24-30. THE SYROPHOENICIAN WOMAN

**From there he set out for the territory of Tyre. And when 24
he went into a house he did not want anyone to recognise
him. He was not able to escape notice; instead, a woman 25
whose daughter had an unclean spirit at once heard
about him, and she came and fell at his feet. The woman 26
was a Greek, by nation a Syrophoenician, and she asked
him to cast the demon out of her daughter. And he said 27
to her, 'Let the children be satisfied first, for it is not right
to take the children's bread and throw it to the dogs'.
But she answered him, 'Yes, sir; yet the dogs under the 28
table eat from the children's crumbs'. And he said to her, 29
'Because of what you have said, go; the demon has gone
out of your daughter'. And she went home and found the 30
child lying on the bed and the demon gone out.**

The evangelist now shifts the scene of Jesus' ministry to
Gentile territory. With the exception of the passage viii. 22-26,
he seems to be predominantly in non-Jewish lands until ix. 30,
and even then he travels incognito. It is understandable that,
after the great controversy with the Pharisees, Jesus should
turn his face toward Judaea and Jerusalem (cf. Luke ix. 51;
in the third gospel the Galilean ministry practically ends with
the Feeding, since Luke omits the controversy). Furthermore,
part of the interval before his departure must have been spent
among the Gentiles, as the mention of Caesarea Philippi indicates (viii. 27).

There are, however, signs that most of the 'Gentile' ministry
is Mark's artificial combination of traditions. (a) The evangelist
follows the pattern of iii. 7-8, where he lists the homes of our
Lord's disciples; thus Jesus carries on a ministry in Galilee
(chaps. i-vi), Tyre, Sidon and the Decapolis (chap. vii), the
tetrarchy of Philip (chap. viii), Peraea and Judaea (chaps. x-xi).

The trip begun here would ostensibly take him north-west to the
Phoenician sea-coast or near it, thence through the Lebanon to
Abilene, the Hauran and Batanaea in the Decapolis; for the geo-
graphical problems, cf. on verse 31. (b) Elijah's flight from Ahab
(I Kings xix. 1-3) may furnish a pattern. (c) Several passages in
chap. viii may be doublets of material in chaps. vi-vii.

vi. 30-44. The Five Thousand	viii. 1-9. The Four Thousand
vi. 45. To Bethsaida	viii. 10. To Dalmanutha
vi. 47-51. Sign of Walking on Water	viii. 11-12. No sign will be given
vi. 53. Crossing of lake; lack of understanding	viii. 13-21. Crossing of lake (verse 13); lack of under-standing
vii. 31-37. The deaf mute (saliva)	viii. 22-26. The blind man (saliva)

This suggests either that Mark has two varying accounts of the
same period in Jesus' ministry, or that he artificially parallels the
Galilean ministry with one in Gentile territory. (d) Much of the
material came to him in oral form, or was thoroughly rewritten
by him. Sir John Hawkins, *OSSP*, pp. 63-66, argues that vi.
45-viii. 26 exhibits the peculiarities of Mark's style to a higher
degree than elsewhere. (e) A further pattern is visible. The discourse vii. 1-23 corresponds to Isa. xxix. 13-14 and the two
miracles vii. 31-37 and viii. 22-26 to the deaf and blind of Isa.
xxix. 18 (cf. the μογιλάλον of Isa. xxxv. 6).

This is the only story in Mark where the person healed is
unambiguously designated as a Gentile. Q also seems to have
contained one such story (Matt. viii. 5-13 =Luke vii. 1-10), and
in both narratives there is emphasis on the faith of the Gentile.
Matt. viii. 10 =Luke vii. 9 explicitly contrasts this with that of
Israel, while in Mark the contrast is implied. Other Marcan
healings perhaps originally involved Gentiles (v. 1-20; vii. 32-
37; viii. 22-26) but the evangelist possibly thinks of twelve healings among Jews and one of a Gentile, corresponding to the
twelve disciples and Levi (cf. on ii. 14).

24   The **territory of Tyre** at this time extended into Galilee as
far as Kedesh; cf. Kraeling, *Atlas*, p. 387. Branscomb, *ad loc.*,
suggests that Jesus **did not want anyone to recognise him**

because he was practically in exile and unable to help his own
people; shall he give to Gentiles that which he cannot give to
his own? (verse 27). The woman's daughter is called θυγάτριον, 25
but the diminutive may be a term of endearment, not an indication that she is a child, since it is occasionally used of a girl of
marriageable age. **The woman was a Greek;** the word prob- 26
ably indicates that she was a pagan. **By nation a Syrophoenician** denotes the political unit to which she was subject.

The **children** are obviously Jews (cf. Hos. i. 10), and the 27
dogs Gentiles. Montefiore remarks that Jews used this term of
opprobrium only occasionally. Commentators have often tried
to soften the harshness of the words. Thus (a) the diminutive
κυνάρια is emphasised, and Jesus is thought to refer playfully
to house-dogs or puppies; but diminutives are used loosely in
late Greek. (b) Or perhaps he says in effect, 'My disciples would
regard Gentiles as dogs, but what have you and I to say to
that?' Neither of these explanations is satisfying, and the remark
remains abrupt and seemingly out of character for Jesus. Would
he have been likely to jest with a woman in so great need? (c)
Matthew's parallel shows that that evangelist thinks of Jesus as
testing the woman's faith. Two other possibilities remain: (d) As
Branscomb says, the word is not intended as an insult but as a
statement of Jesus' perplexity: does he have a right to minister
to the Gentiles? (e) Perhaps the dialogue shows an actual development of Jesus' understanding of his mission; now it is clear
that he must not restrict the Good News to his own nation. This
could follow logically from the teaching of verse 15. It is interesting that the Johannine Christ can say 'salvation is from the
Jews' (John iv. 22) but immediately speak of a new universal
worship (iv. 23-24). This reflects the early Church's twofold
understanding of Jesus: his loyalty to his own people and tradition and the way in which he transcended this.

It is more natural for **bread** to refer to teaching than to healing (Lohmeyer; cf. Matt. vii. 6). Thus the story of the healing
may have grown up around the saying, and it is noteworthy that
Matt. xv. 21-28 makes a number of changes in details of the
story while modifying the dialogue only slightly.

The woman answers with cleverness and good humour (Matt. 28
vii. 7-8 = Luke xi. 9-10; Luke xi. 5-8; xviii. 1-8). One cannot

help admiring her patience and courage, for she must have been desperate. She had no claim on the foreign teacher and healer and makes allowances for what she takes to be his national and professional pride. **Yes, sir:** ναί and the vocative κύριε addressed to Jesus are not found elsewhere in Mark. **The children's crumbs** is a particularly lifelike touch.

29 **The demon has gone out of your daughter.** Whatever lies
30 behind the dialogue, Jesus grants the woman's request. The child is healed at a distance, as in Matt. viii. 13 =Luke vii. 10; John iv. 51-54; cf. P. Fiebig, *Jüdische Wundergeschichten* (Tübingen, 1911), p. 19. For another view, see T. A. Burkill, *ZNW*, lvii (1966), 23-37; *Novum Testamentum*, ix (1967), 161-77.

vii. 31-37. TO THE DECAPOLIS; THE DEAF MUTE

31 **Next he went out of the territory of Tyre and came
through Sidon to the lake of Galilee within the territories
32 of the Decapolis. And they brought to him a deaf and
dumb man and begged him to put his hand on him. And
33 he took him away from the crowd and in private he put
his fingers in his ears and, using saliva, touched his tongue,
34 and he looked up into heaven, uttered a noise, and said
to him, 'Ephphatha', that is, 'Be opened'. And his ears
35 were opened, and at once the impediment of his tongue
was removed, and he spoke plainly. And he commanded
36 them to tell no one; but the more he commanded them,
the more they broadcast it, and they were extremely
37 amazed, saying, 'Everything he does is splendid; he
makes even the deaf hear and the dumb speak'.**

One wonders how well Mark understood the geography
31 with which he deals here. The tradition, if it is a tradition, may have brought Jesus **from Sidon** over the Lebanon and Anti-Lebanon ranges to **the territories of the Decapolis** and thence to **the lake of Galilee**. Or, as Kraeling suggests (*Atlas*, pp. 387 f.), he came back to the lake by a direct route through Galilee. The problem partly concerns ἀνὰ μέσον, here translated **within,** i.e. the last part of the journey was in Decapolis terri-

tory; but the compound preposition can also mean 'between'. The political boundaries of the cities in the Decapolis league are not known to us in detail; some of the 'ten cities' may have been enclaves in the tetrarchies and other realms, as Damascus was, and not all the territory of a given city may have been contiguous. With the exception of Scythopolis (Bethshan), the cities were east of the Jordan.

The story of the deaf mute has a curious character. On the one hand Mark uses it as an example of the fulfilment of OT prophecies (Isa. xxix. 18; xxxv. 6; cf. also Wisd. x. 21) and its language is reminiscent of the LXX. Those who have been hitherto deaf will hear and also proclaim the Good News. The style is rhythmical and concludes with a paean of praise in verses 36b-37. On the other hand, the essence of the story is almost secular. The motif of faith is absent. The use of saliva, the groan uttered by the healer, and the healer's word in the original language, are all marks of ancient miracle tales. Lohmeyer notes that the healing of the man born blind (John ix. 1-7) has the same combination of Christian and (apparently) pagan ideas.

The healing is **away from the crowd and in private,** as 33 in v. 40; for the command **to tell no one,** cf. 1. 43-44; v. 43. 36 This is in accordance with Mark's ideas; it is not yet time for the full proclamation of the Good News (cf. John ii. 4). For the request **to put his hand on him,** cf. on v. 23.   32

The emperor Vespasian is said to have healed a blind man with the use of saliva; cf. Suetonius, *Vesp.* vii; Tacitus, *Hist.* iv. 81.

He looked up into heaven: this may be a gesture of prayer 34 (cf. vi. 41), while the **noise** or groan suggests exorcism. **Ephphatha:** the Aram. form would seem to be *ithpattah* or *ethpattah*; the *th* of the preformative has been assimilated to the following *p.*

The impediment of his tongue was removed, literally 35 'the bond . . . was loosed'.

CHAPTER VIII

viii. 1-10. THE FEEDING OF THE FOUR THOUSAND

1 **In those days there was again a great crowd who had nothing to eat, and he summoned his disciples and said to**
2 **them, 'I am sorry for the crowd, because they have stayed with me for three days already, and they have nothing to eat; and if I send them home hungry they will faint on**
3 **the way'. His disciples answered him, 'Where can one**
4 **get bread enough here in the wilderness to satisfy them?' He asked them, 'How many loaves have you?' They said,**
5 **'Seven'. And he directed the crowd to sit down on the**
6 **ground, and he took the seven loaves and gave thanks and broke them and gave to his disciples to set before them, and they set them before the crowd. And they had a few small fish; and he blessed them and said that these should**
7 **be set before them. And they ate and were satisfied, and**
8 **they picked up the fragments left, seven baskets full. They**
9 **were about four thousand. And he dismissed them. At**
10 **once he got into the boat with his disciples and came to the region of Dalmanutha.**

The close similarity of this story to vi. 34-44 shows that the two are variants of the same account. Both have the following elements: the compassion of Jesus, the questions of how the crowd is to be fed and how many loaves the disciples have, and the phrases in vi. 41-42 = viii. 6-8 εὐλόγησεν (εὐχαριστήσας, εὐλογήσας), καὶ κατέκλασεν (ἔκλασεν), καὶ ἐδίδου, ἵνα παρατιθῶσιν, and ἔφαγον καὶ ἐχορτάσθησαν. The principal differences are that the first Feeding involves teaching as well, while the second is simply a satisfaction of hunger; the numbers are not the same; and different Greek words are used for the baskets. It is not certain whether Mark has two written sources or models the second Feeding on the first.

Nothing in the narrative indicates that the feeding of the Four Thousand is a miracle to benefit the Gentiles. It is in a section mainly devoted to them, but it is possible that Mark thinks of Jesus and his party as having arrived in Jewish territory near the lake. The **wilderness** suggests the same locality as vi. 34-44. 4

Attempts have been made to connect the **seven loaves** and 6 **seven baskets** with the diaconate (Acts vi. 1-6), but in both feedings the disciples act as deacons. If the numbers have any significance—and this is doubtful—the contrast is between the Jewish and Hellenistic parts of the Church, since the Seven in Acts are Hellenists who do much the same work of teaching as the Apostles and do not confine themselves to 'serving tables'.

Jesus **gave thanks** ($\epsilon\dot{\upsilon}\chi\alpha\rho\iota\sigma\tau\dot{\eta}\sigma\alpha\varsigma$) over the loaves and 6 **blessed** ($\epsilon\dot{\upsilon}\lambda o\gamma\dot{\eta}\sigma\alpha\varsigma$) the fish. The verbs are used as synonyms (cf. vi. 41), but the former one may belong to the language of Greek religion; cf. W. L. Knox, *Some Hellenistic Elements in Primitive Christianity* (London, 1944), p. 3.

The **baskets** are $\sigma\pi\upsilon\rho\dot{\iota}\delta\epsilon\varsigma$, not $\kappa\dot{o}\phi\iota\nu o\iota$ as in vi. 43. The 8 word is often used for food hampers.

Dalmanutha is quite unknown. This name, or a variant of 10 it, is read by practically all uncials ($\Delta\alpha\lambda\mu\alpha\nu o\upsilon\nu\theta\alpha$ B; $\Delta\alpha\lambda\mu o\upsilon\nu\alpha\iota$ W). 'Mageda' is read by 28 *e*, 'Magedan' by sy[s], 'Magadan' by one third-century papyrus (cf. Matt. xv. 39), 'Melegada' by D*, and 'Magdala' by Θ. Cod. B of the LXX substitutes 'Magada' in Josh. xv. 37 for the 'Migdal-gad' in the region of the tribe of Gad. The same name is given by Eusebius' *Onomasticon* to a place near Gerasa. If 'Magadan' was the original reading, the tendency would be to substitute the better known name of Magdala, the fishing port on the west side of the lake. Rendel Harris suggested that 'Dalmanutha' arose from *almanutha*, the Aram. equivalent for $\epsilon\dot{\iota}\varsigma$ $\tau\dot{\alpha}$ $\mu\dot{\epsilon}\rho\eta$; Burkitt, *JTS*, xvii (1916), 15 f., conjectured that an original $\epsilon\iota\sigma\tau\iota\beta\epsilon\rho\iota\alpha$-$\delta\alpha\alpha\mu\alpha\theta o\upsilon\varsigma$ (Amathus, the Hamath of 2 Kings xiv. 25, rebuilt by Herod) was changed to $\epsilon\iota\sigma\tau\alpha\mu\epsilon\rho\eta\delta\alpha\lambda\mu\alpha\nu o\upsilon\theta\alpha$. Jack Finegan, *Light from the Ancient Past* (Princeton, 1946), p. 225, derives both 'Magadan' and 'Dalmanutha' from Magdal Nuna or Nunaita ('Magdal of fish').

11 **The Pharisees came out and began to argue with him.
They asked of him a sign from heaven to put him to the**
12 **test. Groaning inwardly, he said, 'Why does this generation look for a sign? I tell you truly, this generation will**
13 **not be given any sign!' Once more he left them, em-
barked, and went to the other shore.**

14   **They had forgotten to take bread and had nothing but**
15 **one loaf with them in the boat. And he commanded them:
'Look out, beware of the yeast of the Pharisees and the**
16 **yeast of Herod'. And they argued among themselves that**
17 **it was because they did not have bread. He recognised
this and said to them, 'Why do you reason that it is because you do not have bread? Don't you think or under-**
18 **stand yet? Have your minds become dulled? "Having
eyes, don't you see? and having ears, don't you hear?"**
19 **And don't you remember, when I broke the five loaves
for the five thousand, how many baskets full of fragments**
20 **did you pick up?' They said to him, 'Twelve'. 'When it
was the seven for the four thousand, how many baskets**
21 **full of fragments did you pick up?' They said, 'Seven'.
And he said to them, 'Don't you understand yet?'**

    Mark connects two pieces of tradition, the refusal of a sign
(verses 11-12) and the saying regarding the yeast of the Pharisees and of Herod (verse 15), adding to them a conversation that
brings out the stupidity of the disciples. This section is a key
to the understanding of viii. 26–ix. 13.

11   A rabbi was sometimes asked to give **a sign** to prove that his
teaching was true; cf. John ii. 18. The rabbinic commentary,
Pesikta Rabbati, taught that the Messiah, when he came, would
stand on the roof of the Temple, and that those who doubted
would see a light from heaven streaming over him (SB, i, 641).
The revolutionary Theudas promised signs to those who followed him (Josephus, *Ant.* xx. 5. 1). Jesus' opponents have in
mind not such wonders as he has already done, but an audible

or visible sign **from heaven.** For a rabbinic anecdote rejecting such signs when they conflicted with the majority opinion, cf. *Baba Meṣia'* 59b, cited by Montefiore and Loewe, *op. cit.* pp. 340 f.

There is abundant evidence for Jesus' teaching that **this 12 generation will not be given any sign.** The phrase εἰ δοθήσεται is a Semitism: 'may this or that happen to me, if . . .'; cf. 2 Sam. iii. 35. The 'sign of Jonah' would seem to be an exception to this, but that sign is Jonah's preaching of repentance (Luke xi. 32) rather than his sojourn in the belly of the whale (Matt. xii. 40). Luke xii. 54-56 teaches that without any special revelation men should be able to recognise the nature of the present time, just as they can predict the weather. Cf. also Luke xiii. 1-5, where the calamities of the Galileans and the fall of the tower of Siloam are not signs that these people were particularly sinful. Finally, the story of the Rich Man and Lazarus (Luke xvi. 19-31) points up the futility of signs: if people will not listen to Moses and the prophets, they will not repent even if one were to rise from the dead!

He **left them,** i.e. the Pharisees, for apparently the disciples 13 went with him to **the other shore.** The locality continues to be uncertain. If he has been at Magdala, he now goes to the eastern shore (the usual meaning of τὸ πέραν). The next stage of the journey is Bethsaida (verse 22).

They had forgotten to take bread. This artificial introduc- 14 tion prepares for the disciples' misunderstanding. **The yeast of 15 the Pharisees** is obviously their evil influence rather than their teachings, for there would be no teaching from Herod. In rabbinical literature yeast is usually a symbol for the evil impulse (*yeṣer ha-ra'*) or the wicked ways and dispositions of humans (SB, i, 728). Paul uses it in this sense in 1 Cor. v. 6-8; cf. Ignatius, *Magn.* x. 2. ('Put away therefore the bad leaven which has become old and sour, and be changed into the new leaven which is Jesus Christ. Be salted in him lest anyone among you be corrupted, since you will be shown up by your savour.') The power of yeast to infect new dough and spread, and the requirement to remove it from the house in Passover season (Exod. xii. 15; xiii. 7) naturally suggested this. When Jesus used it as a figure of the Kingdom of God (Matt. xiii. 33

=Luke xiii. 20-21) it was paradoxical and suggested the intense
power of the Kingdom, whose influence is greater than that of
evil, and perhaps its danger to the old order (cf. on ii. 21-22).

The yeast of Herod is not so much the moral corruption of
the tetrarch's court as interest in royal glory and political privilege. Jesus' attitude to power is seen in x. 42-45; Matt. xi. 8
=Luke vii. 25. He is almost contemptuous of monarchs and
refers to Herod Antipas as 'that fox' (Luke xiii. 32; cf. *JOT*,
p. 109). We do not know why the tetrarch wished to kill him, but
perhaps the motive was the same as in the case of John the
Baptist: he feared any leader who might become too popular.

17   Here, as elsewhere in Mark, more than one layer of meaning
probably ought to be distinguished. **Bread** can refer to teaching,
18 and the disciples do not **think or understand, see** or **hear,**
19 although they have been taught. They also ought to **remember**
that Jesus can provide bread, if it is needed, with several
baskets full of fragments left over. They lack not only understanding but faith; this generation will not be given such a sign
as it expects, but the Feedings, as well as the teaching, are signs
that the disciples ought to recognise.

viii. 22-26. THE BLIND MAN OF BETHSAIDA

22 **They came to Bethsaida. And they brought him a blind**
23 **man and begged him to touch him. Taking the hand of**
the blind man, he led him outside the village, and he
spat into his eyes and laid his hands on him and asked
24 **him, 'Do you see anything?' And he looked up and said,**
'I see men—because I see something like trees walking'.
25 **Then again he put his hands on his eyes, and the man**
looked intently and was restored, and he gazed at every-
26 **thing clearly. He sent him home, saying, 'Tell it to no**
one in the village'.

Since the disciples have not yet learned to see, a miracle is
necessary to open blind eyes. This is a transition section which,
like a theme in a symphony, prepares for a development in full
orchestra. There are three kinds of seeing: the physical restora-

tion of sight in this story; Peter's partial vision which recognises Jesus as Messiah even though he cannot understand the suffering of the Son of Man (verses 27-33); and the vision of the transfigured Son of Man (ix. 2-8).

For the location of **Bethsaida,** cf. on vi. 45. Together with 22 Chorazin and Capharnaum, it rejected Jesus (Matt. xi. 21-23 =Luke x. 13-15); if Mark knew this, his choice of the place for the miracle of seeing is particularly appropriate. 'Bethany' is the reading of D and some OL MSS. This is unlikely unless it is the 'Bethany beyond Jordan' of John i. 28.

The miracle is a twin of vii. 32 and contains some of its secular peculiarities, such as taking the man away from the spectators, the use of saliva and the laying on of hands. It is, 24 however, very lifelike, for the cure is in two stages and at first the man sees **something like trees walking,** even though Mark uses this to prepare for the two stages of Peter's vision. In an Asclepius miracle a blind man believes that he sees trees; cf. Dittenberger, *Sylloge,* 802; 120 ff.

The man looked intently (διέβλεψεν), or perhaps 'opened 25 his eyes wide'. The translation **gazed at everything clearly** is only a conjecture as to the meaning; ἐμβλέπω usually means 'to look at' or 'fix one's gaze on' something. τηλαυγῶς probably means 'clearly'; the variant δηλαυγῶς (S* C L Δ 579) is practically identical in meaning. Rieu translates: 'he could now distinguish even distant objects well'; the adjective τηλαυγής originally means 'far-shining'.

Tell it to no one in the village. This reading of (c) k seems 26 more likely than that of B, 'Do not go even into the village'. A C D N Δ Θ fam 13 contain various combinations of the two readings. That which is adopted corresponds to the other commands not to report the miracles; but cf. also verse 29; ix. 9.

viii. 27-ix. 1. CAESAREA PHILIPPI AND THE FIRST PASSION PREDICTION

Jesus and his disciples went out into the villages of 27 **Caesarea Philippi; and on the road he asked his disciples, 'Who do men say that I am?' They said to him, 'John the** 28

Baptist; but others say Elijah, and others one of the
29 prophets'. And he asked them, 'But you, who do you say
that I am?' Peter answered him, 'You are the Messiah'.
30 And he gave a stern command that they should not speak
of this to anyone.
31   And he began to teach them that the Son of Man must
suffer much and be rejected by the elders and the chief
priests and the scholars and be killed and rise again
32 after three days. He spoke this word plainly. Peter took
33 him to one side and began to reprove him. He turned
around and, seeing his disciples, reproved Peter: 'Get
behind me, Satan, because you are not thinking God's
thoughts but men's'.
34   He summoned the crowd, along with his disciples, and
said to them, 'If anyone wishes to follow behind me, let
him renounce himself and take up his cross and follow
35 me; for whoever wishes to save his life, will lose it; but
whoever loses his life for the sake of the Good News will
36 save it. Why, what gain is it to a man to win the whole
37 world and forfeit his life? What, indeed, might a man
38 give in exchange for his life? For if anyone is ashamed
of me and these words of mine in this adulterous and
sinful generation, the Son of Man will be ashamed of
him when he comes in his Father's glory with the holy
angels.'
ix.1   He said to them, 'I tell you truly: there are some who
stand here who will not taste death till they see the Kingdom of God present with power'.

All commentators recognise that this section introduces the
second half of the gospel. Now Jesus discloses the secret that
the Son of Man must suffer; although he is not yet on his way
to Jerusalem he has set his face in that direction. As Wellhausen says, 'Now for the first time the gospel, as the apostles
proclaimed it, actually begins'. From this point forward, the
story is directed to the Cross and the manifestation of the Son
of Man in glory. The progress is geographical, by way of
Caesarea Philippi, the mount of Transfiguration (ix. 2), and
Capharnaum (ix. 33), through Peraea and Judaea (x. 1), to the

Holy City. Three principal stages are marked by the predictions of the Passion (viii. 31; ix. 31; x. 32-34).

The present section consists of three parts: (*a*) the discussion of Jesus' nature, which in turn divides into verses 27-30 and 31-33; (*b*) sayings on discipleship, verses 34-38; and (*c*) the promise of the Kingdom of God, ix. 1. All these seem to be separate traditions which Mark has brought together.

It is difficult to reconstruct the tradition behind verses 27-33. In Matt. xvi. 13-23, Jesus responds affirmatively to Peter's recognition of him as Messiah, but Luke ix. 18-22 adds nothing to Mark at this point. If there was an answer, it is lost to us; Mark has only the command of silence and the teaching about the Son of Man, unless verse 33 contains the original answer. Indeed the kernel of the dialogue seems to be in verses 29 and 33. The introduction, verses 27-28, corresponds to vi. 14-15, and may be modelled on it. The mention of Caesarea Philippi must, however, be part of the tradition; there is no reason for fabricating it, and it does not fit well with the present frame-work of Mark, for after the journey in the territory of the Decapolis (vii. 31) Jesus has come to the Sea of Galilee and Bethsaida (verse 22), and this necessitates another trip north. The *Gospel of Thomas* (82: 30-83: 14, pp. 9, 11) contains a dialogue parallel to this, in which Jesus asks the disciples to say with whom they might compare him. Simon Peter answers that he is like a 'righteous angel', and Matthew compares him to a 'philosopher', while Thomas says that his mouth is not capable of saying what Jesus is like. The passage, like most of this gospel, is gnostic in its ideas. It is probably based only on the synoptic tradition and throws no light on the original event.

The **villages** are part of the territory of the city-state of 27 **Caesarea Philippi**, i.e. the Caesarea of Philip, so called to distinguish it from the city of the same name on the sea-coast which had previously been called Strato's Tower. The tetrarch Philip rebuilt the city mentioned here and named it in honour of Tiberius (Josephus, *Ant.* xviii. 2. 1; *B.J.* ii. 9. 1). The original name Paneas survives today as Banyas. The city itself lies at the foot of Mount Hermon near one of the sources of the Jordan. The god Pan was worshipped in a grotto near by and the cult of the emperor was also practised in Caesarea. Sir G. A. Smith, *The Historical Geography of the Holy Land*, pp. 475-479, describes the site and notes the contrast between the heathen cults and the recognition of Jesus as the Messiah of the one true God. Nelson Glueck, *The River Jordan* (Philadelphia, 1946), pp. 24-29, develops the same theme eloquently; pictures of the cliff and the Pan niches are given on pp. 21 f.

In rabbinical dialogues, disciples usually ask the questions and the teacher gives answers (cf. iv. 10; x. 2, 17). Here Jesus takes the initiative, as in ii. 8-9; iii. 4; and xii. 35, all of which introduce radically new teachings.

28 The answers **John the Baptist . . . Elijah . . . one of the prophets** are only the opinions of men, even though the first two figures have eschatological significance; Elijah was to pre-
29 pare the way for the Messiah. Jesus presses them for their own answer: **But you . . .** (ὑμεῖς is emphatic). Peter answered him, **You are the Messiah.** The obvious reference is to the Messiah Son of David (x. 47; xi. 10; xii. 35). This type of messianic hope is the earliest in the OT (Pss. xviii; lxxviii. 65-72; lxxxix. 19-37; cxxxii; Amos ix. 11-12; Isa. ix, xi; Hag. ii. 21-23; Zech. iv. 6-10). In the Maccabean period it is partly superseded by the expectation of a priest-king from the tribe of Levi, but the earlier hope revives in Pss. Sol. xvii. 5-8, 23-28; xviii. 6-8; 2 Baruch xxix. 3-8; xxx. 1-2, and is frequently found in rabbinic literature. The Davidic Messiah was expected to be a king of human origin who would establish the political supremacy of Israel over the world. Even though his reign was to inaugurate a new era of righteousness and peace, and was established by God, it was usually believed that this could not be achieved without struggle and war. It seems to be a firm historical fact that in his earthly life some of Jesus' followers expected him to be such a Messiah. This is indicated by x. 47; xi. 10 and also by the anointing in the house of Simon the Leper (xiv. 3-9). It is no doubt this fact which led the high priest and his associates to denounce him before Pilate (cf. especially the form of the charges in Luke xxiii. 2).

30 **And he gave a stern command;** the word can mean 'rebuke'.

31 **And he began to teach:** this might imply that the teaching

was interrupted by Peter's remonstrance (verse 32), or that he now taught this for the first time; but ἤρξατο is often used with no particular force; cf. J. W. Hunkin, *JTS*, xxv (1924), 390-402. Note that the teaching is expressed in indirect discourse, probably because Mark knows no traditional words of Jesus that he can quote. It is actually a kerygmatic statement of faith (Lohmeyer). Our Lord no doubt taught his disciples on some occasion that his mission to Jerusalem might end in suffering and death, but the idea that this was a necessary part of his mission was not realised until after the Resurrection (cf. Luke xxiv. 25-27) when Jesus was identified with the Servant of Isa. xlii.; lii. 13-liii. 12. Now Jesus begins to speak more freely about the **Son of Man.** That it is he who **must suffer** is Mark's contribution to the doctrine; it is absent from the pre-Marcan Son of Man passages in Matthew and Luke. The evangelist's sparing use of the term 'Messiah' must also be observed; Jesus does not accept this title, save perhaps in xiv. 62. On the other hand, while Judaism knew of no suffering Son of Man, it did have the doctrine of a Messiah son of Joseph or son of Ephraim who suffered and died; but he is a warrior Messiah and his death is in battle. The concept may have been drawn from Deut. xxxiii. 17, where Joseph is portrayed as a bull with horns, and from Zech. xii. 10-14, but there is no evidence for it as early as the time of Jesus' ministry. It may possibly be reflected in Rev. vi. 16; xix. 11, where Jesus is the warrior Messiah. The defeat of Simeon bar Kokheba in the Second Revolt, or the failure of the revolutionaries Hezekiah and Judas the Galilean, may be the basis for the Jewish doctrine.

The elders and the chief priests and the scholars are the three groups that make up the Sanhedrin. Cf. Moore, *Judaism*, i. 82: 'In this body, under the presidency of the high priest, besides the heads of the great priestly families, lay elders, men of rank and authority, had seats; among both, probably, there were legal experts, Scribes'.

And rise again after three days. Taken strictly, this would seem to date the Crucifixion on Thursday or the Resurrection on Monday (cf. ix. 31; x. 34; Matt. xxvii. 63; also Matt. xii. 40, 'three days and three nights'), but xvi. 1-6 implies that by Sunday morning the Lord has already risen. Mark's language may not be exact, and Matthew and Luke in the parallel passages regularly correct it to 'on the third day'. The verb ἀναστῆναι implies translation or ascension (cf. Luke ix. 51 and contrast xiv. 28; 1 Cor. xv. 4).

32 **He spoke this word plainly,** or openly. The evangelist wishes to leave no doubt on this point. The disciples had been taught that both the Cross and Resurrection were part of God's predetermined plan. In view of this, only a miraculous stupidity could keep them from understanding. The other Passion predictions are artistic, like the recurrence of an ominous theme in a symphony.

Peter . . . began to reprove him (again the verb ἐπιτιμάω, cf. verse 29), for it was contrary to the conventional idea for the 33 Messiah to suffer. **He turned around;** cf. iii. 34; v. 30. This is Mark's style, but it also describes the gesture of one who is very sensitive to the presence of other people.

Get behind me, Satan. This is the kernel of the tradition and is no doubt an historical reminiscence. The language is Semitic; Bishop, p. 57, remarks that *Yā Shaitān* is common in colloquial Arabic speech, and might be used half playfully in rebuking a younger colleague. ὕπαγε ὀπίσω μου probably means 'get out of my sight', but possibly 'follow me', i.e. 'do not oppose me'; cf. i. 7. **You are not thinking God's thoughts but men's.** The usual concept of Messiahship, like the identification of Jesus with John the Baptist, Elijah, or one of the prophets, is a merely human idea, in opposition to God's purpose. The phrase can mean 'You belong to men's party, not God's'; τὰ 'Ρωμαίων φρονεῖν is used by Polyaenus[1] (viii. 14. 3) in the sense of 'joining the party of the Romans'. Peter is called upon to choose whom he will serve. Jesus may indeed regard Peter's reproof as a temptation from Satan (cf. Matt. iv. 8-10 = Luke iv. 5-8).

34 The short discourse that follows is addressed to the **crowd** as well as **his disciples.** It is thus intended for all who hear the gospel. The words **behind me** now refer to following faithfully in the Way trodden out by Jesus. A man must **renounce himself,** deny his own ambitions and interests. Would Jesus have used the words **take up his cross?** (*a*) It

[1] A historian of the second century A.D.

is often objected that this represents the Church's reflection
on later events; even if Jesus foresaw the possibility of violent
death for himself and any who followed him to Jerusalem, he
would not necessarily have expected death by *crucifixion*, i.e. at
the hands of the Romans. The words at the Last Supper (xiv.
22-24) imply that his body will be broken and his blood poured
out, as though he were to be stoned. (*b*) The saying in this form
must have had a particular value for the Roman church, for
which persecution was a constant danger. Mark's sections on
discipleship are formulated for a martyr church whose members, like their Lord, must be ready literally to carry their
crosses if they are not to renounce him. (*c*) Cod. 2427 omits the
phrase in question, though it is the only known MS. with this
peculiarity.

It may be answered, first, that the authenticity of 2427 is
doubtful; cf. p. 30. This and other omissions in that MS. are
such as a learned modern impostor might make in manufac-
turing a 'more primitive' text of Mark than that of B. Second,
it is not impossible that Jesus should foresee the intervention of
the Roman procurator. Shortly after the death of Herod the
Great, Varus crucified two thousand Jews in putting down a
revolt (Josephus, *Ant.* xvii. 10. 10). Knox, *Sources*, i. 64, cites a
remark of Plutarch (*Mor.* 554A) which may show that 'to carry
one's cross' is proverbial. At the same time, Jesus' saying may
well have been sharpened and pointed up in the tradition.

His willingness to risk and lose his physical life is given as the **35**
supreme example of the true way of salvation. **Whoever wishes
to save his life,** to hoard it and protect it, as though it belonged
to him alone, will **lose** it or destroy it in the true sense of the
word. But to lose it, as Jesus does, in the cause of **the Good
News,** is to preserve it. ἐμοῦ καί is probably to be omitted, with
P[45] D 28 *b c f ff*[2] *k l* vg etc.; the reading is evidently from
Matthew and Luke, who substitute 'for my sake'. One may
question whether 'for my sake' or 'for the sake of the Good
News' belongs to the original saying, since both reflect the
viewpoint of the early Church and 'gospel' is a technical term
in Mark.

Verse 36 is essentially an observation of man's human con- **36**
dition. Many men have apparently won **the whole world,**

i.e. material success, and all in vain, for they die without enjoying it; cf. the story of the rich fool, Luke xii. 15-20. **Forfeit** is, however, stronger; it implies, if not penalty, at least the thought that a man cannot have both the whole world and his life.

37 **What, in fact, might a man give in exchange for his life?** The Greek ψυχή, like the Heb. *nephesh*, draws no distinction between 'soul' and 'life'; it is the animate principle in animals and men. Once a man is faced with the ultimate, either at the Last Judgement or at his death, there is nothing that he can offer to buy back a wasted life.

38   The above sayings are applied to the disciples' attitude to Jesus and his vocation. It was inevitable that many should be **ashamed of** Jesus and his **words.** The Cross had none of the glory with which Paul and later Christian piety invested it; even in Luke-Acts it is almost true that Jesus is regarded as Lord and Messiah in spite of the Crucifixion, not directly because of it; cf., e.g., Acts ii. 23-24. The shame and degradation which in the modern world are associated with the noose, the gibbet and the gas-chamber, belonged to the Cross: 'cursed is everyone who hangs on a tree' (Gal. iii. 13; Deut. xxi. 23). Yet God's purpose for the world is not bound up with the victorious Messiah but with the suffering Son of Man; and if anyone is ashamed of this truth, **the Son of Man will be ashamed of him.** The saying at least belongs to an early stage of the tradition, for Jesus is not explicitly equated with the one who **comes in . . . glory.** This glory is **his Father's;** the Son of Man is also Son of God; it is perhaps Mark who adds this (cf. on i. 9-11; xiii. 32).

CHAPTER IX

He said to them: this marks the saying as belonging to a 1 different source. In the tradition behind the gospels, the ideas of **the Kingdom** of God and of the Son of Man belong to separate cycles; cf. H. B. Sharman, *Son of Man and Kingdom of God* (London, 1943), p. 89. The saying has been regarded as a 'pillar passage' which no one could have invented because it was not fulfilled literally. Indeed, John xxi. 22-23 may be an attempt to correct this embarrassing tradition; Jesus did not say that a certain disciple would not die, but 'if I wish him to remain until I come, what is it to you?' On the other hand, when Mark writes, some of the original disciples may still have been alive; and the evangelist expects the triumphant return of the Son of Man in glory.

No one can deny categorically that Jesus may have given such teaching. His prayer was 'thy Kingdom come', and he shared with his contemporaries the point of view which we call eschatological: God is in control of history, and he can end the world just as he was able to create it. The difficulty with this verse is that other sayings, which are even better attested, warn against calculating times and seasons and teach that there will be disillusioning delays (Luke xvii. 20-22; cf. xii. 38-40). Mark goes so far as to say that, though the end will come within a generation, no one can know just when (xiii. 32-37). The important point, however, is that in Jesus' teaching the weight is not laid on the 'when' of the Kingdom but on the necessity of being prepared for it at all times, in good days as well as bad (Matt. xxv. 1-13; Luke xii. 35-46; xvii. 25-30).

To **taste** (i.e. experience) **death** is apparently a Semitic expression; cf. Heb. ii. 9; 2 Esd. vi. 26. It is used four times in the Qur'an (cf. Bishop, p. 156), and the promise that some 'will not taste death' appears twice in the *Gospel of Thomas* (80:13-14; 84:25, pp. 3, 15). The Kingdom will be **present** (ἐληλυθυῖαν, perfect tense) **with power,** not just in the sense that God's sovereignty is eternally present. The rabbinic expression would be that the Kingdom will be 'revealed', will 'reign', or will be 'established'; cf. the Kaddish in S. Singer, ed., *The Authorised Daily Prayer Book* (London, 1929), p. 37.

ix. 2-8. THE TRANSFIGURATION

2 After six days Jesus took Peter and James and John with him, and brought them up to a high mountain by them-
3 selves, all alone. And his appearance was changed before them, and his clothing became dazzling white, as no
4 fuller on earth could whiten them. And Elijah appeared to them with Moses, and they were talking with Jesus.
5 At this Peter said to Jesus, 'Rabbi, it is good for us to be here, so let us make three tents, one for you and one for
6 Moses and one for Elijah'—for he did not know what
7 response to make, for they were terrified. Then a cloud overshadowed them and a voice came out of the cloud:
8 'This is my Beloved Son, listen to him'. As they looked around at that moment, they no longer saw anyone with them but only Jesus.

The third and climactic revelation of Jesus' nature is the Transfiguration. Mark not only connects it with what goes before—the Baptism, the Blind Man of Bethsaida and Caesarea Philippi—but it leads immediately to the discussion of Elijah's suffering (verses 9-13) and the healing of the epileptic boy (verses 14-29), in which the disciples are unable to act and Jesus reproves the lack of faith of his generation.

There are two principal problems. The first concerns the historic basis of the story. (*a*) Wellhausen and Loisy held that the Transfiguration was originally the account of a resurrection appearance which has been transferred into the earthly ministry of Jesus; for a more recent form of this theory, cf. M. S. Enslin in *Quantulacumque*, ed. by R. P. Casey, S. Lake and A. K. Lake (London, 1937). Enslin holds that this experience is the basis for Peter's confession of Jesus as Messiah. (*b*) It is sometimes thought that there is no historic kernel; it is an epiphany story whose purpose is to express the doctrine of Jesus' divinity, i.e. a creed in narrative form; cf. *FTG*, pp. 275-276. (*c*) Others consider the story historical in the strict sense or at least reflecting an actual experience of the disciples in Jesus' presence; so Eduard Meyer, Harnack and Goodspeed.

The other problem is that of the meaning of the Transfiguration, both for Mark and in the tradition behind his gospel. The story itself can be divided into two main parts: a theophanic vision (verses 2b-4) and a voice from heaven, like the *bath qol* (see on i. 11) of Jewish tradition (verse 7), with Peter's remark (verses 5-6) in between. Verse 8 is the conclusion. The two parts may have been originally connected but have slightly different purposes; the latter revelation interprets the former and bids the disciples listen to Jesus.

Several motifs are suggested by this brief narrative. (*a*) Moses and Elijah are sometimes thought to correspond respectively to the Law and the Prophets, both of which witness to Jesus; but Moses is a prophet, not just a lawgiver (Deut. xviii. 15), and the story contains more than their testimony and that of God to the nature of the transfigured one. (*b*) Elijah was taken up into heaven (2 Kings ii. 11) and the place of Moses' burial was not known (Deut. xxxiv. 6), so that the legend arose that he too had gone directly into heaven; for various forms of this cf. SB, i, 753-755; the pseudepigraphical *Assumption of Moses*; and H. M. Teeple, *The Mosaic Eschatological Prophet* (Philadelphia, 1957), pp. 41-43. Thus Jesus is associated with those who overcame death. (*c*) There are several connexions with the story of Moses on Mount Sinai; the cloud covered the mountain six days and God called to Moses out of the cloud (Exod. xxiv. 16); three men, Aaron, Nadab and Abihu, accompanied Moses (Exod. xxiv. 1); and Moses' face shone so that he put a veil over it (Exod. xxxiv. 29-35). Philo, who develops these motifs, goes so far as to say that God changed Moses' body into a mind-substance like the radiance of the sun and so prepared him for immortality (*Vita Mos.* ii. 51, 288); he also comes near to identifying Moses with the Logos, who is described as God's 'first-born Son' and 'second God'. In the gospel story Jesus thus corresponds to Moses. Cf. Carrington, pp. 173-176, for the connexions of the Moses story with the midsummer festival at which he believes this pericope to have been read. (*d*) The mention of 'tents' or 'booths' suggests some relation to the Feast of Tabernacles. (*e*) Several of the above ideas are developed by Paul in 2 Cor. iii. 12-v. 5. There the fading splendour of Moses' face, which symbolises the old dispensation of condemnation, is contrasted with the enduring glory of Jesus' face and the dispensation of justification. Those who with unveiled face see the glory of Christ reflect that glory; in fact are metamorphosed (the verb used here in verse 3) into his likeness. They die with Christ but are constantly renewed in their inner nature, and their earthly 'tents', i.e. their bodies, are replaced by a new tent, 'eternal in the heavens'. (*f*) The *bath qol* is similar to the voice at the Baptism, i. 11. (*g*) In 2 Pet. i. 16-18 the Transfiguration is thought of as proclaiming 'the power and coming of our Lord Jesus Christ', i.e. it is the foreshadowing of the *parousia* of the Son of Man. (*h*) Toynbee remarks that the story is the supreme example in the gospels of the motif of 'withdrawal-and-return'; cf. *A Study of History, Abridgement*, pp. 222 f.

Recent interpreters have made use of these clues. Harald Riesenfeld, *Jésus transfiguré* (Copenhagen, 1947), regards the narrative as a fundamentally historical account of a vision in which Peter and the others see Jesus enthroned as Messiah and High Priest (this book includes a full bibliography). G. H. Boobyer, *JTS*, xli (1940), 119-140, considers it to be a foreshadowing of the *parousia*, and denies any connexion with the Resurrection appearances. Lohmeyer interprets it as an example of the Son of Man theology, though other motifs are present as well.

2   **After six days** most naturally alludes to Exod. xxiv. 16, but it may possibly symbolise the six days of man's working week, followed by the rest and refreshment of the Sabbath. **Peter and James and John** were present at the raising of Jaïrus' daughter (v. 37) and Mark may think of them as the nucleus of the new Church (Lohmeyer). The **high mountain** is a place of revelation; cf. iii. 13; Matt. iv. 8; v. 1; xxviii. 16. Mount Tabor, which is visible from many parts of Palestine, even from far south in the Jordan valley, is the traditional scene, but Hermon (9,100 feet) is nearer to Caesarea Philippi.

And his appearance was changed (μετεμορφώθη): Paul 3
uses the word in Rom. xii. 2 to denote the renewal of men's
minds, and in 2 Cor. iii. 18, where Christians, seeing the face of
Christ as in a mirror, are transfigured into the same immortal
glory; cf. also 1 John iii. 2-3. In the apocalyptic literature, the
righteous will be changed and become like angels or stars (2
Baruch li. 10, 12; 2 Esdras vii. 97). The **clothing** of **dazzling
white** (cf. Enoch lxii. 15-16) suggests that Jesus is now vested
as the high priestly Messiah (Riesenfeld) or that this is the glory
of the Son of Man (Lohmeyer). The thought of Jesus as priest
is not prominent in Mark, except that in xi. 15-18 he cleanses
the Temple, and in xv. 38 the veil of the Temple is split in two
(cf. Heb. ix. 11-12). **No fuller on earth could whiten the
garments so.** The fuller cleansed and prepared cloth by use of
nitrum, fuller's earth, and human and animal urine from the
latrines; cf. J. Carcopino, *Daily Life in Ancient Rome* (New
Haven, 1940), p. 42 (Pelican edition, 1956, p. 50); Suetonius,
Vesp. 23. After the cloth was well washed and dried it was often
bleached by the fumes of burning sulphur, but this method had
no permanent results. The meanness of the fuller's trade may
have led Matthew and Luke to omit this touch, which (as J. P.
Engelcke remarks in a personal letter) 'is perhaps another illustration of St. Mark's originality, vividness, and contact with the
world about him'.

Elijah and **Moses** were to accompany the Son of Man at his
parousia (Boobyer; cf. 1 Cor. xv. 22-23; 1 Thess. iv. 14-17), as
the prototypes, precursors and attendants of the heavenly king
(Riesenfeld), or as those who are specially related to the chosen
people of God (Lohmeyer). The midrash *Debarim Rabba* contains a saying of R. Johanan ben Zakkai that the two will come
before the last day. On Elijah, cf. *MR*, p. 15.

The Israelites dwelt in **tents** in the wilderness, and this came 5
to be commemorated in the Feast of Tabernacles or Booths
(Lev. xxiii. 39-43); God's worship was also carried on in a tent
(Exod. xxxv-xxxvi; Acts vii. 44). By the first century A.D.
Tabernacles had become the most joyous festival of the year; cf.
Moore, *Judaism*, ii, 43-49. Zech. xiv. 16-19 predicts that in the
coming age all nations will come to Jerusalem to observe the
feast, and there is some reason to think that it was connected

with the hopes of the future triumph of Israel (cf. on xi. 8-10).

6 Peter **did not know what response to make**—he did not understand that what he was seeing was still in the future—and he may have believed that the final age has already come, the events of the Exodus are being repeated, the feast will be celebrated, and Moses and Elijah will remain with them. He wished to erect tents in which they might dwell (cf. Rev. xxi. 3, 'the tent of God is with men').

7 The **cloud** suggests Sinai (Exod. xxiv. 15-18) and also the cloud out of which the Son of Man will be revealed (xiii. 26; xiv. 62; cf. Acts i. 9-11; 1 Thess. iv. 17). 2 Macc. ii. 4-8 contains the tradition that Jeremiah hid the tent, the ark and the altar of incense in a cave, and that the place will not be known until God gathers his people together and the glory of the Lord and the cloud appear. This tends to show that the Transfiguration story is a unity: the three motifs, the glory, the tent and the cloud, are already combined in Jewish thought. When Moses heard Yahweh out of the cloud, the voice gave directions for building the Tent of Meeting, but now its message has to do with God's **Beloved Son.** The Son of Man is also Son of God; and since he is also the 'prophet like Moses' the disciples must **listen to him** (cf. Deut. xviii. 15). Peter had been unwilling to do so at Caesarea Philippi; now God rebukes him, as Jesus had done.

ix. 9-13. DISCOURSE AT THE FOOT OF THE MOUNTAIN

9 **As they were coming down from the mountain he commanded them not to report to anyone what they had seen,**
10 **until the Son of Man should rise from the dead. And they kept the matter to themselves but debated what it meant**
11 **to rise from the dead. They asked him, 'Why do the**
12 **scholars say that Elijah has to come first?' He said to them, 'Elijah comes first and restores all things'.—'And how is it written concerning the Son of Man?' 'That he**
13 **should suffer much and be treated with contempt. But I tell you that Elijah has come, and they have done to him**

whatever they have wished, just as it is written concerning him.'

A revelation or teaching followed by a question and an explanation is a familiar pattern in Mark (cf. iv. 10-20; vii. 17-19; viii. 16-21; ix. 28-29; x. 10-12). The evangelist now makes clear his own understanding of the event: it is the Son of Man whom the disciples have seen; and, since Elijah has now appeared, all is ready for the End.

Verses 11-13 are so apparently confused that many suggestions have been made for their rearrangement. In Matt. xvii. 10-12, Mark's verse 12*b* is taken as a positive statement and placed at the end. Torrey and Rieu take verse 12*a* as interrogative, but in this case the question must be rhetorical, for verse 13 affirms Elijah's coming. C. H. Turner, *Study of the NT, 1883 and 1920* (Oxford, 1920), p. 61, would rearrange as follows: verses 10, 12*b*, 11, 12*a*, 13, and this gives a good sense; another possibility is verses 10, 11, 12*a*, 13*c*, 13*ab*, 12*b* (Grant).

The disciples now have had a chance to learn the full secret, but they are **not to report . . . until the Son of Man should** 9 **rise from the dead;** only then did the Church understand Jesus' suffering (cf. Luke xxiv. 25-27). Jesus' followers, still confused despite viii. 31, **debate** this, just as the Israelites argued 10 with Aaron in Exod. xxxii. 1-6.

That Elijah has to come first is not only the teaching of the 11 **scholars;** it is based on Mal. iv. 5-6. But if Elijah has returned in the person of John the Baptist, he has not succeeded in turning the hearts of the fathers to their children, etc.; he has only made the attempt.

The reference to the Son of Man inserted by Mark in verse 12 12*b* breaks the context so badly that one of the rearrangements noted above seems desirable. Evidently the old tradition contained only the question about Elijah and its answer. It is **written** (in scripture) **concerning the Son of Man** that he must suffer, only if this figure is also the Servant of Isa. liii. 3.

They have done to him whatever they wished (vi. 17- 13 29), but this cannot be **written concerning him** except in the sense that tradition may have identified Elijah with the Servant. Teeple, *op. cit.* pp. 56-58, 100, traces possible connexions

between these two figures and the 'prophet like Moses' but they
are exceedingly tenuous. The identification was probably made
by Christians as a result of reflection on recent events. W.
Bousset, *Die Offenbarung Johannis* (Göttingen, 1906), pp. 317-
324, conjectures that the two witnesses of Rev. xi. 1-12 are
Moses and Elijah.

ix. 14-29. HEALING OF THE EPILEPTIC BOY

14 As they came to the disciples they saw a great crowd
15 around them and scholars in discussion with them. And
as soon as all the crowd saw him they were astonished
16 and they ran to greet him. He asked them, 'What were
17 you arguing with them?' One of the crowd answered
him, 'Teacher, I have brought you my son, who has a
18 dumb spirit. Wherever it sees him it throws him down,
and he foams and grinds his teeth, and becomes stiff. I
told your disciples to cast it out and they were not able
19 to do it.' He answered them, 'O faithless generation!
How long shall I be with you? How long will I put up with
20 you? Bring him to me.' So they brought him to him; and
when the spirit saw him at once it convulsed him and he
21 fell on the ground and rolled and foamed. He [Jesus]
asked his father, 'For how long a time has this happened
22 to him?' And he said, 'Since he was a child. Many times
it has thrown him into fire and into water to destroy him
23 —but if you can, help us, take pity on us!' Jesus said to
him, '"If you can"! All things are possible to one who
24 believes.' The father of the child cried out, 'I do believe
25 —help my unbelief!' When Jesus saw that the crowd was
converging on him, he rebuked the unclean spirit, saying
to it, 'Deaf and dumb spirit, come out of him and enter
26 him no more!' And crying and convulsing him greatly,
it went out, and he became like a corpse so that the
27 majority said he was dead. But Jesus took him by the hand
28 and raised him, and he stood up. And when he had gone
into a house, his disciples asked him privately, 'Why
29 were we not able to cast it out?' And he said to them,

'This kind cannot come out by means of anything except prayer'.

This narrative, like the preceding sections, is in a setting 14 determined by the Exodus story, in which Moses, on coming down from the mountain, finds confusion and faithlessness (Exod. xxxii. 15-24). That the arrangement is artificial is shown by the presence of the **scholars,** who are out of place in the neighbourhood of Caesarea Philippi; it is only in verse 30 that Jesus and his followers go through Galilee, and they do so as secretly as possible. The **arguing** is over the means of healing and the inability of the disciples; as Grant says, the presence of the scribes has no other function.

The boy's illness is ascribed to a **dumb spirit,** i.e. one that 17 refuses to speak (Lagrange); cf. Plutarch, *de Def. Orac.* li, p. 438B. It was part of the technique of exorcism to require the demon to give his name; cf. Campbell Bonner, *HTR*, xxxvi (1943), 43 f. The symptoms of epilepsy, the 'sacred disease', are 18 vividly described here, and Matt. xvii. 15 correctly identifies them; cf. O. Temkin, *The Falling Sickness* (Baltimore, 1945); T. K. Oesterreich, *Possession, Demoniacal and Other* (London, 1930). The seizure may come when the boy is near a **fire,** perhaps a charcoal brazier, or **water,** a cistern or the lake.

Jesus' apostrophe **O faithless generation!** is not addressed 19 to the disciples only but to the whole nation, whose lack of faith frustrates the Good News (cf. Matt. xi. 16 =Luke vii. 31; Matt. xii. 39 =Luke xi. 29). **How long shall I be with you?** The time is short, and how can God's work be accomplished if the disciples cannot even heal this child? The divine patience, which has to **put up with** them, is strained but not exhausted: Jesus says, **Bring him to me.** The nature of the ailment is dramati- 20 cally shown by an immediate seizure, and Jesus' question brings 21 out the long duration of the illness (cf. v. 25).

The father's despairing cry is lifelike: **but if you can, help 22 us, take pity on us!** Jesus throws back the words 'If you can'! 23 It is here, in lack of faith, that the whole trouble resides. **The 24 father** speaks with complete sincerity and insight into the problem of the believer. **I do believe,** I am making the effort of faith—**help my unbelief,** for my faith is not yet sufficient.

25 Jesus drives out the demon by a simple command **to come out . . . and enter him no more,** not a formula of exorcism, for his own authority is sufficient; cf. McCasland, pp. 112-115. As frequently in ancient stories, the demon's departure is marked by an act of physical violence; cf. i. 26; Josephus, *Ant.* viii. 2. 5; Philostratus, *Vita Apollon.* iv. 20. In both of the latter stories the demon is commanded not to return.

27 **Jesus took him by the hand and raised him.** Robinson, *Problem*, p. 39, says that the cure 'is described in terms of resurrection', but this may be far-fetched; cf. the gesture in i. 31.

29 **This kind cannot come out by means of anything except prayer.** This remark is singular in the Marcan healing stories, but it points to the monotheistic principle: this is a work of God, not of man. One may question whether the verse originally stood in Mark, for the point of the story is faith, not prayer. It could scarcely have been present in the MS. of Mark used by Matthew, for Matt. xvii. 21 is omitted by Alexandrian and Caesarean authorities and several versions. When it crept into Matthew's text it was with the addition 'and fasting'; this, like prayer, was regarded as a technique.

ix. 30-32. THE SECOND PASSION PREDICTION

30 **When they went out from there, they made their way through Galilee, and he did not wish anyone to know it,**
31 **for he was instructing his disciples and saying to them, 'The Son of Man is being given over to the hands of men who will kill him; and having been killed, he will rise**
32 **after three days'. But they did not understand the utterance and were afraid to question him.**

As the first Passion Prediction (viii. 31) was followed by teachings on discipleship (viii. 34-38), so the second leads to the dispute over precedence (verses 33-37), and the same pattern is followed in the third (x. 32-34, followed by x. 35-45). All three predictions mark stages of the journey to Jerusalem, which is the Way of the Cross.

A literary comparison of the three shows that viii. 31 and ix. 31 diverge in details though their basic content and structure is the same; they may have been doublets in Mark's tradition (cf. the two Feedings). x. 32-34 appears to have been built up out of the first two, with added touches drawn from the Passion narrative.

The Galilean ministry has ended; when they now **made** 30 **their way through Galilee** it was in secret, and Jesus' work is now with **his disciples.** There is perhaps an irony in the 31 **Son of Man,** who represents God, **being given over to the hands of men,** who are not on God's side (viii. 33). This may be the oldest form of the passion prediction.

ix. 33-37. WHO IS THE GREATEST?

They came into Capharnaum. And when he was at home 33 **he asked them, 'What were you discussing on the road?'** 34 **They were silent; for they had been discussing among themselves which of them was greatest. And he sat down** 35 **and called the Twelve and said to them, 'Anyone who wishes to be first shall be last of all and servant of all',** **and he took a child and set him before them and, em-**36 **bracing him, said to them, 'Whoever receives a child like** 37 **this in my name, receives me; and whoever receives me, does not receive me but him who sent me'.**

Verses 33-48 are based on the theme of 'little ones'. At first the 'little ones' are children (verses 33-37), then those who do Jesus' work even though they are not among the disciples (verses 38-41), and finally those who because of their immaturity and weakness can be led into sin (verses 42-48). Matthew takes up this catechetical device and out of it develops his entire chapter xviii.

The desire to be **greatest** is so natural and universal that 34 Jesus' teaching on humility was difficult to accept, even though it was derived from Judaism; R. Hillel said that his humiliation was his exaltation. Two sayings of Jesus are included here. Verse 35b seems so much of an intrusion that D k omit it, and 35

Matthew and Luke transfer it elsewhere; it may, however, be Mark's anticipation of x. 42-45, by which he binds the two passages together. Montefiore remarks that the combination of humility with service is a new teaching in Judaism.

37 The second saying teaches that to accept or **receive,** i.e. give attention and kindly treatment to, a little child is to accept Jesus himself. The rabbis commended kindness to orphans and waifs and spoke of school children with special affection and interest. The pagan world did not put the same valuation on childhood. The affectionate letter of the Egyptian labourer Hilarion to his wife Alis advises her that if she bears a son she is to rear it but, if it is a daughter, to expose it; P. Oxy. 744, in C. K. Barrett, *The NT Background: Selected Documents* (London, 1957), p. 38. Jesus' saying is given a completely Christian formulation. Children are to be received **in my name,** i.e. at the command of Jesus or for his sake; and to **receive me** is to receive **him who sent me** (the 'apostolic' principle of Matt. x. 40 =Luke x. 16). But Jesus' close identification of himself with those in need may be part of his original teaching (cf. Matt. xxv. 31-46).

ix. 38-40. THE STRANGE EXORCIST

38 **John said to him, 'Teacher, we saw a man casting out demons in your name, and we tried to hinder him, be-**
39 **cause he was not a follower of ours'. And Jesus said, 'Cease hindering him, for no one who will perform a mighty deed in my name will be readily able to speak**
40 **evil of me; for he who is not against us is for us'.**

38 This little anecdote carries on the idea of 'receiving' or acceptance and the theme **in my name.** It is a particularly touching example of an incident that is not strictly historical but is entirely in the spirit and character of Jesus, for it fits with his attitude to Gentiles and Samaritans (Matt. viii. 5-13 =Luke vii. 1-9; Luke x. 29-37).

As the story stands it reflects the perplexity of the later Church when non-Christians undertook **casting out** demons in

the **name** of Jesus. Acts xix. 13-16 tells with considerable relish
of what happened to the seven sons of Scaeva who tried to do
just this. On the growth of tradition regarding exorcism, cf.
Easton, *The Gospel before the Gospels*, pp. 100 f. The kernel of
the story is probably to be found in the two sayings, verses 39*b*
and 40. The first, though it contains the Christian touch **in my** 39
name, expresses Jesus' modest satisfaction that the man will
not be an enemy; cf. Matt. xi. 6 =Luke vii. 23.

He who is not against us is for us is the principle of Matt. 40
xxv. 31-46. It may seem to contradict Matt. xii. 30 =Luke xi. 23,
'He who is not with me is against me'. But in the latter case the
critics of Jesus are bitterly opposed to his casting out demons
and call it the work of Beelzebul. In both instances, one must
choose sides, and to be with Jesus in his battle against the
demonic world is to be on the right side.

ix. 41-48. A CUP OF WATER; SCANDALS

'**For whoever gives you a cup of water to drink in my** 41
**name, because you belong to Christ, I tell you truly, will
not lose his reward.**

'**It would be better for anyone who causes one of these** 42
**little ones who believe to fall into sin, if a millstone were
hung about his neck and he were thrown into the lake.**

'**If your hand causes you to fall into sin, cut it off; it is** 43
**better for you to enter into life maimed than to depart
into Gehenna, into the unquenchable fire, having two
hands. If your foot causes you to fall into sin, cut it off;** 45
**it is better for you to enter into life crippled than to be
thrown into Gehenna having two feet. If your eye causes** 47
**you to fall into sin, gouge it out; it is better for you to
enter the Kingdom of God one-eyed than with two eyes
to be thrown into Gehenna, where "their worm does not** 48
die and the fire is not quenched".'

The concluding sayings in chapter ix are miscellaneous but
all are connected with discipleship.

41   Verse 41 belongs to a late stage of tradition. It introduces the idea of **reward,** common in Matthew, but elsewhere lacking in Mark. Matt. x. 41-42 contains a fuller form of the saying. The phrase **because you belong to Christ** is so foreign to Mark's style that Schmiedel conjectured its absence from the original text. The entire verse, which Luke omits, may, however, be an early addition to the gospel.

42   These **little ones who believe** cannot be readily equated with the Strange Exorcist or with the children of verses 36-37; they are probably immature Christians. **Causes . . . to fall into sin;** cf. on iv. 17. The rabbis used Jeroboam the son of Nebat as an example of the greatest of sinners because he not only did evil himself but caused Israel to sin (1 Kings xiv. 16); cf. Montefiore, *The Synoptic Gospels*, i, 222. The saying may have stood in Q (Matt. xviii. 6-7 =Luke xvii. 1-2) and a form of it is found in 1 Clem. xlvi. 8. This **millstone** is the μύλος ὀνικός, so called because it was so large that an ass was employed to turn it.

The next sayings are directed to the individual and his moral problems. A similar logion is found in Matt. v. 29-30 (possibly
43 from Q). The **hand** is often the member that does the wrong
45 deed; the **foot** suggests going in the direction of temptation, and in Jewish teaching the moral life is often spoken of as a journey
47 (*halakha* is 'the [right] way to walk'). The **eye** can provoke one to sin; cf. Job xxxi. 1 and Propertius, ii. 15. 12, *oculi sunt in amore duces.* But all three are among man's most important members. One must root out whatever is a temptation to sin, no matter how great the sacrifice.

48   The concept of **Gehenna,** common in rabbinic literature, is drawn from the valley of (*gê*) Hinnom, outside the south-west corner of Jerusalem (Josh. xv. 8). At one time it had been a place of human sacrifice; and refuse, particularly from the Temple sacrifices, was burned there. By the first century the idea of Sheol, where both good and bad went after death, had been partially replaced by that of a fiery place of torment (Enoch liv. 1-2; lvi. 3-4; 2 Baruch lix. 10; lxxxv. 13). The imagery of Isa. lxvi. 24 is here connected with it. Jesus employs the notion of Gehenna as part of the conventional eschatology (cf. Matt. v. 22; x. 28 =Luke xii. 5; 'Hades' in Luke xvi. 23) but without giving any positive teaching about it.

'For everyone will be salted with fire.   49
  'Salt is good; but if the salt becomes saltless, with what 50
will you season it? Have salt in yourselves and live at
peace with one another.'

Verse 49 serves as Mark's verbal link between the 'fire' of 49
verse 48 and the 'salt' of verse 50. Its meaning is obscure, and
it is not surprising that the later MSS. add (with some variations) 'and every sacrifice will be salted' (from the rule in Lev.
ii. 13). In this context the saying may mean 'Everyone must
suffer as though in fire in order to avoid sin'. One is reminded
of the saying that Jesus came to cast fire on the earth (Luke xii.
49), a logion which also appears in the *Gospel of Thomas* in two
forms: 'Men possibly think that I have come to throw peace
upon the world and they do not know that I have come to
throw divisions upon the earth, fire, sword, war (83: 34-36, p.
11; cf. 82: 14-16, p. 7). Still more poignant is the saying 'He
who is near me is near the fire' (95: 17-19, p. 45). It is possible,
therefore, that the Marcan saying originally referred to the **fire**
of persecution that is inevitable for a follower of Jesus. The OT
and secular writers, however, use the figure of salt to refer to
that which is useful; in a Talmudic saying it denotes that which
gives value or stimulates the appetite: 'The salt of money is its
scarcity ($h^e\acute{s}er$) but the salt of money is also charity ($he\acute{s}ed$)' (Bab.
Keth. 66*b*). One who is *salted* has had his character tested by the
tribulations of human existence. Thus the saying may be a
simple observation of life.

    Salt, i.e. pure sodium chloride, cannot become **saltless.** The 50
reference may be to impurities in salt, particularly that from the
Dead Sea; the true salt may leach out, leaving a residue. But the
thought may be: it is as paradoxical for a good disciple to change
his character as for salt to lose its taste; but if this should happen,
with what will you restore it? **Have salt in yourselves:** the
present saying applies the figure to that quality which makes
men **live at peace with one another.**

x. 1-12. DIVORCE

1 He arose and went from there into the territory of Judaea
and Transjordan, and the crowds again converged upon
him, and as his custom was he again was teaching them.
2 And Pharisees approached and asked him if it was
lawful for a man to divorce his wife, in order to put him
3 to the test. He answered them, 'What did Moses com-
4 mand you?' They said, 'Moses permitted a man "to
5 write an instrument of divorce and divorce her"'. But
Jesus said to them, 'In view of your hardness of heart he
6 wrote this commandment for you. But from the begin-
7 ning "male and female he created them"; "for this
reason a man will forsake his father and mother, and the
8 two shall become one flesh"; so then they are no longer
9 two but one flesh. Therefore what God has yoked together
10 let not man separate.' When they were back in the house
again, the disciples questioned him about this, and he
11 said to them, 'Whoever divorces his wife and marries
another woman has wronged her by committing adul-
12 tery; and if she, having divorced her husband, marries
another man, she commits adultery'.

Chapter x constitutes a section by itself: the last (and in Mark
the only) journey of Jesus to Jerusalem. Behind the geographical
arrangement, possibly in the pre-Marcan tradition, there are
traces of topical organisation of the material for catechetical
purposes. The NT contains several examples of teaching addressed to various groups in the Church. Col. iii. 18-iv. 1, for
example, deals successively with the duties of wives, husbands,
children, fathers, slaves and masters. Similar patterns can be
observed in 1 Tim. ii. 8-iii. 13; v. 1-vi. 2; Tit. i. 5-9; ii. 2-10;
Eph. v. 22-vi. 9; 1 Pet. ii. 13-18; iii. 1-7; v. 1-5. The principal

theme of the central part of Mark is of course discipleship; it begins in viii. 34-38 and dominates most of chap. ix. The first part of the *Haustafel* or teaching regarding the several groups may perhaps be the pericope on 'little ones', ix. 33-42. In chap. x the pattern becomes more evident: it includes married people (verses 1-12), children (verses 13-16), rich men (verses 17-27), and church leaders (verses 28-30, 35-45).

After the geographical introduction (verse 1) comes a section on divorce. It consists of two parts: a public pronouncement (verses 2-9) and a private explanation to the disciples (verses 10-12). This is Mark's editorial practice (cf. iv. 10-20; vii. 17-19; ix. 28-29); the private teaching, however, is not so much an explanation as a doublet in legal form. It may be drawn from Q, or at least has a parallel in that source (Matt. v. 32 = Luke xvi. 18).

The **territory of Judaea and Transjordan** must be the 1 correct reading; it reverses the order of Mark's narrative and probably belongs to the underlying tradition. διὰ τοῦ πέραν (A N X etc.) is an obvious correction, and so is the Caesarean reading πέραν (omitting καί). Mark probably thinks of the **crowds** as coming to him in Transjordan.

The question of the **Pharisees** appears to be formulated 2 from the Christian, not the Jewish, point of view. Contrast Matt. xix. 3, which expresses the issue debated among Pharisees: whether a man might divorce his wife *for any cause*. All agreed that divorce was legal; the school of Shammai permitted it only if the wife were guilty of unchastity or gross immodesty, while that of Hillel held that a man might divorce his wife even if she spoiled his food. Jewish marriage was not a contract between equals; a woman did not marry, but was 'given in marriage'. It is only fair, however, to add that the Pharisaic rules afforded a certain protection to the more helpless party. Her husband had to give her a writ of divorce that was valid in every respect, written on durable material and with ink that did not fade, and once he had delivered the writ he could not retract it; the woman was free. While a wife could not divorce her husband, she could go before the court and force him to divorce her if he engaged in disgusting occupations such as tanning, had certain diseases, took vows to her detriment, or forced her to take such vows.

Furthermore, the rabbis bitterly condemned indiscriminate divorce even if it was legal: 'the altar itself sheds tears when a man divorces the wife of his youth'.

4 The law attributed to **Moses** (Deut. xxiv. 1) was probably an advance in the rights of woman, for it clarified her status. 5 But in Jesus' view it was at best only something **permitted** because of men's **hardness of heart,** not only their dullness of mind but their rude, uncivilised emotions. It did not correspond 6, 7 to God's purpose, which was lifelong monogamy. The quotations are from Gen. i. 27; ii. 24, principles given in **the beginning** (the Heb. name of Genesis is *bᵉrêshith*) and intended for all humanity.

A similar argument is found in the Damascus Document vii. 1-3 (Rabin, *The Zadokite Documents*, 2nd ed., Oxford, 1958, pp. 16-18): 'The builders of the wall . . . are caught in fornication in two respects: by marrying two women in their lifetime, although the principle of creation is "Male and female he created them", and they who were in the ark, "two and two they went into the ark"'. The context shows that the Essenes forbade polygamy but the argument would apply also to marrying another woman after divorce. If this is so, the issue in verse 2 may be correctly stated: in Peraea, where there were Essenes, the Pharisees ask Jesus whether he sanctions divorce at all. This is one of the very few places in Mark where a parallel to the hitherto published Essene literature may be observed.

9 **Therefore what God has yoked together let not man separate.** Judaism placed a high value on marriage. A man was expected to marry by the age of eighteen and was not considered a complete person until he fulfilled this duty; celibacy was frowned on except in the case of a few students who were so engrossed in the study of the Law that God had, so to speak, granted them a dispensation. A rabbi might forsake his studies to join a wedding party, for God himself presided at Adam's marriage (*Aboth of R. Nathan*, vers. II, viii. 11*b*).

The principle stated here implies no exceptions. A rule to cover a hard case—the premarital unchastity or perhaps the adultery of the wife—is introduced in Matt. v. 32; xix. 9. Paul knows of Jesus' saying forbidding divorce (1 Cor. vii. 12-13) but is constrained to permit it, on his own responsibility as an apostle, when the non-Christian partner insists on a divorce from the Christian. In both instances the Church thought it necessary to modify the principle in actual application, and Matthew believed that the Church had the authority to make legal rulings (Matt. xviii. 18).

Jesus' teaching on divorce is triply attested: by verse 9, by 10, 11 Paul and by the doublet in verses 10-11. This has a parallel in Q and may have been derived from that document. Its oldest and most Jewish form is in Luke xvi. 18; here the man is the active partner and principally responsible, whether he divorces his wife and marries another, or marries the woman who has been divorced. Mark's form of the saying presupposes Roman 12 law, according to which the wife can divorce **her husband;** this idea is absent from Matt. v. 32; xix. 9; Hermas, *Mand.* iv. 1. 6. In all its forms the saying is legal in character and has in mind the **adultery** which in most cases would arise from the divorce; a woman would usually have no choice but to enter upon another marriage.

x. 13-16. CHILDREN

They were bringing children to him for him to touch 13 **them, but the disciples rebuked them. Jesus, when he** 14 **saw it, was indignant and said to them, 'Let the children come to me, stop hindering them, for the Kingdom of God belongs to such. I tell you truly, whoever does not** 15 **receive the Kingdom of God like a child will not enter it.' And he embraced and blessed them, laying his hands on** 16 **them.**

Those who brought the **children** wished Jesus **to touch** 13 **them,** for healing or more probably for blessing. The attitude of the disciples is a conventional trait in Mark (cf. vi. 37; ix. 38) but it would be natural for them to think that Jesus was too busy to be bothered (cf. v. 35).

Let the children come to me; cf. the saying on accepting 14

children, ix. 37: the Good News is directed to them also, they
are the objects of God's love and **the Kingdom of God belongs
to such;** i.e. God's Reign extends to them. The early Church
may well have taken this to mean that children, however young,
can derive benefit from membership in the Church and par-
ticipation in its rites. There is a rabbinic saying that children,
even those whose parents are godless pagans, will have a share
in the age to come. A closer parallel is quoted by Joseph
Klausner, *Jesus of Nazareth* (New York, 1925), p. 306: 'Children receive the presence of the Shekinah', i.e. of God himself.

15 The nucleus of Mark's section is the saying of verse 15, introduced by the solemn *Amen* (cf. iii. 28) which marks it as an
important revelation. To **receive the Kingdom of God** is to
accept the yoke of God's sovereignty, but also to share in its
benefits. Jesus does not explain what it means to receive it
like a child; cf. *Gospel of Thomas* 85: 20-22 (p. 17). Matt.
xviii. 4 applies the concept to humility; but this, as the word is
usually understood, is not a natural characteristic of childhood.
Children can be insistent in their demands, and Jesus assumes
that a child will ask his father for what he wants; cf. Matt. vii.
7-11 =Luke xi. 9-13. Some commentators suggest that a normal
child lives by grace, not works; he does not think that he must
earn his parents' love and care by flattery or good behaviour
but accepts them naturally and responds spontaneously with
his affection. Another possibility is that Jesus thinks of the
unsophistication and freshness of the child, whose world is new
and filled with marvels; he has a great capacity to receive im-
pressions and is not jaded or *blase*; cf. *KGSM*, p. 119. See also
F. A. Schilling, *Exp. Times*, lxxvii (1965), 56-58.

x. 17-31. RICH MEN

17 **As he was going out into the road a man ran to him and,
kneeling to him, asked him, 'Good teacher, what am I
18 to do to inherit eternal life?' Jesus said to him, 'Why do
19 you call me good? No one is good but the One, God. You
know the commandments: "Do not commit murder, do
not commit adultery, do not steal, do not testify falsely,**

do not defraud, honour your father and mother".' He 20
said to him, 'Teacher, as to all these things I have been
careful from my youth'. Jesus, looking upon him, was 21
attracted to him and he said to him, 'One thing you lack;
go, sell whatever you have and give to the poor, and you
will have treasure in heaven, and come, follow me'.
But he was shocked at that saying and went away sorrow- 22
ful, for he was one who had many possessions. And Jesus, 23
looking around, said to his disciples, 'With what difficulty
do those who have money enter the Kingdom of God'.
The disciples were astonished at his words. But Jesus 24
again answered them, 'Children, how difficult it is to
enter the Kingdom of God. It is easier for a camel to pass 25
through the eye of a needle than for a rich man to enter
the Kingdom of God.' But they were extremely aston- 26
ished, saying to themselves, 'Then who can be saved?'
Jesus, looking at them, said: 'With men it is impossible, 27
but not with God, for everything is possible with God'.
Peter began to say to him, 'See, we have left everything 28
and followed you'. Jesus said, 'I tell you truly, there is 29
no one who has forsaken house or brothers or sisters or
mother or father or children or fields for the sake of the 30
Good News who will not receive a hundred times as
much more in this present time of houses and brothers
and sisters and mothers and children and fields—with
persecutions—and in the coming age life eternal. But 31
many of the first shall be last and the last first.'

This is a double dialogue, first between Jesus and the rich
man (verses 17-22), then between Jesus and the disciples
(verses 23-31). In the first part, Jesus is pictured as the teacher,
in the second, as the one who leads his people into the Kingdom
of God. Behind the discourse lies the experience of the early
Church, which heard its Lord's demands for renunciation and
his promise of eternal life. But it is based on sayings of Jesus,
and verses 17-22 may be essentially historical. Verse 25 is
apparently the nucleus of the second part of the discourse.

A man: εἰς, evidently a Semitism; in Mark he is not called 17
'young' (Matt. xix. 20) or a 'ruler' (Luke xviii. 18). **Kneeling**

would not have been customary in the presence of a Jewish
rabbi; the man offers reverence as to his master. Nor is **Good
teacher** the conventional address; only one parallel is given
by SB. One is reminded of the Greek ὦ βέλτιστε (Lohmeyer).
The man's desire to **inherit,** i.e. win or receive, **eternal life**
points in the direction of John. The phrase is found in Dan.
xii. 2 but the more common Jewish phrase is 'the age to come';
cf. C. H. Dodd, *The Interpretation of the Fourth Gospel* (Cambridge, 1953), pp. 144-146.

18 Jesus' response seems so natural and arresting that it can
scarcely have been invented. **Why do you call me good?**
This adjective is appropriate only for **the One.** Bishop, p. 201,
correctly recognises this as a title of the Deity; Mark adds **God**
as an explanation for non-Jewish readers. For goodness as
God's attribute, cf. Ps. cxviii. 1; 1 Chron. xvi. 34; 2 Chron. v.
13; Philo, *Leg. alleg*. i. 47. Here his goodness is connected with
his unity; only God can be good in the absolute sense.

19 **You,** like everyone else, **know the commandments;** there
is no secret as to what God demands. Only the moral, not the
ritual commandments are however cited. They are drawn from
Deut. v. 17-20, 16a, with the insertion **do not defraud.** The
latter clause is perhaps based on Lev. xix. 11, 13, and belongs
to the text of Mark; its omission by B* W sy⁸ etc. is due to
harmonisation with Matthew, Luke and the OT. The citations
are not from the LXX, and therefore the tradition probably
goes back to a Semitic original or the oral gospel.

20 **Teacher, as to all these things I have been careful from
my youth.** This translation adopts the reading ἐφυλαξάμην and
gives it its force as a middle. The man's answer is modest and
proper. A Jew could, however, honestly have said that he had
kept these commandments (cf. 2 Esd. iii. 36; Luke i. 6), and
Jesus takes it for granted that there are 'righteous' men (ii. 17);
the idea is not that of sinless perfection.

21 **Jesus** accepted the answer at face value and **was attracted
to him,** literally 'loved him'; the man was all that he claimed
to be. For a similar response, cf. xii. 34. But, he added, **one
thing you lack.** Cadbury says (*Peril,* pp. 106f.), 'The commands
to almsgiving frequently mention the benefit to be received by
the donor rather than by the recipient. Like mercy "it blesses

him that gives and him that takes," but Jesus is thinking of the
donor: "it is more blessed to give than to receive." . . . And so
when the rich young man is to sell all and give to the poor,
nothing is said about the poor's need, still less is considered the
harm money may do the poor. Perhaps their need is taken for
granted. They may need to get it, but *he* needs to get rid of it.'
The social motive found in the parallel story of the *Gospel
according to the Hebrews* is absent here. As a result, **you will
have treasure in heaven;** cf. Matt. vi. 19-21 =Luke xii.
33-34. Although God's reward is out of all proportion to man's
deeds and is thus a matter of grace (Matt. xx. 1-15), for no one
can claim to have satisfied all God's demands (Luke xvii. 10),
Jesus does not hesitate to teach that there is reward. **And come
follow me.** This may have been an invitation to join the
intimate group of disciples, who could not be burdened with
possessions; Mark no doubt thinks of it as a general rule for
Christians, since he appends the following section, particularly
verses 29-30. The man **was shocked . . . and went away** 22
sorrowful; there is no sequel and he disappears from the
narrative.

The discussion of rich men enshrines two sayings, verses 23
and 25, of which the latter is more vivid and original, and Mark
binds them together with the repetitious verse 24 for the sake
of added emphasis. **The disciples were astonished,** for 24
although Judaism praised the pious poor (Pss. ix. 18; x. 9; xii.
5; xxxiv. 6) and knew of the dangers and temptations of riches,
it was also believed that wealth was a blessing and that the pious
might be rewarded with it (Job xlii. 10; Ecclus. xliv. 6). The
affectionate word **Children** is reminiscent of verse 15 and
implies that the disciples, in contrast to the rich man, can enter
the Kingdom of God in a childlike spirit. Jesus does not deny 25
that a rich man like Zacchaeus may repent and be saved (Luke
xix. 1-10), but he belongs in the company of those biblical
writers who regard riches as a source of spiritual danger (cf.
Luke i. 53; Jas. ii. 1-7; v. 1-6). **It is easier for a camel to pass
through the eye of a needle . . .** This is the authentic oriental
hyperbole that marks several of Jesus' sayings (cf. xi. 23; Matt.
vii. 3-5). Attempts to explain it away are unsuccessful; it is
doubtful, for example, if there was an actual Greek word κάμιλος

('rope') for which κάμηλος might have been substituted (cf. Liddell-Scott-Jones, *s.v.*), and the change would not help matters much. The suggestion of a gate called 'the Needle's Eye', through which a camel could barely squeeze, is only fanciful.

26, 27 The disciples ask, **Then who can be saved?** The answer comes out of strict monotheism and confidence in God's grace: **everything is possible with God.** Cf. *Problem*, pp. 54 f.

28 The last part of the section is loosely connected to the foregoing by verse 28. This reflects the sacrifices made by members of the early Church **for the sake of the Good News;** the words 29 'for my sake' should probably be omitted, as in viii. 35. In 30 return for their losses they will receive **a hundred times as much** in hospitality and the love of the new family (cf. iii. 35) but **with persecutions;** and the crowning gift **in the coming age** is **life eternal** (cf. verse 17).

31 **But many of the first shall be last and the last first.** This saying on the 'reversal of roles' is found also in Matt. xx. 16. Its original context cannot be determined, but the idea is frequent in the Bible, cf., e.g., Luke i. 52-53; 1 Sam. ii. 4-5. It is an affirmation of God's sovereignty and overruling judgement.

x. 32-34. THE THIRD PASSION PREDICTION

32 **They were on the road going up to Jerusalem, and Jesus was preceding them, and they were stunned, and those who followed were afraid. Again taking the Twelve to one side he began to tell them the things that were about to** 33 **happen to him: 'See, we are going up to Jerusalem, and the Son of Man will be handed over to the chief priests and the scholars, and they will condemn him to death** 34 **and hand him over to the Gentiles, and they will mock him and spit on him and scourge him and kill him and after three days he will rise again'.**

32 Jesus is pictured as a rabbi whose disciples literally walk behind him **on the road going up.** The whole Jordan valley south

of Lake Huleh lies below sea level, while **Jerusalem** is at an elevation of about 2,550 feet. The disciples were **stunned** and **afraid;** Mark expresses the sense of the numinous which they may have felt in his presence. They were shocked by the teaching he had given and his steadfast resolution to go to the Holy City, where danger and death awaited him, yet they could only follow; cf. R. Otto, *The Idea of the Holy* (London, 1923), pp. 84 f.; *Problem*, pp. 68-73.

The third passion prediction draws details from xv. 1, 15-20; for its literary connexions, cf. on ix. 31.

x. 35-45. LEADERS AMONG THE DISCIPLES

James and John, the sons of Zebedee, approached and 35 **said to him, 'Teacher, we want you to do for us whatever we ask you'. He said to them, 'What do you want me to** 36 **do for you?' They said to him, 'Grant us that in your** 37 **glory we may be seated, one at your right and one at your left'. Jesus said to them, 'You do not know what you are** 38 **asking. Can you drink the cup that I drink and undergo the baptism that I undergo?' They said to him, 'We can'.** 39 **And Jesus said to them, 'You shall drink the cup that I drink and undergo the baptism that I undergo, but to sit** 40 **at my right or left is not mine to grant; instead, it is for those for whom it has been prepared'. When the ten** 41 **heard it they were indignant about James and John. Jesus** 42 **summoned them and said to them, 'You know that those who are recognised as ruling the Gentiles lord it over them and their magnates exert authority over them. It is** 43 **not so among you; instead, whoever wishes to be great among you shall be your servant, and whoever wishes to** 44 **be first among you shall be slave of all; for even the Son** 45 **of Man did not come to be served but to serve, and to give his life as a means of freeing many.'**

This is a fitting climax to the theme of discipleship, which was introduced early in the gospel (i. 16-20) and developed most thoroughly from viii. 34 on. Jesus' teaching on humble service is nowhere more beautifully expressed than in verses 43-45, and it is characteristic of Mark that the pattern is the Son of Man: he is not just the apocalyptic judge but the one who has healed the sick, embraced children and patiently taught his disciples.

The evangelist has anticipated the teaching of this section in ix. 34-35, which fits poorly into its context. His method is to introduce a theme and develop it later; cf., e.g., the Kingdom of God, i. 15; iv. 1-30; the Son of Man, ii. 10, 28; viii. 31-38; xiii. 3-27. This section exhibits still another of his editorial habits: it is in two parts, the discussion with James and John (verses 35-40) and the explanation to the disciples (verses 42-45), as in the story of the Rich Man above, and viii. 27-ix. 1.

35 **James and John** are the 'sons of thunder' (iii. 17) and their request is an example of their impulsive abruptness, possibly their presumption. The demand for an unspecified boon is well known in folk tales; cf. vi. 22, where Antipas offers such a gift unasked. Why are these two men singled out? The tradition may have originally connected them with the story, but it could have been told of others. As early as Paul's ministry in Corinth there were groups of Christians for whom Paul, Apollos or Cephas was the greatest hero (1 Cor. i. 12). Peter's followers must be responsible for the special tradition in Matt. xvi. 17-19, and note how the saying, that flesh and blood has not revealed the truth to Peter, is countered by Paul's statement in Gal. i. 11-12. James (evidently the brother of the Lord), Cephas and John were 'pillars' of the Jerusalem church (Gal. ii. 9; cf. 1 Cor. ix. 5). The brother of the Lord presides over the Church of Jerusalem in Acts xv, and so great is his authority that he is traditionally regarded as the first bishop of that city and is prominent in the Clementine literature and the (in part gnostic) *Gospel of Thomas* 82: 25-30, p. 9. In the last-named passage, the disciples ask who will be great among them and Jesus answers, 'You will go to James the righteous, for whose sake heaven and earth came into being'. Although James the son of Zebedee is not prominent in such traditions, his brother John is no doubt the Beloved Disciple, who is the ideal of the Fourth Evangelist (John xiii. 23; xix. 26-27; xx. 4; xxi. 20-24). Mark has no single apostolic hero.

36 **What do you want me to do for you?** Note the colloquial

use of the subjunctive without ἵνα, here and in the following verse.

The two, having witnessed the Transfiguration, realise that 37 Jesus will come in **glory;** yet they cannot rise above the concept of earthly messiahship and they ask to **be seated** at his **right** and his **left** as the two principal members of his cabinet. That such ideas could be entertained is shown by Matt. xix. 28 = Luke xxii. 28-30; Rev. xiv. 8, 10; indeed the choice of a twelfth apostle to succeed Judas (Acts i. 15-26) was no doubt due to the belief that in the coming age the Twelve would be the Sanhedrin of the new Israel.

Jesus asks in turn, **Can you drink the cup that I drink?** 38 Does Mark think of this dialogue as taking place near Jericho, perhaps as they crossed the Jordan where John baptised? The tension heightens here: the two disciples have Jerusalem and Jesus' glory in mind, their teacher thinks of the crisis that he must meet in the Holy City. The OT speaks of a cup of joy or salvation (Pss. xvi. 5; xxiii. 5; cxvi. 13) and also a cup of suffering or punishment (Pss. xi. 6; lxxv. 8; Isa. li. 17, 22; Jer. xxv. 15, 17, etc.). Something like the **baptism** of tribulation and death is mentioned in Ps. xlii. 7; Isa. xliii. 2; for Paul, the Christian rite is the identification with the Lord in his death which is followed by rising to new life (Rom. vi. 3-4). The saying must be connected with the two sacraments, which are prominent in Mark's thought. (Cf. Knox, *Sources*, i. 71, where the cup saying is thought to be more natural and the saying regarding baptism a later addition.) If the disciples are to have the privileges of them, they must share the vocation of the suffering Son of Man who gives them. Even though they **do not know what** they **are asking,** they reply, **We can.** James certainly underwent martyr- 39 dom (Acts xii. 2). The fate of John is uncertain. According to the tradition, he lived to a great age, but a fragment of Papias preserved in Philip of Side says that 'John the theologian and James his brother were put to death by Jews'.

As Lohmeyer remarks, verse 40 has no inner connexion with 40 the preceding story, but it may already have been combined with it in the pre-Marcan tradition. The privilege **is not mine to grant; instead, it is for those for whom it has been prepared,** i.e. by God. In place of ἀλλ' οἷς **(for those for whom),** a b d ff k aeth read ἄλλοις (for others), and the Old Syriac has a similar reading, but this would not accord well with Jesus' teaching. He elsewhere refuses to make exact predictions of the future; to do so is to invade God's prerogative (cf. xiii. 32; Luke xvii. 20-22).

42   There are **those who are recognised as ruling the Gentiles** (δοκοῦντες), possibly 'reputed as ruling' or 'seem to rule'; for although men recognise their rule, only God is the ultimate sovereign. Such men **lord it over them,** and this was expected in the ancient world; cf. Stewart Perowne's comments on the speech of Agrippa II, *The Later Herods* (London, 1958), pp. 124 f. It is still true in political and economic life that the exercise of power impresses men, but Jesus was an exception to the rule; cf. Matt. iv. 8-10 =Luke iv. 5-8; Matt. xi. 8 =Luke vii.

43 25. **It is not so among you; instead, whoever wishes to be great among you shall be your servant.** διάκονος soon became a technical ecclesiastical term, certainly as early as 1 Tim. iii. 8-13, and possibly in Phil. i. 1, though elsewhere in the genuine letters of Paul it means 'servant', 'minister', in a general sense. Here the diaconate is not the lowest order of ministry, but

44 the highest, and the **first . . . shall be slave of all,** *servus servorum Dei* not merely in title but in attitude and deed, for this is the nature of **the Son of Man** himself; cf. Phil. ii. 5-11. δοῦλος (Heb. 'ebed) often denotes a worshipper of God (Ps. xxxiv. 22) or one called by God to a special service (Josh. i. 1; Jer. vii. 25; Rom. i. 1).

45   The phrase **to give his life as a means of freeing many** (λύτρον ἀντὶ πολλῶν) is often thought to be due to the influence of Pauline ideas (Rom. iii. 24-25; 1 Cor. vii. 23; Gal. iii. 13). Certainly the idea of ransom is not prominent in the gospels, and the word is not used elsewhere in the NT save in the parallel Matt. xx. 28; on λύτρον and the corresponding Heb. *kopher*, cf. R. Otto, *KGSM*, pp. 256-259. This may be part of the theology of the Gentile church; it must, however, be remembered that vicarious suffering is a native idea in Judaism; cf. 2 Macc. vii. 37-38; 4 Macc. vi. 28; xvii. 21-22; Montefiore and Loewe, *Rabbinic Anthology*, pp. 225-232; and one need not look further than Isa. lii. 13-liii. 12 for the background of this verse (cf. the 'many' in liii. 12).

x. 46-52. TRANSITION SECTION: BLIND BARTIMAEUS

They came into Jericho. And as he and his disciples and 46
a considerable crowd were coming out from Jericho,
Bartimaeus (that is, Timaeus' son), a blind beggar, sat
alongside the road, and when he heard that it was Jesus 47
the Nazarene he began to shout, 'Son of David, Jesus, 48
pity me'. A number of people commanded him to be
quiet, but he kept crying out all the louder, 'Son of David,
pity me'. Jesus halted and said, 'Call him'. And they 49
called the blind man, saying to him, 'Courage, get up,
he is calling you'. He cast away his cape, leaped up, and 50
came to Jesus. Jesus said, 'What do you want me to do 51
for you?' The blind man said to him, 'Rabbouni, I want
to see again'. Jesus said to him, 'Go, your faith has healed 52
you', and immediately he saw again; and he followed
him on the road.

Jericho lies a little west of the Jordan and a little north of the 46
Dead Sea. The OT site, Tell es-Sultan, is north of the modern
town (which is still called *Erîḥa*) near the spring 'Ain es-Sultan,
which supplied its water. The excavations, which reach back
into the pre-pottery Neolithic period, show that Jericho is the
oldest continuously inhabited city known to exist. But the town
through which Jesus and the disciples passed after crossing the
Jordan lay west of Erîḥa, where the Wady Qelt opens out into
the river valley. This was developed in splendid style by Herod
the Great and Archelaus and has been partly excavated; cf. J. B.
Pritchard, *The Excavation at Herodian Jericho, 1951* (New
Haven, 1958).
Bartimaeus is known to us only by his patronymic, which
Mark explains for Gentile readers as **Timaeus' son**. The latter
is a Greek name; its Aramaic form would be Timai, which might
be an abbreviation of Timotheus; for the use of Greek names
by Jews, cf. on iii. 13-19. The man addresses Jesus as **Son of** 48
David, i.e. the messianic king. This is particularly dramatic, for
the people of Jericho must have been disillusioned with the

Herodian family, and after Archelaus' exile the city was part of the Roman province of Judaea. Curtis Beach, *The Gospel of Mark* (New York, 1959), p. 98, notes that the man gives Jesus this title *while he is still blind*; like James and John, he does not yet see his true nature. For Jesus' rejection of the term, cf. xii. 35-37. Lohmeyer objects that a Jew would not say **pity me** (ἐλέησόν με) to an earthly messianic king, for the words would be used in addressing God or a divine Lord; thus the phrase shows a mingling of theologies in the story. It is true that κύριε ἐλέησον ('Lord, have mercy') was a shout of acclamation to the emperor; cf. Epictetus, ii. 7. 12, where it is spoken to an augur as though he were a god. But Josephus (*Ant.* ix. 4. 4) employs it in the address of a woman to Joram. **A number of people commanded** Bartimaeus **to be quiet,** for the words could be construed as seditious.

49 **Courage:** Rieu, 'All is well'; Phillips, 'It's all right now'.

50 **He cast away his cape,** thus showing his eagerness and faith; Bishop, p. 205, remarks that the reading of 565 sy[sin], ἐπιβαλών, 'putting on', seems more lifelike; the blind man acted out of innate courtesy and sensitivity.

51 **What do you want me to do for you?** Note the θέλεις ποιήσω without ἵνα; this is colloquial Hellenistic Greek.

Rabbouni, found only here and in John xx. 16, 'my Lord' or 'my master'; *rabban* is a heightened form of *rab*, and the personal pronoun is added at the end.

Dibelius, *The Message of Jesus Christ* (New York, 1939), p. 167, regards the story as a paradigm which shows how the man 52 risked everything to reach Jesus. The concluding saying, **Go, your faith has healed you** (cf. on v. 34), is characteristic of paradigm style. The cure is not described in detail (contrast viii. 22-25).

He followed him on the road. The road led up the south side of the Wady Qelt. It can be travelled today but is no longer the principal highway. Jesus was now on the last stage of his journey, and Jerusalem lay about fifteen miles away. It was a long uphill trip which might have required twelve hours.

———

xi. 1-11. THE TRIUMPHAL ENTRY: A NIGHT IN BETHANY

When they came near to Jerusalem, to Bethphage and 1
Bethany at the Mount of Olives, he sent two of his dis- 2
ciples and said to them, 'Go into the village opposite you,
and as soon as you enter it you will find a colt tied, on
which no one has ever sat; untie it and bring it. If anyone 3
says to you, "Why are you doing this?" say, "The master
needs it, and he will send it right back here".' They 4
went away and found the colt tied at the door, outside,
in the street, and they untied it. Some of those who were 5
standing there said to them, 'What are you doing, un-
tying the colt?' And they said to them just what Jesus had 6
said, and the men permitted them. So they brought the 7
colt to Jesus, and they put their garments on it and he sat
on it. Many people spread their garments on the road, 8
others spread branches which they had cut in the country.
Those who went ahead and those who followed kept 9
crying out,

> 'Hosanna!
> Blessed is he who comes in the name of the Lord!   10
> Blessed is the coming kingdom of our father
>   David!
> Hosanna on high!'

He went into Jerusalem, into the temple enclosure, and, 11
when he had looked around at everything, the hour now
being late, he went out into Bethany with the Twelve.

Chapters xi-xiii comprise a major section of the gospel, devoted to Jesus' ministry in Jerusalem, but chap. xiii stands somewhat by itself as the final and climactic discourse addressed to
the disciples. Mark gives the clear impression that this is Jesus'

first visit to the Holy City during his ministry, but several considerations make this unlikely. Jesus had friends in the city (verses 2-3; xiv. 13-16), he was apparently known to Simon the Leper (xiv. 3), other visits are implied by Matt. xxiii. 37 =Luke xiii. 34, and, finally, the Fourth Gospel recounts two other visits; cf. *JOT*, pp. 84-88.

The length of this visit to Jerusalem is another problem. The triumphal entry is conventionally dated on Palm Sunday; the Sabbath would thus have been spent just east of Jericho, and Jesus would have arrived in Jerusalem on Sunday evening. On this assumption, verses 12-19 recount the events of Monday, and the story of Tuesday begins at verse 20. Nothing is said of the ending of this day, and it is necessary to assume that xiv. 1 refers to Wednesday, with the Last Supper taking place on Thursday night.

The mere recital of the above shows that the notes of time are not definite, and xiv. 49 speaks of Jesus having taught 'daily' in the Temple. The details of the triumphal entry suggest that he is welcomed as a pilgrim coming for a festival, but the waving of branches and the use of Ps. cxviii are observances connected with Tabernacles and Hannukah (Rededication), not Passover, so far as one can learn from the Jewish sources. Furthermore, the half-shekel Temple tax, which made money-changing necessary (verse 15), had to be paid nearly two weeks before Passover. Branscomb, *ad loc.*, therefore suggests that Jesus came to the city in the autumn, while Burkitt prefers to think of December; cf. *Jesus Christ: An Historical Outline* (London, 1932), pp. 42 f. If one of these hypotheses is not adopted, it is necessary to make two assumptions: that Jesus entered the city two or three weeks before Passover, and that some of the ceremonies of Tabernacles had been added to the Passover celebration as well as to that of Hannukah. Carrington, pp. 192 f., regards this section as the second lesson in the Tabernacles season, the healing of Bartimaeus being the first.

1   **Bethphage and Bethany** are approximately **at the Mount of Olives,** but if the traditional identifications of the two villages are correct, they are mentioned in the wrong order. Jesus would first have come to Bethany, now known as el-'Azarîyeh because of the reputed tomb of Lazarus which is displayed there. This

lies south-east of the mountain on the present automobile road, out of sight of Jerusalem. The statement of John xi. 18, that it was 15 stades from Jerusalem (almost two miles), fits the location fairly well. Bethphage is on the north slope of Ras esh-Shiyah, and nearer, more precisely at the mount itself. 'Bethphage' is omitted by D 700 a b c ff² i k aur vg Origen. It may have crept into Mark's text from Matt. xxi. 1, which has only Bethphage; Luke xix. 29 includes both villages, but this may also be due to conflation. For a full discussion, including the suggestion that Bethany lay farther north than Bethphage, on the western slope of the Mount of Olives, cf. K. Lake in *BC*, v, 475 f.; map in Kraeling, *Atlas*, p. 396. 'Bethphage' apparently means 'house of figs'; it is reckoned by the Mishnah as an outlying part of Jerusalem (Menahoth xi. 2). The etymology of 'Bethany' is doubtful; Jerome says, *domus adflictionis eius vel domus obedientiae*.

The **colt** found in **the village** need not be an ass's colt; 2 Walter Bauer, *JBL*, lxxii (1953), 220-229, shows that in Greek literature πῶλος means 'young animal' when another animal is mentioned in the context, but 'horse' when no other animal is named. It is likely that villagers would ride on asses, but there is no evidence that Mark has the prophecy of Zech. ix. 9 in mind, as does Matt. xxi. 5; cf. Knox, *Sources*, pp. 77 f. This is one **on which no one has ever sat;** to the evangelists this suggests that it is intended uniquely for Jesus' honour, almost as if it were a sacrificial animal (Deut. xxi. 3; Num. xix. 2). The Zechariah prophecy is based on the blessing of Judah in Gen. xlix. 9-12: this 'lion's whelp' will have the sceptre and will bind 'his foal to the vine and his ass's colt to the choice vine'; cf. *ANET*, p. 482, for the use of 'foal of an ass' at Mari as early as the eighteenth century B.C.; such an animal was sacrificed at the making of a treaty. In this instance the colt is found tied **in the street** (ἐπὶ τοῦ ἀμφόδου); but evidently Justin (*Apol.* i. 54) and Clement (*Paid.* i. 5. 15) read ἀμπέλου ('vine') not ἀμφόδου in their texts of Mark; whether or not the reading is original, it shows that early Christians perceived a reminiscence of the prophecy of Judah's royal power.

The directions to the disciples to bring the animal, with the 3 answer to be made if a question is raised, suggest that Jesus had

friends in the village, although Mark may think of Jesus' knowledge as supernatural. The triumphal entry seems to be
planned; it is not convincing to say that Jesus was fatigued from
the long journey, for the further distance into Jerusalem was not
great. Two questions naturally arise: what was Mark's theological interpretation of the incident, and what was the original
meaning of Jesus' action?

7   The shouts and actions of the people imply that they welcomed him as the Messiah son of David; and, if there are allu-
sions to OT passages, these are messianic. This is in disharmony
with Mark's theology, but he may have considered the welcome
accorded Jesus only one more example of the people's blindness,
like the demand of James and John and the words of Bartimaeus.
Lohmeyer, however, attempts to connect the story with the Son
of Man tradition by citing Sanh. 98a, 'R. Yehoshua ben Levi
[c. 250] said, "See, the Son of Man comes on,the clouds of
heaven", and "poor and riding on an ass". If they [Israel] are
worthy of him, he comes on the clouds; if they are not worthy
of him, poor and riding on an ass.' The entry, on this theory,
is outwardly only the acclamation of a rabbi beloved by a small
group of Galileans, who see in this the humble coming of the
Son of Man, whom the public as a whole ignores. Lohmeyer's
idea is attractive, but the parallel is late; there is no evidence
from the first century that Jews other than the followers of Jesus
would have connected the two prophecies with one another.

In view of Mark's tendencies, the story is surprising enough;
it must have come from the tradition. The charges against Jesus
before the Sanhedrin and Pilate do not mention the incident, but
it might nevertheless have contributed to the suspicions of the
authorities; in Luke xxiii. 2 he is accused of 'calling himself
Messiah king'. The original meaning of this solemn entrance
into the city must be bound up with Jesus' purpose in coming
to Jerusalem. This was not merely in order to suffer and die (cf.
the Gethsemane pericope, xiv. 33-36, and the cry from the
Cross, xv. 34); it was part of a larger vocation to proclaim the
Kingdom of God and give the nation a final opportunity to
accept it. Like the cleansing of the Temple, the triumphal entry
was a sign of Jesus' prophetic leadership; cf. F. C. Grant, *The
Gospel of the Kingdom* (New York, 1940), pp. 72 f. He came into

the city with peace and humility but with the authority of God.

The incident, however, turned into a messianic demonstra- 8
tion. **Many . . . spread their garments on the road,** thus
receiving Jesus as a monarch (cf. 2 Kings ix. 13). The word translated **branches** might mean reeds, grasses, or foliage from trees.
John xii. 13 speaks of palm branches; palms will grow in shel-
tered spots in Jerusalem but are not native as they are in Jericho.
Mark does not say that the people carried the branches, as
though they were the *lulab* of Tabernacles, but perhaps they had
cut them for that festival, and now **spread** them on the way.
There is one place on the Mount of Olives where the group
would suddenly come in view of the city; cf. Bishop, pp. 211 f.

The shout of **Hosanna** ('Save now') and **Blessed is he who** 9, 10
comes in the name of the Lord! (Ps. cxviii. 25-26) suggest
the ritual of the Temple at the time of Tabernacles. The wor-
shippers carried the *lulab*, myrtle and willow with a spray of
palm leaf, and the *ethrog* or citron, and at certain points in the
recitation of the Hallel (Pss. cxiii-cxviii) they waved these in
concert. After the supplemental sacrifices of the day they
marched in procession around the altar carrying the branches and
citrons and singing the Hosanna; cf. Moore, *Judaism*, ii, 43 f.

Blessed is the coming kingdom of our father David!
Jewish sources do not ordinarily call David 'our father'; the
'fathers' are the patriarchs; and it would be more natural to
think of David's kingdom as being 'established' or 'returning'.
The words, however, preserve the memory of messianic enthu-
siasm. **Hosanna on high,** i.e. 'Save now in the highest', must
be a misunderstanding of the Hebrew, as though it meant 'Glory
to God in the highest' (Luke ii. 14; cf. the parallel Luke xix. 38),
unless Mark meant 'Save now, O thou who dwellest in the
heights', or, as Burkitt suggests, 'up with your wands', since the
lulabs were sometimes called Hosannas. It is probable, however,
that when Mark wrote the meaning of the word had been forgotten by Christians; it was, as in the later Church, a liturgical
formula.

Matt. xxi. 12 gives the impression that the cleansing of the 11
Temple followed immediately, but Mark is more lifelike; Jesus
merely visited **the temple enclosure, . . . the hour** was **late,**
at least six or seven o'clock in the evening.

xi. 12-14. THE CURSING OF THE FIG TREE

12 **The next morning as they were coming out of Bethany**
13 **he got hungry. Seeing a fig tree far off, with leaves on it,**
he went to see if he would find anything in it, and when
he came to it he found nothing but leaves; for it was not
14 **the season for figs. He said to it, 'May no one ever eat**
fruit from you!' His disciples heard this.

12   The narrative begins in a lifelike fashion—**he got hungry**—
for ancient orientals ate very little breakfast. In the warm climate
of the Sea of Galilee, fig trees bore fruit for ten months of the
year (Josephus, *B.J.* iii. 10. 8), but in Jerusalem the figs would
13 not ripen until summer; thus if this incident occurred at Passover time **it was not the season for figs,** and the story seems
pointless. If, however, the time is Tabernacles, one could expect
the crop of late figs and the words are a gloss; cf. Carrington,
p. 194. also *MR*, p. 122, *n.* 14.

14   Ancient people may not have felt much difficulty in the story;
the rabbis taught that even the idle curse of a righteous man was
effective (Mishnah Aboth ii. 10). Nevertheless, this is the only
curse miracle attributed to Jesus in the gospels, it reminds one
of the apocryphal infancy stories (e.g. Greek *Gospel of Thomas*
iii-v in James, *Apocryphal NT*, p. 50), and it seems to conflict
with Jesus' character. The simplest explanation is that the parable of the barren fig tree (Luke xiii. 6-9) has been turned into
a miracle which symbolises the rejection of Israel or of the
priesthood. In Luke xix. 41-44 this incident is replaced by
Jesus' weeping over the city and his prophecy of destruction.
The cleansing of the Temple follows immediately.

xi. 15-18. THE CLEANSING OF THE TEMPLE

15 **They entered Jerusalem. And he went into the temple**
area and began to drive out those who were selling and
buying there and he overturned the money changers'
16 **counters and the seats of those who sold doves, and he**

did not permit anyone to carry a vessel through the temple area. He taught them: 'Isn't it written, "My house 17 shall be called a house of prayer for all nations"? But you have made it a "cave of bandits".' The chief priests and 18 scholars heard this and sought a way to destroy him, for they were afraid of him because all the crowd was astonished at his teaching.

John places this narrative at the beginning of Jesus' ministry (ii. 13-22), probably for symbolic reasons; it seems likely that Mark has chosen the proper location. There is no trace of the Son of Man theology, except in the very general sense that the Son of Man is judge. Here Jesus acts as a prophet. Just as Isaiah went naked (Isa. xx. 1-6), Jeremiah buried his loincloth (Jer. xiii. 1-11) and the Christian prophet Agabus bound Paul hand and foot with his belt (Acts xxi. 11-12), so the Galilean by a prophetic sign proclaims God's intention to purify the Temple or destroy it. This was a high-handed and dangerous act; he could not have controlled the Temple precincts more than temporarily, even though the authorities were at the moment afraid to touch him. There is no indication that he intended to raise an armed revolt, though the leaders certainly must have considered this as 'stirring up the people' (Matt. xxi. 10; cf. Luke xxiii. 1), and the incident no doubt formed part of the basis of the charge that he planned to destroy the Temple (xiv. 58).

Jeremiah had prophesied that God would do to this Temple what he had done to Shiloh (Jer. vii. 1-16), and this section is quoted in verse 17, along with Isa. lvi. 7. The Book of Malachi is principally a denunciation of the priesthood; here the messenger of the covenant will purify the sons of Levi and God himself will come to judgement (Mal. iii. 3, 5); thus Jesus acts as the forerunner or symbolically in the place of God. Bacon, *Story*, p. 232, cites a midrash from *Debarim Rabba* which combines the Malachi prophecy with that of Isa. xlix. 14-l. 1, 'A certain king was angry with his wife and forsook her. The neighbours [i.e. the Gentiles] declared: He will never return. Then the king sent word to her: Cleanse my palace, and on such and such a day I will return to thee. He came, indeed, and was reconciled to her.'

Jesus' protest was not against the Temple worship as such (cf. verse 16; Matt. v. 23-24 contains no objection to offering gifts at the altar) but against the abuses that had been tolerated or encouraged by the high priest and his associates. The Talmud records curses on the Sadducees for their greed, and not long before the fall of Jerusalem a rabbi relaxed the rules for purification sacrifices because of the extortionate prices charged for doves; cf. SB, i, 851, 853; ii, 570. According to Josephus (*Ant.* xx. 8. 8; 9. 2), about the same time the priestly leaders seized the tithes with the result that some of the poorer priests died of starvation. Hence the quotation **cave of bandits** may have been apt, though we are not to suppose that the Temple was continually undergoing desecration; despite abuses, the true worship of God went on. Lightfoot, *GM*, p. 63, sees in the pericope the vindication of the rights of the Gentiles, for whom it is also a place of worship.

15   Those who **were selling and buying there** maintained booths in the Court of the Gentiles, surrounding the main courts on three sides. Sacrificial animals and wine were sold. Annas and his family owned such markets, which were destroyed by a mob about the year 67.

The **money changers** (κολλυβισταί) were men who changed other currencies into the coinage of Tyre, in which the half-shekel tax had to be paid (Mishnah Shekalim i. 1-3); for this service they received a fee or *qôlbôn*; cf. Israel Abrahams, *Studies in Pharisaism and the Gospels*, 1st Series (Cambridge, 1917), pp. 82-89. Their **counters** or tables were set up in the Court of the Gentiles from 25 Adar to 1 Nisan. We have no record of abuses of this privilege or protests against it, and it is possible that in the general confusion the counters were overturned.

16   Jesus enforced a rule that is recorded in the Mishnah (Berakhoth ix. 5): **he did not permit anyone to carry a vessel through the temple area** and so make it a short-cut from one
17 part of the city to another. This is in accordance with the principle of Isaiah that **My house shall be called a house of prayer for all nations**; it was to the Court of the Gentiles that his action applied.

18   **The chief priests and scholars . . . were afraid of him.**

Undoubtedly the people were on Jesus' side, and to have seized him now might have resulted in a bloody riot, however little Jesus wished it, and this in turn would have led to the intervention of Roman troops. The gospels tend to minimise the numbers who were attracted to our Lord, but Acts ii. 41 speaks of the later baptism of three thousand people, and Tacitus' words suggest that early Christianity was a mass movement (*Annals* xv. 44).

xi. 19-25. THE FIG TREE WITHERS; FAITH AND PRAYER

When it was evening they went out of the city. As they 19, 20 **came past early in the morning they saw the fig tree withered from the roots up. Peter, remembering, said to** 21 **him, 'Rabbi, see! the fig tree that you cursed is withered'. Jesus answered, 'Have faith in God. I tell you truly, if** 22, 23 **anyone says to this mountain, "Be removed and cast into the sea", and does not doubt in his mind but believes that what he says will happen, it will happen for him. There-** 24 **fore I tell you, whatever you pray and ask for, believe that you have received it, and it will happen for you. And** 25 **whenever you stand at prayer, forgive anything that you have against anyone, so that your Father who is in the heavens will forgive your wrongdoings.'**

The cleansing of the Temple and the night, spent presumably 20 in Bethany, provide the necessary lapse of time for **the fig tree** to be **withered.** Mark's connexion of this with the cleansing of the Temple is deliberate.

The evangelist now makes the transition from the prophetic action of Jesus to his teaching. As in the healing of the epileptic boy (ix. 19, 23-24), the first lesson is faith (verse 23), and to it is appended a teaching on prayer (verse 25; cf. ix. 29). The two sayings, which were originally independent, are connected by verse 24.

The figure of the **mountain** being **cast into the sea** has the 23 same hyperbolical character as the camel through the eye of the needle (x. 25) and the speck and the log (Matt. vii. 3-5). This was the natural style of an oriental teacher and would not have been misunderstood by Jesus' original hearers; cf. the stories of Elijah and Elisha (1 Kings xviii. 20-39; 2 Kings vi. 8-23). Knox, *Sources*, p. 83, notes that 'moving a mountain' is a conventional phrase for performing a difficult task; cf. SB, p. 759. The saying originally has nothing to do with prayer but with the **faith** of the man of God, and the connexion of this with the fig may have been suggested by Hab. iii. 17-18, 'Though the fig tree do not blossom . . . yet will I rejoice in the Lord'. Mark adds,

24 **Therefore I tell you, whatever you pray and ask for,** etc.; this is fundamentally the same teaching as in Matt. vii. 7-8 = Luke xi. 9-10, which is more Semitic in form.

25　**And whenever you stand at prayer**—the usual posture for both Jews and Greeks (Matt. vi. 5; Luke xviii. 11), kneeling or prostration being a special act of penitence or reverence—**forgive anything that you have against anyone.** It was a standard Jewish teaching that he who seeks God's forgiveness must be ready to forgive others (Ecclus. xxviii. 2; T. Gad vi. 3-7) and Jesus brought it into high prominence (Matt. vi. 12, 14-15 =Luke xi. 4; Matt. xviii. 21-35 =Luke xvii. 3-4). The words **your Father who is in the heavens** and **wrongdoings** are in Matthew's style, not Mark's, and the text here may be influenced by Matt. vi. 14-15; the original form was perhaps: 'that you also may be forgiven'.

xi. 27-33. CONTROVERSY OVER AUTHORITY

27 **They entered Jerusalem again. And while he was walking in the temple area the chief priests and scholars and**
28 **elders came to him, and said to him, 'By what authority are you doing these things? Who gave you authority to do**
29 **these things?' Jesus said to them, 'I will ask you one thing; answer me, and I will tell you by what authority**
30 **I am doing these things. John's baptism—was it from**
31 **heaven or from men? Answer me.' They discussed it among themselves, saying, 'If we say "from heaven",**

he will say, "then why didn't you believe him?" but if 32
we say, "from men"!'—they were afraid of the crowd,
for they all held John to be actually a prophet. So they 33
answered Jesus, 'We do not know'. And Jesus said, 'I
will not tell you, either, by what authority I am doing
these things'.

Once more there appears to be a reminiscence of Jeremiah,
whose prophecies were challenged by the priests (Jer. xxvi. 7-15)
and by the prophet Hananiah (Jer. xxviii).

As in verses 15-18, Jesus again appears as prophet, though the
form of the dialogue, with its question and counter-question, is
rabbinic. These two aspects of Jesus as teacher appear again and
again in the gospel tradition.
The chief priests and scholars and elders who **came to** 27
him were not the whole Sanhedrin (cf. on viii. 31) but a delegation from it. **These things,** i.e. the cleansing of the Temple. 28
Jesus might have answered as did Amos to the priest of 29
Bethel (Amos vii. 14-15), namely that God had called him to
prophesy; but he answered by another question, that of the
authority of the most famous prophet of his own time. **John's** 30
baptism was on the authority of a prophet; thus if he was a true
one it was **from heaven,** i.e. God, not **from men** (cf. Gal. i. 1,
where Paul insists that his apostleship is not dependent on men).
The question does not evade the issue, for the authority of
John and that of Jesus were the same—was the (apparently)
new word of God a true one?—but it had the effect of putting 31
the opponents on the horns of a dilemma; for the popularity of 32
John, cf. Josephus, *Ant.* xviii. 5. 2. The representatives of the 33
highest legal and religious authority in the nation were not willing to discuss the matter and **answered** weakly, **We do not
know.** Like many officials, they might have answered: 'The
matter requires further study'. Jesus, by his final statement,
rejected their authority to examine him; if they could not make
a decision regarding John the Baptist, their own authority was
negligible.

xii. 1-12. THE PARABLE OF THE WICKED TENANTS

1 He began to speak to them by figures. 'A man planted a vineyard, and he enclosed it with a wall and dug a vat and built a tower, and rented it out to tenants, and went 2 away. At the agreed time he sent a slave to the tenants so that he might receive some of the fruit of the vineyard 3 from them. They seized him, beat him, and sent him 4 away empty-handed. Again he sent another slave to them, and they beat that man on the head and insulted him. He 5 sent another, and that one they killed. He sent many 6 others; some they beat, and some they killed. He had no one left but his only son; finally he sent him to them, say-7 ing, "They will respect my son". But those tenants said to one another, "This is the heir; come, let us kill him, 8 and the inheritance will be ours". So they seized him and 9 killed him and threw him out of the vineyard. What will the owner of the vineyard do? He will come and destroy the tenants and give the vineyard to others.

10 'Haven't you read this text?

"The stone which the builders rejected
Has been made into the keystone;

11 This is the Lord's doing,
And it is admirable in our eyes".'

12 They considered seizing him, but they feared the crowds, for they knew that he had spoken this figure with them in mind; and they left him and went away.

The evangelist probably thinks of this as an allegory. Thus God is the owner of the vineyard, the tenants are the priests (possibly the scribes, less likely the whole Jewish people), the slaves are the prophets, the only son is Jesus the Son of God, and the 'others' are the Christian apostles or the Gentiles. Mark adds a quotation from Ps. cxvii. 22-23 LXX (Ps. cxviii, Heb.) which typifies the rejection and exaltation of Jesus and connects the teaching with the Triumphal Entry. But if 'the son' is not taken allegorically, and parts of verses 6-7 are eliminated, the story can be thought of as a simple prophetic parable, like that of the barren fig tree (Luke xiii. 6-9). The parable in the *Gospel of Thomas* (93: 1-16, p. 39) must be close to the original form. Cf. also Matt. iii. 9 = Luke iii. 8.

The **man,** who **planted a vineyard and . . . enclosed it 1 with a wall** made out of stones gathered from the soil, cared for it as Yahweh did in Isa. v. 1-7; the house of Israel is God's vineyard. The **vat** is the lower trough into which the juice is filtered after the grapes have been trodden; cf. Bishop, p. 223. The **tower,** which was sometimes a leaf-covered wooden booth, was on a high place so that it served as a look-out, and was occupied by the family (in this case by the tenants) during the vintage season; stone towers are also to be observed in Palestine.

Agricultural lands were frequently **rented out to tenants** on a share-cropping agreement. The farmer paid his own expenses and returned to the owner from one-quarter to one-half the crop. There were men who owned properties in Judaea and Galilee, with a wife and a household in each place; cf. Gittin 34b, cited by Finkelstein, *The Pharisees*, i, 41.

With the mention of **his only son,** the parable becomes an 6 allegory. Surely a father who knew that they **beat** and **killed** the slaves would not put his son in such danger. Only God might reasonably expect them to **respect my son;** the allegory is anthropomorphic and there is no reflection on God's omniscience. Similarly the slaves are stupid to suppose that **the in- 7 heritance will be ours;** this could occur only if the man died without heirs, the vineyard was in a distant country, and the property was practically abandoned to them; cf. Jeremias, *The Parables of Jesus* (London, 1954), pp. 58 f. The added note, **and 8 threw him out of the vineyard,** implies religious rejection or excommunication of Jesus.

The midrash of the **stone** was a favourite theme in Christian 10, 11 preaching. Cf. Acts iv. 11, where this passage from the Psalm is used, and 1 Pet. ii. 4-8, where it is combined with Isa. xxviii. 16 (also used in 1QS viii. 7-8 to refer to the council of the Essene community) and Isa. viii. 14-15; cf. also the name Peter (iii. 16) and especially Matt. xvi. 18. For Christians, Jesus is the **key-stone**; so Jeremias, Ἄγγελος, i (1925), 65-70; *ZNW*, xxix (1930), 264-280; or 'corner-stone' (cf. the 'foundation', 1 Cor. iii. 11). God has reversed the judgement of men by exalting him; there is no reference to the resurrection in this parable, but it may be implied here.

12 **They considered seizing him, but they feared the crowds.** This editorial note is modelled on xi. 18.

xii. 13-17. CONTROVERSY OVER THE POLL TAX

13 **They sent some of the Pharisees and Herodians to him to**
14 **trap him by what he might say. So they came and said to him, 'Teacher, we know you are a true man and do not care about anyone's opinion, for you pay no attention to personalities but teach God's Way truthfully—is it permissible to pay a tax to Caesar or not? Shall we pay or**
15 **not pay?' He, knowing their hypocrisy, said to them, 'Why are you testing me out? Bring me a denarius so that I may**
16 **see it.' They brought it; and he said to them, 'Whose picture and inscription is this?' They said to him, 'Caesar's'.**
17 **Jesus said to them, 'Pay Caesar what is Caesar's and God what is God's'. They were completely astonished at him.**

The poll tax incident is the first of four dialogues. D. Daube, *JTS*, n.s. ii (1951), 45-48, cites a rabbinic parallel for the arrangement. R. Joshua ben Hananiah (A.D. 90) was asked four types of questions, as follows: (*a*) questions on points of rabbinic law; (*b*) haggadic or religious questions involving apparent contradictions in scripture; (*c*) *boruth* ('vulgarity'), i.e. mocking or teasing questions; and (*d*) *derekh 'eres*, principles of moral life. The four questions found here conform to these types, though not in the same order: verses 13-17 are legal, verses 18-27 are mocking, verses 28-34 have to do with *derekh 'eres* and verses 35-37 are haggadic.

The essence of the first, which is a paradigm or pronouncement story, is in its concluding saying, verse 17. At the same
time, it is very lifelike, and deals with an issue that was of the
highest importance to Palestinian Jews in the first century, for
the revolutionary wing of the Pharisees, led by Judas the
Gaulonite, Josephus' 'fourth philosophy', taught that only God
could be the lord and ruler of the Jews, and that taxation was
the first step toward slavery (*Ant.* xviii. 1. 1, 6; *B.J.* ii. 8. 1).

The **Pharisees** who came to Jesus apparently represented 13
the non-political section of the party. The words they addressed
to him could have been spoken sincerely, but Mark thinks of
them as **hypocrisy,** and his inclusion of the **Herodians** (i.e.
partisans of Herod Antipas, cf. iii. 6; viii. 15) is an ominous note;
such people might have been eager **to trap him.** These details
do not belong to the kernel of the dialogue, and we do not know
the original situation. It appears that Jesus had to be asked the
question, for his position was not known.

The **tax** (κῆνσος) is evidently the *tributum capitis* or poll tax 14
which was imposed on provincials; it was this which Judas of
Galilee had resisted. In Galilee, taxes would have been paid to
the government of Herod Antipas; this story presupposes the
situation in Judaea, where the tax was for **Caesar.**

Bring me a denarius: Jesus did not have one in his posses- 15
sion. This silver coin was approximately the weight of the Greek
drachma which in turn equalled one-quarter of the Jewish shekel
(Josephus, *Ant.* iii. 8. 2). It was first minted for the purpose of
paying soldiers in the Roman army, and analyses of hoards of
coins found in Syria show that it cannot have circulated widely
among the civilians of Palestine; cf. J. S. Kennard, *Render unto
God* (New York, 1950), pp. 53-60. Kennard urges further that
the possession of a denarius showed the connexions between
Jesus' opponents and the Romans; indeed the tribute would not
ordinarily have been paid in this coinage (p. 51). Yet the word
is used fourteen times in the gospels, and 'drachma' only twice
(Luke xv. 8-9); and in Matt. xx. 2, 9 f., 13, it is the labourer's
daily wage.

Jesus asks, in effect, who is *de facto* the sovereign in Judaea. 16
The concession to Simon Maccabaeus of the right to coin money
was an acknowledgement of his position as ethnarch and high

priest. If the money of the emperor is legal tender, it is he to whom taxes should be paid. The **picture and inscription** were those of Augustus or Tiberius; coins of either might have circulated. Like the standards of the legions which led to demonstrations in Palestine (Josephus, *B.J.* ii. 9. 2 f.), these bore the picture of one who was worshipped as a god, at least in the eastern provinces. The Jews did not object to the image of the god Melkart on the coins of Tyre, in which the temple tax was paid, but the image of the emperors had direct political significance. The inscription gave the emperor's name and titles: some examples say 'son of God' or 'son of the deified Augustus'.

17 **Pay Caesar what is Caesar's.** Of one thing there is no doubt: Jesus permitted the tax to be paid. But what were the implications of his ruling? Some theologians have thought mistakenly that he assigned the state a sphere of life in which it was to be supreme, i.e. the political and economic order, while God (as represented by ecclesiastical institutions) dealt with the 'spiritual' or 'religious' aspects of society. Even Paul in Rom. xiii. 1-7 cannot have meant to go as far as this, though he regards the empire as the bringer of positive blessings. The other extreme is represented by Kennard, who holds that Jesus contemptuously told the partisans of Rome to pay their denarii to the emperor—let Caesar have back his own, but we who have no such coinage in our purses will not pay the tax! This view assumes that during the Jerusalem ministry Jesus embraced the doctrine of Judas the Gaulonite, and presses the saying far beyond its natural meaning. The only evidence for it is the charge made against Jesus in Luke xxiii. 2.

The clue to the correct interpretation is in the words **and God what is God's.** The Reign of God is universal, permanent and absolute (cf. on i. 14-15). God is directly concerned with everything in human life, and whatever resists him will finally be brought to an end. God is supreme, even in Caesar's realm, but in the world as it is now constituted, certain men are permitted a limited and contingent sovereignty, and it is not an infringement of God's rights to pay them the taxes that they exact. In a real conflict of loyalties, Jesus would undoubtedly have said, as did his disciples afterward, 'We must obey God rather than men' (Acts v. 29). Indeed his cleansing of the Temple

and continued teaching had some of the aspect of civil disobedience, and he could have saved his own life by keeping
silent. Thus the attitude of Jesus was almost precisely that of
the moderate rabbis. They held that the existing government
must be obeyed, though they often counselled their disciples not
to become involved in its affairs, but when it was a question of
idolatry they chose martyrdom rather than submission. Some of
them must have applauded the words of Jesus; in view of the
false rumours in circulation they may have been **completely
astonished.**

The application of the principle is by no means easy. The
subjects of the Roman empire did not have the rights and
accompanying responsibilities that mark citizenship in many
modern states. Even where church and state are in theory separate, the separation can never be complete, and the demands of
governments often impose difficult problems of conscience on
the loyal Jew or Christian who takes seriously the basic doctrine
of the Kingdom of God.

xii. 18-27. CONTROVERSY WITH THE SADDUCEES

Sadducees—who say that there is no resurrection—came 18
to him and questioned him: 'Teacher, Moses wrote for us 19
**that "if someone's brother dies" and leaves a wife be-
hind, "and leaves no child, his brother must take the wife
and raise up offspring for his brother". There were seven** 20
**brothers; the first took a wife, and when he died he left
no offspring; the second took her, and died leaving no** 21
offspring behind; the third, the same way; and the seven 22
left no offspring. Last of all the woman also died. In the 23
**resurrection, whose wife shall she be? For all seven had
her as wife.' Jesus said to them, 'Isn't your error due to** 24
**this, that you know neither the Scriptures nor the power
of God? For when they rise from the dead, they neither** 25
**marry nor are given in marriage, but are as angels in the
heavens. As for the dead rising, haven't you read in the** 26
book of Moses, in the section on the Bush, how God said

to him, "I am the God of Abraham and God of Isaac and
27 God of Jacob"? He is not a God of dead men but of
living. You are greatly in error.'

The theory adopted by Montefiore, that the story of the
adulteress (found in some MSS. between John vii. 52 and viii.
12) belongs before the dialogue with the Sadducees, is one of
the most interesting conjectures in the history of criticism. If it
is correct, another day of teaching begins here and ends at xiii.
37; but it is no more than a learned guess.

The controversy now recorded is another example of Jesus as
rabbi and prophet. It starts out humorously, with the opponents
propounding the kind of hypothetical question that divinity
students in all cultures are apt to debate, but Jesus raises the
argument to a higher level.

18   The party of **Sadducees** is mentioned only here in Mark, and
not often in the other gospels. Little is known of them except for
Josephus' account in *Ant.* xviii. 1. 4 and sparse notices in rabbinic writings; cf. E. Schürer, *Geschichte des jüdischen Volkes*
(4th ed., Leipzig, 1910-11), ii, 452-454, 475-489. There are two
reasons for this: our information comes entirely from their
enemies, and after the destruction of the Temple they disappear
from history. To Mark and his readers they were little more than
names. They were, however, the most dangerous of Jesus'
opponents; the high priest and the group associated with him
belonged to this party. The Sadducees were politically and re-
ligiously conservative. The Maccabean monarchs John Hyrcanus, Aristobulus and Alexander Jannaeus adhered to them,
and later the Sadducees supported the Roman administration.
Many of them were wealthy landowners who had little education and only scant interest in religion. They held that only the
Pentateuch was binding and interpreted it literally and strictly,
opposing the innovations of the Pharisees. Their doctrine **that
there is no resurrection** was well known. The name of the
party was probably derived from Zadok, Solomon's priest (1
Kings i. 38-39); thus they claimed to be his spiritual de-
scendants.

19   Their quotation from **Moses** is a free paraphrase of Deut.
xxv. 5-6 with a phrase drawn from Gen. xxxviii. 8. This rule of

'levirate marriage' was designed to insure that the deceased
brother should have **offspring** that would be counted as his
own, so that the family would not die out. That the law was
modified at an early time is shown by Deut. xxv. 7-10 and Ruth
iii. 9-iv. 12; cf. M. Burrows, *JBL*, lix (1940), 23-33, 445-454.
Later developments are to be seen in the Mishnah tractate
Yebamoth.

The Sadducees may often have cited this hypothetical case in
controversy, in order to show that the Pharisaic resurrection
doctrine was absurd. Had Jesus wished to answer them on their
own premises, he might have said that only the first brother was
the true husband, for the others were only 'doing the part of the
next of kin' (Ruth iii. 13). But he deals directly with the issue
of resurrection.

The error of his opponents is that they **know neither the** 24
Scriptures nor the power of God. It is on the latter that the
hope of life after death must rest. The conditions of the future 25
life cannot be compared to man's life on earth, and Jesus'
answer is reminiscent of the saying in the Talmud (Berakhoth
17a): 'Rab used to say: In the world to come there is no eating
or drinking or marrying or envying or hate; but the pious rest
with crowns upon their heads, and are satisfied with the glory
of God'.

The second saying, which refers to **the section on the Bush** 26
(Exod. iii. 6), is a verbal argument that may ultimately come
from the Pharisaic tradition: God speaks of himself as **the God
of Abraham . . . and Isaac . . . and Jacob** as though they are
living and he is their God; therefore they must be alive. Though 27
the argument is not persuasive, it points to the basis of the
resurrection faith: the living God who does not desert his people.

xii. 28-34. THE GREAT COMMANDMENT

One of the scholars, when he heard them disputing and 28
knew that he had given a fine answer to them, came up
and asked him: 'Which commandment is most important
of all?' Jesus answered, 'The most important is, "Listen, 29

30 Israel, the Lord our God is one Lord; and you shall love
the Lord your God with all your heart and all your life and
31 all your mind and all your strength ". The second is, "You
shall love your neighbour as yourself". No other com-
32 mandment is greater than these.' The scholar said to him,
'Well said, sir! You said truly that "he is one and there is
33 no other but he " and "to love him with all one's heart "
and "all one's understanding and all one's strength" is
better than all "the burnt offerings and sacrifices".'
34 Jesus, seeing that he had responded intelligently, said to
him, 'You are not far from the Kingdom of God'. No one
after that dared to ask him a question.

In spite of his general hostility to the Pharisees, Mark for the
third time includes a dialogue which shows Jesus' agreement
with them. His traditions of the days in Jerusalem thus have a
character distinct from much of the record of the Galilean ministry. This 'summary of the Law' need not have been original
with Jesus. In Luke x. 25-28 it is an unnamed 'lawyer' or scribe
who utters it, and R. Aḳiba (martyred about A.D. 135) said that
Lev. xix. 18 was the great principle of the Law.

Other such summaries of the Law, or expressions of the
essence of religion, are well known in Judaism. For example,
'R. Simlai said: Six hundred and thirteen commandments were
given to Moses, 365 negative commandments, answering to the
number of the days of the year, and 248 positive commandments, answering to the number of a man's members. Then
David came and reduced them to eleven [Ps. xv]. Then came
Isaiah, and reduced them to six [Isa. xxxiii. 15]. Then came
Micah, and reduced them to three [Mic. vi. 8]. Then Isaiah
came again, and reduced them to two, as it is said, "Keep ye
judgement and do righteousness". Then came Amos, and reduced them to one, as it is said, "Seek ye me and live'. Or one
may then say, then came Habakkuk [ii. 4], and reduced them
to one, as it is said, "The righteous shall live by his faith"'
(Makkot 23b-24a, cited by Montefiore and Loewe, op. cit.
p. 199).

The 'golden rule' (Matt. vii. 12 =Luke vi. 31) is another
summary of the Law attributed to Jesus. This kind of popular

ethical wisdom is certainly a feature of his teaching, although it is not the most distinctive one.

Listen, Israel, the Lord our God is one Lord. The *Shema'*, 29 with which these words begin (Deut. vi. 4-9; xi. 13-21; Num. xv. 37-41), is perhaps the most eloquent expression of Israelite monotheism. A pious Jew was expected to recite it three times a day (for some of the rules, cf. Mishnah Berakhoth i-ii), and by doing so took upon himself the yoke of the Kingdom of God. On God as the One, cf. on ii. 7; x. 18.

You shall love the Lord your God, etc. The quotation from 30 Deut. vi. 5 is similar to the LXX, but differs from it in reading 'heart' (καρδίας) for 'mind' (διανοίας), in adding the phrase 'and all your mind' after 'life', and in substituting ἰσχύος for δυνάμεως. It may go back to the oral tradition of Jesus' saying, not to a written translation of the OT.

It is difficult to determine the relation of the Summary of the Law to Jesus' teaching as a whole, and to know whether it had the same meaning to him as to a Pharisaic rabbi. The pericope suggests no context for it except the scribe's question. It may be that such a principle was the touchstone by which our Lord tested specific enactments of the written or oral Law: were they, or were they not, truly love of God and love of neighbour? On the other hand, a rabbi might have said that all the Law taken together constituted such love; one does not completely love God and neighbour unless one obeys the whole Law. The Pharisees 33 would, however, have meant more by it than this: love is more important than other commandments, such as **burnt offerings and sacrifices.** Because of their view of the Torah, they could not have repudiated the sacrificial system, but numerous sayings of theirs parallel the remark made here; e.g. 'It happened that R. Johanan ben Zakkai went out from Jerusalem, and R. Joshua followed him, and he saw the burnt ruins of the Temple, and he said, "Woe is it that the place, where the sins of Israel find atonement, is laid waste". Then said R. Johanan, "Grieve not, we have an atonement equal to the Temple, the doing of loving deeds", as it is said, "I desire love, and not sacrifice"' (*Aboth of R. Nathan*, quoted by Montefiore and Loewe, pp. 430 f.).

The scholar accepts the answer with warm approval, and 32 Jesus recognises him in turn as genuinely religious, **not far** 34

from the Kingdom of God, i.e. prepared to enter it or receive it. This is a counterpart to the idea that it has drawn near (i. 15). In Mark's account of the Jerusalem ministry, Jesus speaks of the Kingdom only here and in xiv. 25. Does this mean that in this period he ceased to teach its imminent coming? If so, the reason may possibly be that his teaching of the sole sovereignty of God was in danger of being confused with the programme of the revolutionists. But, whatever the form of his teaching, it is all related in one way or another to the concept of God's Reign. It seems more likely that the Galilean tradition, or one part of it, was interested in the Kingdom of God idea, while the teachings remembered by the Jerusalem disciples were more of the rabbinic variety.

xii. 35-37. CONTROVERSY OVER THE SON OF DAVID

35 **As he was teaching in the temple, Jesus said, 'How is it**
36 **that the scholars say the Messiah is son of David? David himself said, in the Holy Spirit,**

> **"The Lord said to my Lord, sit at my right**
> **Until I put your enemies under your feet".**

37 **David himself calls him Lord; in what way is he his son?'**

This brief saying is the climax of the series of anecdotes. It is rabbinical in form and probably arises out of Christological debates in the Palestinian Church. Mark finds in it the answer to the salutation of Bartimaeus and the shouts of the people
35 at the triumphal entry. The standard doctrine of Pharisaic **scholars** was of course that **the Messiah is son of David;** this was based on many OT passages (cf. on viii. 29), and the alternative notion that he would come from the tribe of Levi had been generally abandoned because of disillusionment with the later Maccabees.

36   Here Jesus is depicted as citing **David himself,** the traditional author of the Psalms, against this doctrine. Ps. cx may be as late as the Maccabean period, but most Jews accepted the

tradition without critical reflection. The psalm is quoted almost exactly in the LXX form. It was a favourite text in early Christian preaching, and here its divine inspiration is explicitly emphasised; cf. Acts ii. 33, where it is said that, in contrast to David, Jesus was exalted to the right hand of God (cf. also Heb. i. 13; x. 13). If he is David's **Lord** he is not **his son**, or not 37 *merely* his son, for a son honours his father as superior. The logion need not imply actual denial of the strong and probably correct tradition that Jesus was descended from David (Matt. i. 6; Luke ii. 4; iii. 31; Rom. i. 3), but Mark is quite uninterested in it; he regards it as irrelevant to Jesus' true nature as the exalted Son of Man and he would ignore or deny it rather than confuse Jesus with the conventional Messiah.

xii. 38-40. DENUNCIATION OF THE SCRIBES

The great crowd listened to him with pleasure. In the 38 **course of his teaching he said, 'Beware of scholars who wish to go about in long robes, who want greetings in the market-places, and places of honour in the synagogues** 39 **and at dinners; men who eat up widows' houses and** 40 **make long prayers out of pretence. These men will receive a very severe punishment.'**

Another form of this satire was preserved in Q, and expanded by Matthew into a kind of litany of woes (Matt. xxiii. 1-36 =Luke xi. 39-52) .There is no reason to doubt that Jesus spoke 38 against certain **scholars** whose life did not accord with their profession; the rabbis themselves hold such persons up as evil examples; cf. the seven classes of Pharisees in the Talmud, Jer. Berakhoth 14*b*; Jer. Soṭah 20*c*; Bab. Soṭah 22*b*; and Montefiore and Loewe, pp. 487 f. That Jesus did not include all scribes in this condemnation is clear from verses 28-34.

The **long robes** (στολαί) were the outer garment, reaching nearly to the feet, worn in the cities of Palestine by government officials and religious dignitaries down to modern times. **Greetings** were apt to be ceremonious, as in parts of the Arab world

today; elsewhere Jesus' disciples are told not to waste time on
them (Luke x. 4). Professional religious men (and not only the
Pharisees!), like most other people, often enjoy being addressed
39 by honorific titles and like **places of honour in the synagogues.** Special seats for the more important members of the
community were often provided; cf. E. L. Sukenik, *Ancient
Synagogues in Palestine and Greece* (London, 1934), pp. 57-61.
Elsewhere a rule of modesty **at dinners** is attributed to Jesus
(Luke xiv. 7-10).

40 All of the foregoing weaknesses may have marked certain
Pharisaic scholars, but **men who eat up widows' houses and
make long prayers out of pretence** sounds more like a denunciation of the high-priestly group. 'One of the lacunae in the
Gospels', says Branscomb, 'is the absence of any such criticism
of the priestly class'; cf. also Abrahams, *Studies in Pharisaism
and the Gospels*, 1st Series, chap. x. The Pharisees taught that it
was the spirit of the prayer that counted, not its length or short-
ness; cf. Montefiore and Loewe, pp. 342-349; and Jesus' teaching
in Matt. vi. 7.

xii. 41-44. THE WIDOW'S MITE

41 **As he sat facing the treasury, he saw how the crowd was
giving money to the treasury. Many rich men gave a great
42 deal; and a poor widow came and put in two *lepta*, that is
43 a *quadrans*. He summoned his disciples and said to them,
'I tell you truly, this poor widow has put in more than
44 all the people who have put money into the treasury, for
all of them gave out of their wealth, but she has given
out of her poverty everything she had, all she had to
live on.'**

The link between this incident and the foregoing seems to be
the word 'widow', but both sections deal in a general way with
appearances. The outward show of piety has no significance;
it is the inner disposition of mind, and in this case the depth
of the sacrifice, that count. B. S. Easton remarks, *What Jesus*

Taught (New York, 1938), p. 81, that the poor woman serves as a good contrast to the rich fool of Luke xii. 16-20.

The **treasury** may be one of the thirteen receptacles placed 41 in the Court of the Women for money given to the Temple. They were known as Shofar-chests because of their trumpet-like shape, and six of them were for free-will offerings (Mishnah Shekalim vi. 5). **Many rich men gave a great deal;** this would have been known because there were priests present to inspect the coinage. The **poor widow came and put in two** 42 *lepta,* the smallest bronze coins. Mark explains this in terms of Roman coinage as equalling **a** *quadrans,* i.e. one-quarter of an *as.* The *as* was one-sixteenth of a denarius, so that her gift amounted to one-sixty-fourth of a labourer's daily wage (Matt. xx. 2). In modern equivalents she gave a farthing, or one-fourth of an American cent, or a Jordanian *fil,* though the purchasing power of such coins was greater in antiquity. The *lepta* mentioned here were probably the small bronze coins minted by procurators, or even by Herod or the Maccabean kings. Various issues are found in Palestinian hoards; cf. A. Reifenberg, *Ancient Jewish Coins* (Jerusalem, 2nd ed., 1947), Plate ii, Nos. 14-17; p. 41.

CHAPTER XIII

THE APOCALYPTIC DISCOURSE

In this gospel the climax of Jesus' teaching ministry comes in chap. xiii. The Passion Narrative contains teaching only by example and in the form of brief remarks on the events leading up to the Crucifixion.

Thus the chapter is the last of a series of formal teachings, the others being iv. 1-34; vi. 7-11; vii. 1-23; viii. 31-ix. 1; ix. 33-x. 45. The theme is not the Kingdom of God, but the coming of the Son of Man. Except for the actual events of the Cross and Resurrection, the full secret of Jesus' nature is now disclosed. He is both Son of Man and Son of God; and before he comes in glory the Good News of his coming must be proclaimed to all nations (verse 10). Those who bear the message must be prepared for a cosmic disaster and also for the most severe persecution imaginable. The discourse provides our only clue to the exact dating of the gospel, but it is unfortunately difficult to interpret. The book may be written at the height of the Jewish War, or very soon after the catastrophe, when Mark knew that the time had been shortened and not all flesh would perish (verse 20). But the date cannot be much later than this, for although the day and hour cannot be calculated (verses 32-37) the evangelist insists that the Son of Man will come within this generation (verse 30). In contrast to this, Matt. xxiv. 9-14 finds it necessary to explain the delay of the Parousia, and Luke xxi. 20-24a rewrites the prophecy of Daniel to make it refer primarily to the destruction of Jerusalem, which will be followed by the 'times of the Gentiles'; thus the coming of the Son of Man will be much delayed.

So important is this Coming to the evangelist that it is to this, rather than the Resurrection, that his gospel points forward. The Resurrection is of course presupposed, but perhaps it is the glorified Son of Man whom the disciples are to await in Galilee (xiv. 28; xvi. 7). It is not certain what this meant to the earliest readers of the gospel. Had the Galileans already seen him risen in his homeland, as Matthew says (Matt. xxviii. 16-20), in an anticipation of the Parousia similar in nature to the Transfiguration? Or was the return to take place there, even though Peter and certain other disciples had already died?

This chapter emphasises, as perhaps nothing else can, the vast mental difference between the earliest Christians and those who came later. Not only is it difficult for the modern Christian to imagine this as the culmination of our Lord's teaching; it was not even possible for the Fourth Evangelist. John climaxes his gospel with a farewell discourse of Jesus to the disciples (chaps. xiii-xvii), but the Coming is reinterpreted as the return of Christ through the Holy Spirit and the eschatology is completely 'realised'.

The nucleus of the chapter, as many critics agree, is the so-called Little Apocalypse (verses 5-8, 14-20, 24-27; Marxsen, pp. 108 f., assigns to it verses 7, 8, 12, 14-22, 24-27). This is a piece of Christian prophecy (though some regard it as purely Jewish) originally spoken in connexion with the events of Caligula's reign. When Herod Agrippa I visited Alexandria in 38, anti-Jewish riots took place, and the enemies of the Jews called for the setting up of statues of the emperor in all the synagogues. Order was restored only with difficulty, and almost immediately further troubles broke out in Palestine. In Jamnia the Jews destroyed an altar in honour of Caligula, whereupon the mad emperor gave orders that his statue should be erected in the Temple at Jerusalem. To the Jews this was a repetition of the disaster of 168 B.C., when Antiochus IV Epiphanes profaned the Temple by making it a sanctuary of Olympian Zeus (1 Macc. i. 54-64; Josephus, *Ant.* xii. 5. 4). The Book of Daniel called this the 'abomination of desolation' (*shiqquṣ shomêm*, a play on the name *Ba'al shamayim*, which corresponds to Zeus Olympios, Dan. ix. 27). What had originally been a prophecy after the event was of course regarded as a prophecy now about to be fulfilled, and Palestinian Christians were as deeply shaken by the crisis as were their fellow-Jews. Petronius, the legate of Syria, who had received Caligula's orders, gave command for the making of the statue and went to Ptolemais. There a delegation of Jews pleaded with him, weeping and mourning. He wrote to Caligula asking for a delay and went down to Tiberias where thousands of Jews besought him not to desecrate their holy place. Finally he sent a letter to the emperor requesting that the plan be abandoned. Meanwhile Caligula had decided not to proceed with his plan, but on receiving the letter he ordered Petronius to kill himself. Fortunately the news of the emperor's assassination arrived in Palestine before the emperor's letter, and the crisis passed.

At the height of this crisis a Palestinian Christian wrote the Little Apocalypse. First, he believed, there would come the birth-pangs of the new age, then the desecrating abomination itself with a persecution in Judaea, and finally the cosmic disasters inaugurating the coming of the Son of Man, who was to gather his elect together from all parts of the earth. This is the purest Jewish apocalyptic, applied without change to the belief in Jesus' return. It is probably the work of a Galilean, and it was widely enough circulated so that St. Paul in 2 Thess. ii adapts it to a new crisis occurring about the year 50; cf. Bacon, *Mark*, pp. 129 f. In the present gospel the abomination seems to have been given a new meaning; it may refer to the standards bearing the emperor's image, or to a profanation of the Temple accompanying the destruction of Jerusalem.

Around this old prophecy has been built a complete discourse on the last days and their meaning for Christians. The stage is set by the prophecy of the Temple's destruction (verses 1-2) and the request of the four disciples to know when this will take place (verses 3-4). After the first part of the Apocalypse (verses 5-8) come a warning of persecution and a direction for the behaviour of martyrs (verses 9-13). Between the second and third parts is a warning against false Messiahs and false prophets (verses 21-23), and the chapter is concluded by three sections: the figure of the fig tree (verses 28-29), a prophecy with the solemn assurance of the authority of Jesus' words (verses 30-31), and the exhortation to watch, in which the prophecy is slightly modified (verses 32-37).

Marxsen, in dealing with the structure of the chapter (*op. cit.* pp. 101-128), notes that the first ταῦτα in verse 4 looks back to verse 2, while the second points forward to verses 29-30; βλέπετε in verse 5 perhaps refers to verse 2 and is resumed in verses 9

and 33; time notes throughout the chapter indicate the sequence
of the prophecy. Lightfoot, *GM*, pp. 51 f., finds that the chapter
is closely connected with the Passion Narrative, e.g.: verse 9
= xiv. 53-xv. 15; verses 22-23 = xiv. 33-46, 50, 66-72; verses 32-
33 (the 'hour') =xiv. 35, 37; verse 35 =xiv. 17, 43, 72; xv. 1;
verse 26 =xiv. 62. Robinson, *Problem*, pp. 61-67, notes the
oscillation between the language of prophecy and that of Jewish
apocalyptic, and the reference to the trials in which Christians
are now involved. The struggle of the Gentile Church for sur-
vival is thus made part of the apocalyptic event.

Cf. Carrington, pp. 202, 206-209, for his view of the liturgical function of the chapter; for other theories, see J. Lambrecht,
Die Redaktion der Markus-Apokalypse (Rome, 1967).

xiii. 1-2. PROPHECY OF DESTRUCTION OF THE TEMPLE

**As he was going out of the temple area, one of his dis- 1
ciples said to him, 'Teacher, look! What stones and what
buildings!' Jesus said to him, 'Are you looking at these 2
great buildings? Not a stone will be left on stone—there
is nothing that will not be destroyed.'**

The picture is dramatic. From the Kidron ravine the **dis- 1
ciples** could see the tremendous foundation **stones** of the
Temple area, laid under Herod's direction. Some of them, as
much as 14 feet in length, beautifully dressed and fitted, can
still be seen at the south-east corner of the *Ḥaram esh-Sherîf*
and also at the Wailing Wall on the west side. The **buildings,**
not yet complete in Jesus' time, were magnificent, particularly
the Holy of Holies, with its eastern face covered with golden
plates. Some of the monolithic columns in the colonnade were
thirty feet high. For descriptions, see Josephus, *Ant.* xv. 11. 3-7,
and tractate Middoth in the Mishnah; Sir G. A. Smith, *Jerusalem* (New York, 1908), ii, 497-520; Kraeling, *Atlas*, pp. 399-
401. The prophecy was almost completely fulfilled: **not a stone 2
was left on stone** except for the foundations.

R. Joḥanan ben Zaḳḳai is said to have made a similar prophecy at almost the identical time, forty years before the Temple's destruction (B. Yoma 39b). At his hearing before the high priest, Jesus' prediction was twisted into a threat that he himself would destroy it, but the witnesses did not agree (xiv. 58-59); cf. Acts vi. 14, where Stephen is charged with having made a similar statement. Later forms of the tradition are found in John ii. 19-21; *Epistle of Barnabas* xvi.

These verses, like the story of the cleansing of the Temple, are part of the tradition of Jesus' prophetic-rabbinic teaching in Jerusalem; note that the disciples address him as **Teacher**.

xiii. 3-8. THE LITTLE APOCALYPSE I: BIRTH-PANGS

3 **When he was seated on the Mount of Olives facing the temple, Peter, James, John and Andrew asked him pri-**
4 **vately, 'Tell us, when will these things happen? What is the**
5 **sign to show when all these things will be concluded?' Jesus**
6 **began to say to them, 'Be careful that no one deceives you. Many will come in my name, saying, "I am", and**
7 **they will deceive many. But when you hear of wars and rumours of wars, do not be upset; "it must happen", but**
8 **the end is not yet. For "nation will rise against nation and kingdom against kingdom". In some places there will be earthquakes; there will be famines. These are the beginning of the birth-pangs.'**

Verses 3-4 are the evangelist's introduction to the first part
3 of the Little Apocalypse. The prophecy of the Temple's destruction was part of Jesus' well-known teaching; the remainder was given **privately** to the four chief disciples (cf. iii. 16-18; ix. 2; x. 35); as they were the first to be called (i. 16-20), so they receive the final instructions. The fall of the Temple is made part of the events of the end.

4   **What is the sign . . .?** In contrast to viii. 11-13, a sign is now given. This was necessary in order to understand the future;

Jesus' own authority did not require a sign. **Concluded**: the verb is almost a technical term in apocalyptic.

Many will come in my name, saying, 'I am', i.e. the 6 Son of Man, who bears God's authority; on the special force of ἐγώ εἰμι, cf. on vi. 50, and note the anticipation of xiv. 62. As early as A.D. 40 the Christians were no doubt in danger of being confused by false prophets and false Messiahs such as Simon Magus (Acts viii. 9-11; cf. Justin, *Apol.* i. 26); later there were Menander and el-Kesi; cf. Weiss, *HPC*, 756-766.

The phrase **wars and rumours of wars** might apply to the 7 troubles late in Caligula's reign; in any case there was periodic turmoil from this time until the outbreak of the Jewish War; cf. *JOT*, pp. 98-102. **'It must happen'** is apparently a reminiscence of Dan. ii. 28, 'the things that must happen in the last of days'. **The end is not yet**; cf. 2 Thess. ii. 1-2. **For 'nation 8 will rise'**, etc.; quoted freely from Isa. xix. 2. **Earthquakes** are a frequent feature of apocalyptic, particularly in the Sibylline Oracles; **famines** were known all too often in Palestine, and there was a serious one in the time of Claudius (Acts xi. 28); on its date, see *BC*, v, 452-455; K. S. Gapp, *HTR*, xxviii (1935), 258-265.

The birth-pangs later became a technical apocalyptic term for the woes preceding the advent of the Messiah or the new age. The idea goes back as far as Isa. xxvi. 16-19; Mic. iv. 9-10; Hag. ii. 6, and is reflected in 2 Esd. ix. 3; cf. Bousset, *Religion*, pp. 250 f. It is especially vivid in the Essene Hymns of Thanksgiving (1QH iii. 3-18) and in Rev. xii. 1-6.

xiii. 9-13. PERSECUTION

'You must watch out for yourselves. They will hand you 9 over to sanhedrins and you will be beaten in synagogues, and you will stand before governors and kings, to bear witness against them, for my sake. But the Good News 10 must first be proclaimed to all the nations. When they 11 hand you over and lead you captive, do not worry beforehand about what you are to say, but say the very thing

that is given to you at that hour, for it is not you who are
12 speaking but the Holy Spirit. A brother will betray his
brother and a father his child, and "children will stand
13 up against parents" and put them to death, and you will
be hated by everyone on account of my name; but the
one who holds out to the end will be saved.'

9   **You must watch out for yourselves.** This may mean 'Do
not put yourselves unnecessarily in danger' or 'you must guard
against weakness in the face of persecution'. The **sanhedrins**
are presumably the local ones, with 33 members each, located
in cities other than Jerusalem (Mishnah Sanhedrin i. 6). Flog-
ging was administered in **synagogues,** the basis being the law
of Deut. xxv. 1-3; the rabbis reduced the forty to 39 lashes, and
Paul received this punishment five times (2 Cor. xi. 24). Usually
the *ḥazzan* or attendant inflicted the whipping, but Paul is said
to have performed it himself (Acts xxii. 19). **You will stand
before governors,** as Paul stood before Felix and Festus (Acts
xxiv. 1-xxv. 12), **and kings,** such as Herod Agrippa (Acts xii.
1-3). The background is Palestinian, but even here the note of
witness comes in; the Church is already conscious of the responsibility of martyrdom for Jesus' sake. Strathmann, *TWNT*,
iv, 508, understands the witness as a justification of the martyr
and a sign that the opponents are guilty of his blood.

10   Mark interrupts the section to emphasise that the witness
must be to **all the nations. Good News** and **proclaimed** are
among his technical words.

11   A martyr or confessor need not **worry beforehand** and prepare a careful defence, for it is **the Holy Spirit** who speaks.
This is one of Mark's few references to the Spirit (cf. on i. 4-8);
he who undertakes the witness is endowed with the truth and
authority which Jesus possessed.

12   **A brother will betray his brother,** etc. Such incidents undoubtedly occurred, as they did later in Christian history. At the
same time, this is part of the apocalyptic expectation; cf. Enoch
xcix. 5; c. 1-2; Jub. xxiii. 59; 2 Esd. vi. 24; 2 Baruch lxx. 6; the
idea is developed from Mic. vii. 6, which is quoted here. A
similar saying stood in Q (Matt. x. 34-36 = Luke xii. 51-53).

13   **You will be hated by everyone**; Tacitus (*Annals* xv. 44)

speaks of Christians as 'a class hated for their abominations' and
their religion as 'a most mischievous superstition'. Christians
interpreted this as being **on account of** the **name** of Jesus; cf.
1 Pet. iv. 12-16. Certainly at a later time they were persecuted
for the name itself; cf. Pliny, *Epistles* xcvi-xcvii.

He **who holds out to the end will be saved**: the thought
is probably that his physical life will be preserved.

xiii. 14-20. THE LITTLE APOCALYPSE II: THE TRIBULATION

'When you see "the sacrilege that makes desolate" 14
standing where he should not' (the reader must use his
mind) 'then those who are in Judaea must flee to the
mountains. Whoever is on the roof must not come down 15
and go into his house to take anything, and whoever is in 16
the field must not turn back to take his cape. Alas for the 17
women with child and the nursing mothers in those days!
And pray that it will not be in the winter. For those days 18, 19
will be a time of "pressure such as has not happened
from the beginning of creation even till now"—and there
will be nothing like it again. If the Lord had not shortened 20
the days, no living thing would be saved; but because of
the elect whom he chose he has shortened the days.'

'**The sacrilege that makes desolate**' (Dan. xii. 11) was 14
originally the statue set up in the Temple by Antiochus Epiphanes, together with the sacrifice of swine on the altar (cf.
general note on chap. xiii), and in the original form of the Little
Apocalypse the statue of Caligula. Mark reinterprets the sacrilege by adding **standing where he should not**; ἑστηκότα is a
masculine participle and therefore most naturally refers to a
person, not a thing. It is often suggested that this is the Antichrist (cf. 2 Thess. ii. 1-12); on this conception, cf. Bousset,
Religion, pp. 254-256, and Frame, *Thessalonians, ad loc.* Another
possibility is that the emperor himself or the standards bearing
his image is thought of as appearing in the Temple, or in the

Holy Land. Pompey had profaned the Holy of Holies by enter-
ing it (Josephus, *Ant.* xiv. 4. 4). The evangelist's parenthetic
phrase, **the reader must use his mind,** indicates that the
teaching is cryptic.

When this occurs, **those who are in Judaea** (this shows the
place of origin of the Little Apocalypse, but cf. Marxsen, p. 123)
must flee to the mountains (cf. 1 Macc. ii. 28; 2 Macc. v. 27),
for it was safer there. Eusebius tells of an oracle given to the
Church in Jerusalem which commanded the Christians there to
leave the city and go across the Jordan to Pella (*H.E.* iii. 5. 3);
this may be reflected in Rev. xii. 6, where the woman who has
borne the Messiah has a place of refuge for 1,260 days or nearly
three and a half years, the approximate length of the Jewish War.

15 **Whoever is on the roof** must flee, probably by the ladder or
outdoor stairway, and not **go into his house to take anything;**
17 there is no time for one to do more than to save his life. The
tribulation will be particularly severe for **women with child**
18 **and the nursing mothers. Winter** is not always severe in
Judaea, but snow falls in many years. Bishop, p. 234, remarks
that in February, 1950, seventeen people were found frozen to
death one morning in Ramallah.

20   But **the Lord** has **shortened the days.** Behind this lies
the concept of a fixed time, which God can nevertheless alter;
cf. 2 Baruch xx. 1-2; lxxxiii. 1; *Epistle of Barnabas* iv. 3; and the
idea of the 'Restrainer' in 2 Thess. ii. Cf. also Bacon, *Mark*,
p. 116.

xiii. 21-23. FALSE MESSIAHS AND FALSE PROPHETS

21 '**And then if anyone says to you, "See, here is the**
22 **Messiah"—"see, there he is"—do not believe it, for**
there will arise false messiahs and "false prophets" and
"they will do signs and wonders" to try to deceive the
23 **elect if they can. As for you, watch out; I have told you**
everything beforehand.'

21   The mention of **the Messiah** may indicate that Mark took
this saying from the tradition, for one would expect 'Son of

Man', as fitting better with the point of this chapter. There is a parallel in Q, Matt. xxiv. 26 = Luke xvii. 23; in Luke this is in a Son of Man context. The words **false messiahs** are omitted 22 by D and a few other MSS., but they fit the situation well; there were several figures, mainly Jewish revolutionists, to whom the term might apply; cf. W. R. Farmer, *Maccabees, Zealots and Josephus* (New York, 1956). On the **signs and wonders** of **false prophets,** cf. Acts viii. 9; 2 Thess. ii. 9-12; Rev. xiii. 13; *Didache* xvi. 4.

xiii. 24-27. THE LITTLE APOCALYPSE III: COMING OF THE SON OF MAN

'But in those days after that pressure "the sun will be 24 darkened and the moon will not give its light, and the 25 stars will be falling" from the sky. "And the powers in the heavens" will be shaken. And then they will see "the 26 Son of Man coming in the clouds" with great power and glory. And then he will send the angels and "gather" the 27 elect "from the four winds, from the height" of earth "to the height of the sky"'.'

The coming of the **Son of Man** (cf. Dan. vii. 13-14) is pre- 24-26 ceded immediately by disasters in the heavens, the imagery being drawn from Isa. xiii. 10; xxxiv. 4, not in the LXX version. The Little Apocalypse may originally have been composed in Aramaic.

The gathering of the dispersed people of Israel is a standard 27 feature of apocalyptic. Its OT basis was such passages as Isa. xi. 12; xxvii. 13; xlix. 22; Ps. cxlvii. 2, and it is developed in Ecclus. xxxvi. 11; Enoch xc. 32; Ps. Sol. xi; xvii. 26, 31; Test. Naphtali vi and the tenth of the Eighteen Benedictions in the synagogue liturgy. The idea lived on in Christianity; cf. the prayers in *Didache* ix. 4; x. 5. The **four winds** is a reminiscence of Zech. vi. 5; **'the height' of earth** is the mountainous east of Palestine and **the height of the sky** (cf. Deut. xxx. 4) denotes the sea and the sky at the west; the outlook is Palestinian.

28 'Learn this example from the fig tree; when its branch
   becomes soft and puts out leaves, you know that summer
29 is near; just so you, when you see these things happening,
30 know that it is near—at the doors. I truly tell you that this
   generation will not pass away before all these things hap-
31 pen. Heaven and earth will pass away, but my words will
32 not pass away. But no one knows that hour or day, neither
   the angels in heaven nor the Son, but only the Father.
33 Take heed, keep awake, for you do not know when the
34 right time is. It is as when a man away from home has left
   his house and has given his slaves the authority, and
   assigned each man his task, and has commanded the
35 doorkeeper to keep alert. So, then, keep awake, for you
   do not know when the lord of the house is coming, at
36 evening or midnight or cockcrowing or dawn—lest he
37 come suddenly and find you asleep. And what I tell you
   I tell all: keep alert.'

As was said above, the concluding section is composite.
Verses 28-29 are a little parable on the signs that are available
for everyone to see; cf. Luke xii. 54-56. As B. T. D. Smith
remarks, *Parables*, pp. 89-91, this could have been spoken in the
'springtime' of our Lord's ministry: when the blind receive
their sight and the poor have the Good News preached to them,
you know that the Kingdom of God is near (cf. Matt. xi. 2-6
= Luke vii. 18-23). Mark, however, uses it to refer to the woes
preceding the end.

28   The **fig tree,** except for the evergreens, is the commonest in
   Palestine. It **puts out leaves** in April or May, and hot weather
   may come very soon afterward.
30   **I truly tell you,** etc. This solemn affirmation may be a re-
   writing of ix. 1, which referred to the Kingdom of God; here
31 the idea is stated in more general form. Mark adds an eloquent
   affirmation of the eternal validity of Jesus' **words;** this expresses the faith of the early Church, but it is especially applied
   here to the apocalyptic predictions.

At the same time, Mark must know that Jesus had a certain 32
reticence about predictions of the future. This is clearly shown
by Luke xvii. 20-37 and the undoubtedly genuine sayings which
reject signs (cf. on viii. 11-13). Therefore the evangelist restricts
the prediction slightly: at least so far as the exact **hour or day**
is concerned, not even **the Son** knows, but only **the Father;**
the phraseology is reminiscent of Matthew and John, and shows
that already in Mark the Son of God theology has developed to
some degree.

It is hard to escape the following conclusions: (*a*) Jesus shared
with his contemporaries the general eschatological outlook. God
had made the world and could bring its history to an end when
he chose; and the Kingdom of God would surely come. (*b*) Jesus
predicted the destruction of the Temple and the fall of Jerusalem, at least in general terms; the 'signs of the times' that anyone could see made this plain. (*c*) He did not make the definite
predictions that are embodied in chap. xiii, for to do so would
be to infringe upon God's prerogatives; cf. *JOT*, chap. viii. (*d*)
But he did teach men to be ready at all times for God's judgement and the coming of his Kingdom. This moral imperative
is the essential truth in the eschatological outlook.

This last point is now developed. For Mark it is summed up 33
in the verbs ἀγρυπνεῖτε (verse 33) and γρηγορεῖτε (verses 35-
37), both of which mean **keep alert** or awake. The figure of the 34
householder **away from home** is found also in Q, Matt. xxiv.
43-51 = Luke xii. 35-46, and is closely related to the parables of
Matt. xxv. 1-13, 14-30 (=Luke xix. 12-27). Here the figure is
the apt one of the **doorkeeper** rather than the steward. Smith,
Parables, pp. 104-106, quotes a Jewish proverb: 'Of the ten
measures of sleep that came down into the world, slaves received
nine, and the rest of the world only one'. The porter sat at the
gate of the walled courtyard and controlled access to the house.
On the figure of the absentee master, cf. Cadbury, *Jesus: What* 35
Manner of Man, p. 42. Mark adopts the Roman time-reckoning
by which the night was divided into four watches, approximately 6-9 p.m., 9 p.m. to midnight, midnight to 3 a.m. and
3-6 a.m.; cf. vi. 48. Lightfoot sees a connexion between this and
the events of Jesus' night of arrest; cf. above, p. 211.

CHAPTER XIV

THE PASSION NARRATIVE

The story of Jesus' suffering and death, and the events immediately preceding it, may have formed a unit at an early stage of the gospel tradition. In Mark it is generally straightforward and self-contained. Except where the evangelist has inserted independent traditional material, it shows few traces of his theology or individual habits. The later evangelists edit it and supplement it—Luke more freely than Matthew—but its basic structure remains the same. Dibelius remarks acutely (*FTG*, pp. 197-201) that Matthew adds touches of Christological significance tending to show that Jesus as Son of God was conscious of the meaning of the events, while Luke presents the Passion as a martyrdom. The Fourth Evangelist, who elsewhere deals so freely with his narrative materials, tells a straightforward story with relatively little Johannine colouring. His Passion Narrative is independent of the one used by Mark but illuminates it at several points; evidently it is a piece of very old tradition.

The evangelists, and their anonymous forerunners, do not tell the story for its historical or biographical interest. Their concern, as always, is to show that the events were in accordance with the will of God and served his overruling purpose. The shameful story of the Cross, not yet glorified by a long tradition of worship and piety, took its meaning from its sequel in the Resurrection and—particularly in the instance of Mark—from the hope of the coming of the Son of Man. A clue to the early Christians' processes of thought is seen in Luke xxiv. 19-27. Had it not been for the Resurrection, all that would have been left to them was the memory of a martyrdom: 'We had hoped that he was the one who would redeem Israel'. It was the experience of the Risen Lord, together with the searching of the Scriptures 'beginning with Moses and all the prophets', that illuminated the way of the Cross and provided the motive for telling the story.

It is impossible to determine just how the Passion Narrative was first used in teaching and worship. Carrington makes the attractive conjecture that xiv. 3-xv. 41 made up ten of the fourteen lessons read in the paschal cycle on 14 Nisan (*op. cit.* pp. 152 f.). Almost nothing is actually known of Christian liturgical customs in the first century, but it may be significant that Melito, second-century bishop of Sardis, in his *Homily on the Passover*, devotes most of the space to the Hebrew *pascha* and its types, dwelling largely on the details of the Passion, while the peroration is an address of the risen Christ to the faithful. The OT was still uniquely the Bible of the Christians, but it is not impossible that in some churches the Passion story was read along with it.

There is considerable agreement on the passages to be assigned to the pre-Marcan Passion Narrative, and the reconstruction of Grant, *Gospels*, p. 79, serves as a good example: xiv. 1-2, 10-11, 17-18a, 21-27, 29-31, 43-53a; xv. 1-15, 21-22, 24a, 25-27, 29a, 32b-37, 39. This is very similar to the list given by Dibelius, *Message*, pp. 30-34.

The theology of the reconstructed document is very simple. 'Son of Man' appears in but one verse (xiv. 21). The cup of the Last Supper is the 'blood of the covenant'; Jesus promises to drink it again with them in the Kingdom of God (xiv. 24-25). The falling away of the disciples is connected with the prophecy of Zech. xiii. 7 (xiv. 27), and the fulfilment of Scripture is emphasised at the time of Jesus' arrest (xiv. 49). Judas addresses him as 'Rabbi' (xiv. 45). In the trial before Pilate the charge is that Jesus is King of the Jews (xv. 2, 9, 12; cf. verses 26, 32). The cry from the Cross quotes Ps. xxii. 1 and a reference is made to Elijah (xv. 34-35). The centurion speaks of Jesus as a 'son of God' (xv. 39). Elsewhere the evangelist adds a theological interpretation to some of these elements, but here they are quite undeveloped. In other words, the old narrative seems to stand at the beginning of a theological development; Mark as a whole represents a later stage, and Matthew and John still later ones.

Historically the narrative deserves the highest respect. It is simple and unadorned, and gives the course of events with considerable objectivity, including elements that could not possibly serve a tendentious purpose and that sometimes raised difficult theological problems. Above all, it makes clear that the motive for the Crucifixion was political; the opponents of Jesus intended to destroy anyone who could conceivably become a king of the Jews.

The earliest Christians in telling the story inevitably found that certain OT passages suggested themselves. The last word of Jesus, for example, was drawn from Psalm xxii. As the result of further reflexion on the Scriptures, the tradition gathered to itself elements from Pss. xxii, lxix and elsewhere, and these were included in Mark's narrative. The later gospels exhibit the continuation of this process; see, e.g., Matt. xxvii. 5-10, 34; Luke xxiii. 46; John xix. 24, 28.

Some of Mark's additions may indeed have historical value, but they belong to later stages of the tradition and in a few instances their original context is probably lost. Here and there they show signs of Mark's own interests; e.g., the terms κηρύσσω and εὐαγγέλιον in xiv. 9, and the preparations for the Passover, which parallel the arrangements for the Triumphal Entry (xiv. 12-16; cf. xi. 2-6). It is probably Mark, not the compiler of the old narrative, who is responsible for identifying the Last Supper as a Passover. The Fourth Gospel contains a different tradition.

xiv. 1-2. THE PLOT AGAINST JESUS

1 **The Passover and the feast of Unleavened Bread were two days later. The chief priests and scholars tried to find a way to seize him by trickery and kill him, for they said,**
2 **'Not on the feast day, lest there be turmoil among the people'.**

1   **The Passover** was celebrated on the 15th day of the month Nisan, and the eight-day **feast of Unleavened Bread** began on the same day (Exod. xii. 14-20). The Jewish day ran from sundown to sundown, and the paschal meal actually took place on what we might regard as the evening of the 14th, the lambs having been slain in the Temple earlier in the afternoon. The

statement of verse 12 is thus, from the Jewish point of view, inexact; the paschal lamb was not killed on the first day of Unleavened Bread or *maṣṣoth*. The festival is said to be **two days later**: Mark thus thinks of the plot as taking place on the 13th, which according to his reckoning would be a Wednesday, for all the evangelists agree that the Crucifixion occurred on Friday.

Not on the feast day, lest there be turmoil among the 2 people. The plan is to **seize** Jesus **by trickery** (D and some OL MSS. omit this and also 'and the feast of Unleavened Bread' in verse 1, but both readings probably belong to the original text) before sundown at the end of 14 Nisan. Mark's account does not fit with this, since he regards the Last Supper as a Passover. If he is correct, one must assume that the original plan miscarried; otherwise this is an indication that Jesus was crucified before the Passover; cf. on verses 12-16.

xiv. 3-9. THE ANOINTING IN BETHANY

When he was in Bethany in the house of Simon the Leper, 3 as he was at table, a woman came. She had an *alabastron* **of pure, extremely precious nard ointment, and she broke the *alabastron* and poured it on his head. Some of 4 them were inwardly indignant: 'What is the purpose of this waste of ointment? This ointment could have been 5 sold for more than 300 denarii and given to the poor.' They began to scold her. But Jesus said, 'Let her alone; 6 why do you make her unhappy? She has done something 7 beautiful for me. You have the poor with you always, and whenever you wish you can do good to them; but as for 8 me, you do not always have me. What she had in her power she has done; she has anointed my body for burial 9 beforehand.—I tell you truly, wherever the Good News is proclaimed in the whole world, this thing that she has done will be mentioned as a memorial to her.'**

At this point Mark interrupts the story of the plot to tell of 3 the anointing of Jesus. The scene is in **Bethany,** where he seems to have spent his nights (xi. 11-12; cf. verse 19). This may belong to the same tradition as xi. 1-10, since it contains a messianic motif. Nothing else is known of **Simon the Leper.** Possibly he had been healed; if not, this is an indication of Jesus' willingness to associate with such people (cf. i. 40-44).

The **woman** is not to be confused with the sinful woman of Luke vii. 36-50, which is a very different story. Here there is no thought of penitence. The *alabastron* was a long tube-like flask of the type sometimes called a 'tear-bottle'; it may have been made of alabaster, but more probably of glass; **nard** or spikenard was an aromatic oil extracted from the root of the plant, which was native to India. She **poured it on his head,** not his feet, as in Luke vii. 38; he and his companions were no doubt seated cross-legged on the floor, eating out of a common bowl.

This was a secret anointing for kingship, as in 2 Kings ix. 1-13; 1 Kings i. 38-40; the woman was an enthusiast who hoped that Jesus would rule over the nation. It is not certain whether verses 4-7 belong to the original story, since they contain the usual misunderstanding on the part of the disciples and introduce the idea, so natural for Christians, that personal devotion to Jesus is praiseworthy. But the ironic remark of verse 8 may well be historical.

5   **This ointment could have been sold for more than 300 denarii,** a year's wages for a workman. The lavishness of the gift suggests John ii. 1-11, where a tremendous quantity of water is changed into wine.

7   **You have the poor with you always . . . but . . . you do not always have me.** Bishop notes that the claim of the passing guest was greater than that of those who were always there (p. 243). This is not indifference to the needs of the poor, but a rebuke to those who criticised the woman for an act of devotion and loyalty. In Mark and the tradition behind the gospel, the words also had Christological significance: the hidden Son of Man will be here for only a short while.

8   Jesus may, however, have spoken the words **she has anointed my body for burial beforehand:** anyone who is regarded as the King of Israel cannot escape death; the well-meant gesture will not have the result that she hopes.

9   The phrase **I tell you truly** indicates an addition to the source; **the Good News** is of course a favourite Marcan word.

xiv. 10-11. JUDAS' PLAN TO BETRAY

Judas Iscariot, one of the Twelve, went off to the chief 10
priests to betray him to them. When they heard it, they 11
were glad and promised to give him money. And he tried
to find a way to hand him over at a convenient time.

Here the basic Passion Narrative is resumed. There are two 10
problems: what did he betray, and why? The word **betray**
translates a verb meaning 'to hand over', and verses 44-45 show
that Judas' part in the proceedings was to identify Jesus, perhaps also to indicate where he could be found. The motive can 11
scarcely have been **money** alone. The sum is not specified but
it may have been greater than the thirty pieces of silver of Matt.
xxvi. 15, which depends on the prophecy of Zech. xi. 12. It is
difficult, however, to imagine that one of the most intimate disciples could do this act even for a great amount of money.
Various suggestions have been made; e.g., that Judas was disillusioned when he found that his Master rejected earthly
messiahship; that he thought this act would force God to reveal
his Messiah and vindicate him by a miracle; or even that Judas
was tricked into believing that the chief priests would protect
Jesus against his enemies. The motive is, however, unknown;
there is only a double tradition of Iscariot's violent death (Matt.
xxvii. 3-10; Acts i. 18-19).

A convenient time would not be on the feast day (verse 2).

xiv. 12-16. PREPARATIONS FOR PASSOVER

On the first day of the Unleavened Bread, when they were 12
accustomed to kill the paschal lamb, his disciples said to
him, 'Where do you want us to go and make preparations
for you to eat the Passover feast?' He sent two of his dis- 13
ciples and said to them, 'Go into the city, and a man will
meet you who is carrying a pot of water. Follow him, and 14
where he goes in say to the head of the house, "The
teacher says, 'Where is my dining-room, where I may

15 eat the Passover with my disciples?'" He will show you
a large upstairs room ready and furnished; so make ready
16 for us there.' The disciples went out, came into the city,
and found things just as he had told them, and they prepared the Passover feast.

As noted above, part of the story of the Last Supper (verses
17, 18*a*, 21-27, 29-31) may belong to the original Passion Narrative; but in Mark this is preceded by the present incident, which
recalls the preparations for the Triumphal Entry. Is Mark right
in regarding the Last Supper as a Passover? Several considerations make this very doubtful.

(*a*) Although the Fourth Evangelist agrees that the Crucifixion took place on a Friday ('the day of preparation', John xix.
31, 42), this was also the day of preparation for the Passover
(John xviii. 28; xix. 14). Thus Jesus died at approximately the
time when the paschal lambs were slain, and the statement of
Paul that 'Christ our paschal lamb has been sacrificed for us'
(1 Cor. v. 7) may indicate that he accepts a similar tradition. The
Quartodecimans of Asia Minor celebrated the Crucifixion and
Resurrection as the Christian Pascha on 14 Nisan; cf. the letter
of Polycrates in Eusebius, *H.E.* v. 24. 2-7. They may have de-
pended on the Fourth Gospel for this, but Polycrates refers only
to the traditions current in Asia; cf. B. Lohse, *Das Passafest der
Quartodecimaner* (Gütersloh, 1953).

(*b*) The Talmud (Sanh. 43*a*) contains a tradition that Jesus
was hanged on the eve of Passover.

(*c*) The early Church celebrated the Eucharist at least weekly;
had its principal precedent been a Passover meal, an annual
observance might have been more appropriate.

(*d*) A trial conducted by the Sanhedrin could not be held on
the eve of a Sabbath or the eve of a festival, and sentence could
not be pronounced on the same day as the vote to convict (Mishnah Sanhedrin iv. 1; v. 5). The hearing before the high priest
(verses 53-64) was in no sense a legal trial, but it is unlikely that
an informal examination of this sort, and the arrest in Gethsemane, would take place on Passover night. It is true, of course,
that the rule of remaining in the house after the paschal meal
was not observed at this time, and that Gethsemane was con-

sidered part of the city of Jerusalem. But if Mark's dating is
accepted, it is necessary to assume that Jesus's enemies abandoned their original plan (verses 1-2) and in desperation took
the risk of stirring up a disturbance among the people.

(e) It is possible to fit the account of the Last Supper into the
framework of a Passover, if one accepts the tradition in this
section that such careful preparations were made. The hymn at
the end could have been one of the Hallel psalms, and it is possible to use the word ἄρτος in referring to the maṣṣoth or unleavened bread; cf. J. Jeremias, *The Eucharistic Words of Jesus*
(Oxford and New York, 1955), pp. 14-57. But the account does
not itself demand this, and there is no mention of the lamb, the
bitter herbs, or the maṣṣoth as such. The notion that the Last
Supper was a ḳiddush or preparatory meal celebrated the day
before Passover has been adequately disposed of by Jeremias
(pp. 24 f.). Perhaps more is to be said for the theory that this
was a solemn meal of a ḥaburah or religious fellowship; cf. F. L.
Cirlot, *The Early Eucharist* (London, 1939), pp. 1-16, and literature there cited. Such a meal might take place at any time of
the year.

Attempts have been made to reconcile the dating of Mark and
John by supposing that the Pharisees and Sadducees celebrated
the Passover on different days or disagreed as to the reckoning
of the calendar; for arguments, see A. Arnold, *Der Ursprung des
christlichen Abendmahls* (Freiburg im Breisgau, 1937), pp. 70-73.
For the theory of Julian Morgenstern that the Galilean Jews
followed strictly the procedure of Exod. xii. 1-4 and ate the
Passover one day earlier than did the Jews of Jerusalem, cf.
JOT, p. 20. An ingenious harmonisation of Mark and John
is attempted by Mlle A. Jaubert, *Revue de l'histoire des religions*,
cxlvi (1954), 140-173, who supposes that Jesus followed the
example of the Qumran community and celebrated the Passover
on Tuesday night, three days before the Crucifixion and the
ordinary date of the festival. This, however, assumes a closer
connexion of Jesus with the Essenes than the sources will permit—particularly since the Gospel of Mark shows so few contacts with the Qumran literature—and it puts the Last Supper
one day earlier than one would suppose from verses 1-2.

The absolute dating of the Passover and Crucifixion in terms of our modern calendar involves many difficulties. A plausible case has been made out for assigning the date of Friday, April 7, A.D. 30, for the Crucifixion on the basis of the Neo-Babylonian calendar and the Fourth Gospel (i.e. on 14 Nisan); cf. A. T. Olmstead, *Jesus in the Light of History* (New York, 1942), pp. 279 f. Jeremias, *op. cit.* p. 13, argues, on the basis of astronomical calculations, that the same date is correct but to be equated with 15 Nisan. But the beginning of the month may have been determined by observation of the new moon, in which case neither a conventional calendar, such as the Neo-Babylonian, nor the calculation of astronomers, will necessarily fix the date. M. H. Shepherd, Jr., *The Paschal Liturgy and the Apocalypse* (London, 1960), pp. 36 f., notes that in the Diaspora the Jews followed a fixed calendar (Philo, *De spec. leg.* ii. 28; Josephus, *Ant.* iii. 10. 5). 'It is quite possible', he says, 'that in the year Jesus was crucified, the Palestinians observed Passover on Saturday, whereas the Jews of the Dispersion celebrated it on Friday.' Cf. *JBL*, xxx (1961), 123-32. In this case, the Fourth Gospel preserves the original chronology, while Mark mistakenly corrects the account to make it conform to the Roman tradition. This appears to be a simple and logical solution of the problem.

12   Mark's language is not precise; they were not **accustomed to kill the paschal lamb** on **the first day of the Unleavened Bread,** but on the afternoon before, since the new day began at sundown. The evangelist must think of the Roman day, which like ours began and ended at midnight, so that both events were part of the same day. The Passover and Unleavened Bread were in theory separate festivals, but Josephus combines the two into an eight-day celebration (*Ant.* ii. 15. 1).

Where do you want us to go and make preparations . . .? Note the colloquial ποῦ θέλεις ἀπελθόντες ἑτοιμάσωμεν without ἵνα.

13   **Go into the city, and a man will meet you who is carrying a pot of water.** Women usually carried water, and the man could easily be noticed; but water is occasionally carried by men in Arab Palestine. It is possible that arrangements had been made secretly beforehand, because of danger to Jesus and his disciples; but Mark thinks of Jesus as possessing supernatural knowledge.

The **large upstairs room** would be **furnished** with rugs 15
and cushions, and perhaps a low table.

xiv. 17-25. THE LAST SUPPER

**When evening had come he came with the Twelve. As 17, 18
they were at table and eating, Jesus said, 'I tell you truly,
one of you will betray me—"he who eats with me"'.
They began to be sorrowful and to say, one by one, 'Surely 19
it cannot be I?' He said to them, 'One of the Twelve, a 20
man who dips with me into the common bowl. For the 21
Son of Man is going away, just as it is written about him;
but alas for that man through whom the Son of Man is betrayed. It would be good for that man if he had not been
born.' As they were eating, he took a loaf, blessed it, broke 22
it, and gave it to them and said, 'Take this; this is my
Body'. He took the cup, gave thanks over it, and gave it 23
to them, and they all drank of it. He said to them, 'This 24
is my "Blood of the Covenant" which is being poured out
for many. I tell you truly, I will no longer drink of the 25
fruit of the vine until that day when I drink it new in the
Kingdom of God.'**

The tractate Pesahim in the Mishnah describes the main
features of the Passover celebration, as it is observed in Judaism
to this day, and many of the customs must go back to the time
of our Lord. In addition to the roast lamb, the meal included
unleavened bread, bitter herbs, usually a sauce known as *haro-
seth*, and at least four cups of wine. The father of the family
presided. The ritual involved blessings over the festival, the
wine and the bread, explanations of the elements of the meal,
and two of the *Hallel* psalms (Pss. cxiii-cxiv), ending with the
Ge'ullah, which praises God for rescuing his people out of
Egypt.

If the Last Supper was not a Passover, the prayers and blessings would have taken a simpler form. The *kiddush* used in
present-day Judaism begins with blessings over the cup, the
festival or Sabbath, and then the bread. The meal is then eaten,

and at the conclusion Ps. cxxvi is said, followed by a thanks-giving; cf. S. Singer, *The Authorised Daily Prayer Book*, pp. 124, 230 f. The only other type of Jewish meal with which the Last Supper can be compared is the cult meal of the Essenes, directions for which are given in 1QSa ii. 17-22 (cf. 1QS vi. 1-6 and Josephus, *B.J.* ii. 8. 5). K. G. Kuhn in K. Stendahl (ed.), *The Scrolls and the NT* (London and New York, 1957), pp. 65-93, finds certain similarities between the two: only men are present, and only those who belong in the inner circle; the one who presides is the appointed leader of the community, not simply a *pater familias*; and at the beginning of the meal he pronounces both the blessings over the bread and the wine. This does not indicate, as Kuhn says, that Jesus was influenced by the Essenes; rather that both reflect Jewish religious practices.

17   **When evening had come**: this was the beginning of 15 Nisan, if this was Passover; otherwise 14 Nisan.

18   **One of you will betray me.** It is not necessary to think, as Mark does, of supernatural knowledge, for Jesus may have been able to observe peculiarities in the behaviour and attitude of

20   Judas. **One of the Twelve** emphasises the irony and tragedy of the betrayal; **a man who dips with me** does not single out Judas; it is merely that it is one of the group present, who are bound together with the most sacred of ties. The **common bowl** may have contained the *ḥaroseth* sauce of almonds, figs, dates, spices and vinegar, into which the bitter herbs were dipped.

21   There is further dramatic irony in the fact that it is **the Son of Man** who is betrayed; cf. Matt. viii. 20 = Luke ix. 58, where the Son of Man has nowhere to lay his head. It is not **written about him** in the OT that he must go away to death, unless the Son of Man is also the Servant of the Lord; cf. on ix. 12. The phrase **alas for that man** is reminiscent of the Q saying on scandals, Matt. xviii. 7 = Luke xvii. 1-2, and may be drawn from it.

22   Matt. xxvi. 26-28; 1 Cor. xi. 23-25; and Justin, *Apology* lxvi. 3, follow Mark's order in the words of institution: first the bread, then the cup. The shorter text of Luke xxii. 15-19a, followed by D and several OL MSS. and *Didache* ix. 1-4, have the cup and bread in reverse order, as in the present-day Jewish *ḳiddush*

prayers. The longer text, read by most other MSS., includes verses 19b-20, which add a second cup and also touches which are found in Paul's account. Luke's shorter text is probably the original one and indicates that the third evangelist had a tradition independent of Mark; cf. Leaney, *St. Luke*, pp. 72-75, against J. Jeremias, *op. cit.* pp. 87-106. It is impossible to say which tradition is more primitive, that of Mark or of Luke; but, as compared to that of Paul, Mark's is clearly more Palestinian. It contains no command to repeat the action, and the covenant is not called 'new'.

He took a loaf: Mark thinks of the *maṣṣoth* of Passover, but it may have been a flat cake of leavened bread. He **blessed it,** possibly using the words now customary in Judaism: 'Blessed art thou, O Lord our God, king of the world, who hast brought forth bread from the earth'; he then **broke it,** as the host or the father of the household still does, and **gave it to them,** adding the words **Take this; this is my Body.** This interpretation of the breaking and giving the bread suggests that he expected to be stoned to death and his body thus broken. Crucifixion did not necessarily involve the breaking of bones (John xix. 31-33), which was an added torture. His death, furthermore, is to be for the benefit of his disciples; as they are nourished by the bread, so they are to participate in the blessing to result from the giving of his life (cf. x. 45).

He took the cup, gave thanks over it: εὐχαριστήσας is 23 here a synonym for εὐλογήσας (cf. on vi. 41), and the traditional thanksgiving is: 'Blessed art thou, O Lord our God, king of the world, who hast created the fruit of the vine'. **They all drank of it:** it is not certain whether the evangelist has Judas specifically in mind; this theme is developed in John xiii. 21-30; cf. 1 Cor. xi. 27-29.

This is my 'Blood of the Covenant'. In the phrase τὸ αἷμά 24 μου τῆς διαθήκης, the last two words may have been added at an early stage of tradition; cf. the simple formula above 'This is my Body'. In Jewish tradition the 'blood of the covenant' usually refers to circumcision, but here the allusion must be to Exod. xxiv. 8; Zech. ix. 11. A new relation is to be inaugurated, or an old relation restored, between man and God. Jesus' blood will be **poured out**—again the figure suggests death by stoning, not crucifixion—and it will be **for many** (cf. x. 45), probably 'for all', not merely for those present. The words go back to Jesus himself or at least to the earliest Palestinian Church.

25   The concluding verse makes the Cup a pledge of the coming banquet **in the Kingdom of God.** If the Last Supper was not a Passover, it was at least held not long before, and the ideas of the festival must have been in the minds of everyone. The Jewish paschal ritual contains this promise: 'This year here, next year in the land of Israel; this year as slaves, next year as free men'. The eschatological nature of the Eucharist is expressed by Paul as proclaiming 'the Lord's death until he come' (1 Cor. xi. 26), while in the *Didache* the Cup is connected with the Vine of David, and the Bread, which was scattered on the mountains and became one, represents the Church which will be gathered from the ends of the earth into the Kingdom of God. The words of Jesus thus point beyond his self-giving to the sure coming of the Kingdom; there he will **drink** the wine **new** (καινόν, 'afresh'), since everything in the coming age will be a new creation.

xiv. 26-31. TO THE MOUNT OF OLIVES; PROPHECIES

26 **When they had sung the hymn they went out on to the**
27 **mount of Olives. Jesus said to them, 'You all will fall away tonight, because it is written, "I will strike the**
28 **shepherd, and the sheep will be scattered". But after I**
29 **am raised up I will go before you into Galilee.' Peter said**
30 **to him, 'Even if all fall away, still I will not'. Jesus said to him, 'I tell you truly, today—tonight—before the cock**
31 **crows twice, *you* will disown me three times'. But he said emphatically, 'Even if I have to die with you, I will not disown you at all'. They all said the same thing.**

26   The **hymn** may have consisted of Pss. cxiii-cxiv, or possibly Ps. cxxvi, depending on the occasion. **The mount of Olives** begins to rise as soon as one crosses the Kidron ravine, and Gethsemane (verse 32) is on its western slope.

A group of prophecies now follows. The first is that **You all** 27 **will fall away tonight,** perhaps 'give up your faith' (σκανδα-λισθήσεσθε, cf. on iv. 17). This prepares for the prediction of Peter's denial. The quotation is drawn from Zech. xiii. 7, in a form different from that of the LXX. The figure of **the shepherd** and **the sheep** suggests an army that has lost its king (cf. 1 Kings xxii. 17).

But after I am raised up I will go before you into Galilee. 28 This saying breaks the context, and is actually omitted by the third-century Fayyum fragment in Vienna. It corresponds to xvi. 7, which can also be regarded as interrupting the narrative. Both verses may, however, be Mark's addition to the tradition, indicating his belief that the Son of Man will return to Galilee, where he had first revealed himself; but cf. Grant's view, in note on xvi. 7. The translation **will go before you** is as ambiguous as the Greek προάξω ὑμᾶς; the words may mean 'I will precede you' or 'I will lead you'; cf. J.Weiss, *HPC*, p. 18. The evangelist thinks of the scattering of the sheep as only temporary; as in Ezek. xxxiv. 11-16, where God will feed his sheep and seek the lost, so the risen Lord will reassemble the disciples. Marxsen, pp. 70, 75 f., argues that this is the oracle which led to the removal of the Church to Pella (Eusebius, *H.E.* iii. 5). Lightfoot, *GM*, pp. 106-116, sees in this the idea that the disciples have a work awaiting them in Galilee; Jesus will lead the way there, as he did before.

Peter is as ready to promise as were the sons of Zebedee (x. 29 39). His affirmation that he will not **fall** away, and Jesus' prediction that *you* **will disown me three times,** are equally 30 emphatic; note the σύ and the σήμερον ταύτῃ τῇ νυκτί. 'Disown' is almost a technical term in the gospels; cf. the Q saying, Matt. x. 32-33 = Luke xii. 8-9. The idea is found in viii. 38. The evangelist has a clear motive for including the account of Peter's denial. It serves as a warning example to any Christian who wavers in the face of persecution, but also as an encouragement, for Peter was restored and became head of the church in Rome. The story may have been sharpened and touched up, but it is entirely possible that the evangelist heard it from the great apostle himself.

32 They came to a place whose name was Gethsemane, and
33 he said to his disciples, 'Sit here while I pray'. He took
with him Peter and James and John, and began to be in
34 deep amazement and anxiety, and he said to them, 'My
mind is extremely sad, so sad I am near death; stay here
35 and keep alert'. He went forward a little and fell on the
36 ground. And he prayed that if it were possible the Hour
might pass from him, and he said, 'Abba (Father), everything is possible for you; take this cup away from me—yet
37 not what I will but what you will'. He came and found
them sleeping, and said to Peter, 'Simon, are you asleep?
Weren't you strong enough to keep alert for one hour?
38 Stay awake and pray that you do not undergo trial. The
39 spirit is eager, but the flesh is weak.' Again he went away
40 and prayed, saying the same thing; and when he came
again he found them sleeping, for their eyes were
weighed down, and they did not know what answer to
41 make to him. He came the third time and said to them,
'Are you still sleeping and resting? It is all over; the Hour
has come; see, the Son of Man is given up into the hands
42 of sinners. Rise, let us go; see, the man who has given me
up is approaching.'

This powerful scene, which has so profoundly influenced
Christian piety in all generations, continues the theme of discipleship. Hoskyns noted that it has coloured the entire
portrayal of Jesus' ministry in the Gospel of John; cf. *Fourth
Gospel* (2nd ed., London, 1947), pp. 81 f. It has a deeper emotional tone than the rest of the Passion Narrative, and it contains
the motifs of the Son of Man and the Hour.

The form of the story seems to be influenced by the Lord's
Prayer; note the *Abba* and the submission to God's will (verse
36) and the prayer that the disciples will not enter into trial
(verse 38). It is also a counterpart to the Transfiguration, for the
same three disciples accompany him (verse 33) and they do not
know what to answer (verse 40). Thus it is a revelation of the

nature of the Son of Man, in this case the glory of his stead-fastness in the face of suffering and death. Jesus is held up before the Church as the supreme example for the Christian martyr.

The 'rule of three' also governs the form; as there are three disciples, so he comes to them three times; cf. the predicted three denials (verse 30) and the Resurrection 'after three days' (viii. 31, etc.). This indicates that the story is traditional, not a recent pious invention; Grant, *ad loc.*, points to the way in which it is reflected in Heb. v. 7-10. As it stands, however, it contains one difficulty: the disciples are said to have been asleep, yet the words of Jesus' prayer are reported.

The name **Gethsemane** is usually interpreted as meaning 32 'oil press' or 'olive grove', and in the Latin Garden, nearest to the Kidron ravine, there are some very old olive trees. The derivation is, however, uncertain, and Jerome gives the name as *Gesamani*, connecting it with the 'fat valleys' (*gê' shᵉmânîm*) of Isa. xxviii. 1. Different parts of the western slope of the mount, all identified with Gethsemane, are occupied by the Latin Catholics, the Armenians, the Greek Orthodox and the Russian Orthodox.

The words translated **in deep amazement and anxiety** 33 (ἐκθαμβεῖσθαι καὶ ἀδημονεῖν) are so strong that it is difficult to express them in English; cf. Rieu, 'consternation and desola-tion'; Phillips, 'began to be distraught with horror'; Moffatt, 'appalled and agitated'. Thus the evangelist expresses Jesus' realisation of what is about to take place. The words **so sad I** 34 **am near death** are in the strongest possible contrast to the Fourth Gospel, where Jesus foresees the future completely and contemplates it unperturbed (John xii. 27). Mark here must pre-serve an actual memory of the event; cf. Heb. v. 7.

Keep alert: the reason for the command is not given; it is one of the maxims of discipleship that Christians should be ready to watch with Christ; cf. xiii. 34, 37. Possibly the disciples are to watch for the approach of others, more likely to give him human companionship in his most difficult hour.

He . . . fell on the ground: prostration is the supreme 35 gesture of supplication. For **the Hour,** cf. John ii. 4; xii. 27; xvii. 1.

36 **Abba,** Aram. 'father'; Mark explains it as ὁ πατήρ; cf. Rom. viii. 15. The **cup** is the cup of suffering; cf. x. 38.

38 **Pray that you do not undergo trial.** Neither here nor in Matt. vi. 13 = Luke xi. 4 does Jesus reflect on why trials or ordeals must come; he accepts them as a fact of human existence, not necessarily sent by God (cf. Jas. i. 13-14), and considers it appropriate to pray for deliverance from them.

The spirit is eager, but the flesh is weak. The contrast between flesh and spirit, artistically set forth with the particles μέν and δέ, is reminiscent of Gal. v. 16, and appears to be a Hellenistic Christian reflexion; cf. W. L. Knox, *Some Hellenistic Elements in Primitive Christianity*, p. 3.

41 **It is all over.** This translation of ἀπέχει is conjectural and based on the context. Arndt-Gingrich, *s.v.*, suggest 'the account is closed', basing this on the commercial use of the verb, 'to receive a sum in full'; J. de Zwaan, *Expositor*, 6th ser., xii (1905), 459-472, 'he [i.e. Judas] has received the money'; Klostermann, following the Vulg. *sufficit*, 'it is enough'; i.e. 'enough of sleep; stand up'.

The Son of Man is given up into the hands of sinners: cf. the irony of verse 21; for the form, cf. ix. 31.

42 The words **Rise, let us go,** artistically impart movement to the scene and prepare for the action of verse 43.

xiv. 43-52. THE ARREST OF JESUS

43 **Just as he was speaking, there arrived Judas, one of the Twelve, and with him a crowd with swords and clubs,** 44 **come from the chief priests and scholars and elders. The one who had betrayed him had given them a signal, saying, 'The man whom I kiss is the one; seize him and lead** 45 **him away under guard'. When he came he at once approached him and said, 'Rabbi', and greeted him with** 46, 47 **a kiss. They laid hands on him and seized him. And one of the bystanders drew a sword, struck the slave of the** 48 **high priest, and cut off his ear. Jesus said to them, 'Are you come out as against a bandit, with swords and clubs,**

to arrest me? I was with you daily in the temple area 49
teaching, and you did not seize me; but let the Scriptures 50
be fulfilled.' They all left him and fled. And a certain 51
young man followed him, who wore a linen cloth over
his naked body. They seized him, but he left the linen 52
cloth behind and fled naked.

Grant and others regard all of this section and verse 53*a*,
which follows, as belonging to the original Passion Narrative.
There are, however, slight differences in style. Verses 43-46 are
written in smooth idiomatic *koine*; note the genitive absolute
(verse 43), the pluperfect and ὃν ἄν (verse 44), and the οἱ δέ
(verse 46). On the other hand, verses 47-52 appear more Semitic,
e.g. εἷς δέ τις and εἷς τις (verses 47, 51). The evangelist's
hand may have been more active in the first part of the section.

It is again emphasised that **Judas** was **one of the Twelve;** 43
cf. verses 10, 20.

The **crowd** is said to **come from the chief priests and**
scholars and elders, i.e. the Sanhedrin, though perhaps it was
sent only by certain members of the court. John xviii. 3 speaks
of Roman soldiers and some ὑπηρέται, by which the Temple
police may be meant. This is conceivable on the night before
Passover, but Mark gives the impression that the people **with**
swords and clubs were gathered especially for the arrest; one
of them was a slave of the high priest (verse 47).

A **signal** would be necessary in the dim light, even if there 44
were full moon, for there were probably trees in the garden.
Otherwise the wrong man might be seized, and the conspirators
also feared that Jesus' disciples would make trouble.

Judas addressed Jesus as **Rabbi,** 'my Lord'; this honorific title 45
was now coming into use; cf. ix. 5; x. 51; xi. 21. Mark sometimes
translates it as διδάσκαλε. The **kiss** was a normal greeting of
affection between teacher and pupil; Judas may have kissed his
hand or his head.

The precautions were justified; **one of the bystanders,** not 47
necessarily a disciple, but one who was on Jesus' side, **cut off**
the **ear** of the **slave of the high priest.** The narrative is restrained and objective; Luke xxii. 50 adds that it was the right
ear, and John xviii. 10 that the man's name was Malchus.

48   Jesus protests being dealt with as though he were a **bandit** (λῃστής); the word is used by Josephus to denote the semi-messianic revolutionary *banditti*, such as Judas the Galilean, Theudas and Eleazar, who from time to time arose in Palestine.

49 His activity had been that of a public prophet and teacher. It is not explained what **Scriptures** are to be **fulfilled;** cf. ix. 12; xiv. 21.

51   The next incident may well have been told by an eye-witness, for it is the kind of story that would be photographed on someone's memory and told without any particular motive. Matthew and Luke omit it, perhaps because they see no point in it. It has been suggested that it contains reminiscences of Amos ii. 16 and Gen. xxxix. 12, but the latter parallel has to do only with literary form. One popular theory is that, if the evangelist is John Mark (Acts xii. 12, 25; xiii. 5, 13; xv. 37-39), he has included himself in the gospel, much in the fashion of a renaissance painter who puts his own portrait on one of the faces of a crowd. But Papias said that Mark neither heard the Lord nor was he a follower of his (Eusebius, *H.E.* iii. 39. 15), and there is no further evidence to support this attractive fancy. John Knox, in S. E. Johnson (ed.), *The Joy of Study* (New York, 1951), suggests that here the story of the Empty Tomb (xvi. 1-8) is anticipated. In both narratives there is a νεανίσκος περιβεβλημένος; here he wears a σινδών, while in xv. 46 this unusual word is used to denote the sheet in which Jesus is to be wrapped; cf. also the fragment of the *Gospel according to the Hebrews*; *Acts of Pilate* xv. 6; *Gospel of Peter* vi. 24. (These texts are translated in James, *Apocryphal NT*, pp. 3, 111, 92.)

There can be no doubt that some connexion exists; one of the stories is modelled on the other, and both have the tone of a dream-sequence. In the original tradition was the young man of this section an angel, who later appears to instruct the women, or is the young man of chap. xvi a disciple?

52   The word γυμνός can mean **naked,** but also 'clad only in a chiton'; in the latter case the **linen cloth** was not a tunic but an added covering.

They led Jesus to the high priest, and all the chief priests 53
and elders and scholars convened. Peter followed him 54
from far off and as far as inside the high priest's courtyard, and was sitting with the servants and warming
himself near the fire.

The chief priests and the whole Sanhedrin tried to find 55
evidence against Jesus so as to put him to death, and did
not find it; for many testified falsely against him, but their 56
testimony did not agree. Some stood up and testified 57
falsely against him, saying, 'We heard him saying, "I 58
will destroy this sanctuary made with hands and within
three days I will build another made without hands"'.
But not even so did their testimony agree. The high priest 59, 60
stood up in front and questioned Jesus: 'Don't you answer
anything to what these men testify against you?' But he 61
kept mute and answered nothing. Again the high priest
questioned him: 'Are you the Messiah, the Son of the
Blessed?' And Jesus said, 'I AM; and you will see "the 62
Son of Man seated at the right side of Power" and "coming with the clouds of heaven"'. The high priest ripped 63
his garments apart and said, 'What more need do we
have of witnesses? You have heard the blasphemy. What 64
do you think?' And they all condemned him as worthy of
death. Some began to spit at him and to cover his face 65
and beat him and say to him, 'Prophesy!' And the servants took him and slapped him.

While Peter was below in the courtyard, one of the 66
maids of the high priest came; and when she saw Peter 67
warming himself she looked at him and said, 'You too
were with that man of Nazareth, Jesus'. He denied it, 68
saying, 'I don't know, I don't even understand what you
are talking about'. Then he went out into the gateway, 69
and the cock crew; and the maid, seeing him, again
began to say to the bystanders, 'This is one of them'. 70
And he again denied it. After a little while once more the
bystanders said to Peter, 'Certainly you are one of them;

71 **why, you are a Galilean too'. But he began to curse and
to swear, 'I don't know this man you are talking about'.**
72 **At once the cock crew the second time. And Peter remembered the word that Jesus had spoken to him,
'Before the cock crows twice you will deny me three
times'. And he burst into weeping.**

The account of Peter's denial must have been told by that
apostle himself. Even though in itself it is an edifying story, it
might well have been suppressed or forgotten if he had not made
it known to the church in Rome. It is lifelike and circum-
stantial, and perhaps only the evangelist himself is the middle-
man between Peter and the reader. If this is so, it tends to
confirm the tradition that Jesus was taken into the house of the
high priest.

It is more difficult to establish the accuracy of the account of
the hearing before the high priest, which needs to be considered
in relation to the narrative of Jesus' trial as a whole. Mark tells
of three meetings: one of the Sanhedrin at night (verses 55-65),
another in the morning (xv. 1), and a trial before Pilate (xv.
2-15). At the night meeting, the original charge is based on an
alleged threat of Jesus to destroy the Temple, but the proceedings result in a charge of blasphemy and a condemnation. The
Sanhedrin does not, however, proceed to an execution. Instead,
after a morning session of this body, Jesus is handed over to
Pilate, who conducts a trial and condemns Jesus to be crucified
on the charge of pretending to be 'king of the Jews'. Matthew's
version is largely dependent on that of Mark. Luke xxii. 66-71
pictures a morning meeting of the Sanhedrin, in which Jesus is
condemned for saying that he is the Son of God. Afterward he
is given hearings before Pilate and Herod Antipas and is handed
over to be crucified. The Fourth Gospel has an independent
narrative, in which Jesus is examined by Annas and Caiaphas
at night and then led to the Praetorium for a hearing before
Pilate. In both hearings the dialogue is very different from what
is contained in the Marcan accounts.

Several problems immediately appear.

(*a*) The Sanhedrin is said to have condemned Jesus, but it did
not execute the sentence. According to the Talmud, execution

might be by stoning, fire, beheading, or strangulation; but Jesus was crucified, and at that by the Roman authorities after a trial before Pilate. Is this because at this time the Romans did not permit the Sanhedrin to inflict the death penalty? Several pieces of evidence seem to point in this direction; cf. F. Büchsel, *ZNW*, xxx (1931), 202-210; xxxiii (1934), 84-87. (1) In John xviii. 31 the Jews are quoted as saying, 'It is not lawful for us to put anyone to death'. (2) The Jerusalem Talmud states (Sanh. i. 1; vii. 2) that forty years before the destruction of the Temple the power to pass capital sentence had been removed. (3) Another Jewish source, the *Megillath Ta'anith*, says that after the outbreak of the Jewish War the Jews were again able to put evildoers to death. (4) The story of the woman taken in adultery (John vii. 53-viii. 11) is sometimes thought to reflect a situation in which the court could not execute sentence; thus the accusers try to get Jesus to say whether Jewish or Roman law should have jurisdiction. (5) The Roman authorities kept custody of the vestments of the high priest. It may have been necessary for him to wear certain insignia in order to pass judgement; thus the court was prevented from exercising jurisdiction.

It may be answered, however, (1) that John xviii. 31 is apologetic in purpose; the evangelist aims to show that the Jewish leaders tried to shift their responsibility to Pilate. In any case it does not outweigh the evidence to be given later. (2) The statement in the Jerusalem Talmud may rest on a misunderstanding of an earlier tradition, according to which the Sanhedrin at one time changed its place of meeting to the bazaars; and according to Pharisaic ideas, the sentence of death could not legally be passed except in the regular meeting place in the Temple precincts. (3) The tradition in *Megillath Ta'anith* may merely mean that during the Jewish War the authorities were able to punish those who supported the Roman cause. (4) The essence of the story of the adulteress has nothing to do with the competence of the Sanhedrin; it is designed only to illustrate Jesus' forgiveness of sinners. (5) The procurator kept custody of the high priest's vestments, but if this restricted the activities of the court, it does not necessarily imply the removal of jurisdiction in capital cases; it merely meant that a valid session could not be held without the governor's knowledge.

On the other hand, several pieces of evidence indicate that the Sanhedrin possessed and exercised the power. (1) Josephus tells of several instances (*Ant.* xiv. 9. 3; xx. 10. 5; *B.J.* ii. 8. 1; 11. 6; vi. 2. 4), the most notable being the death of James the brother of the Lord (*Ant.* xx. 9. 1). In this last case a protest was made, but it seems to have been against the injustice of the sentence, not because the court was incompetent. (2) Stephen was stoned to death, and according to Acts vi. 12 this was an act of the Sanhedrin. (3) The Mishnah (Sanhedrin vii. 2) tells of a priest's daughter who was burnt to death for adultery. Although it has been objected that this may have occurred in the reign of Agrippa I (A.D. 41-44), a date as late as 53 is possible. (4) The right to inflict the death penalty is implied by Agrippa's letter to Caligula, quoted in Philo, *Legatio ad Gaium* xxix, and perhaps also by the inscription set up between the Court of the Gentiles and the Court of the Men of Israel, warning that a Gentile who passed beyond would immediately be put to death (cf. Acts xxi. 29). (5) Paul Winter argues further that the curious provision in the Talmud for death by strangulation probably came into being after A.D. 70, when the court could no longer act openly but had to carry out its executions in secret. Cf. H. Lietzmann, *ZNW*, xxx (1931), 211-215; xxxi (1932), 78-84; *Sitzungsberichte Akad. Berlin, phil.-hist. Klasse* (1931), 313-322; T. A. Burkill, *Vigiliae Christianae*, x (1956), 80-96; Paul Winter, *On the Trial of Jesus* (Berlin, 1961); Gerard S. Sloyan, *Jesus on Trial* (Philadelphia, 1973).

(*b*) Another question concerns the night trial. It has already been remarked (cf. note on verses 12-16) that if this was the night of Passover, a legal meeting of the Sanhedrin could not be held. Even if the dating of John is correct, Jesus could not have been legally condemned to death in a night trial (Mishnah Sanhedrin iv. 1, 'In capital cases they hold the trial during the daytime and the verdict also must be reached during the daytime'). The Mishnah no doubt reflects the jurisprudence of first-century Pharisees, but one can say, with Winter, that the Sadducees may have followed a different procedure. Probably they were governed by ancient custom which was never written down. Thus we cannot rule out a night meeting as utterly impossible.

(*c*) The original charge was that Jesus had uttered a threat against the Temple, but this was apparently not pursued because the evidence was not conclusive. The questioning then turned to the issue of Jesus' messiahship, and, according to Mark, it was because of his answer that he was condemned for blasphemy. In the rabbinic tradition, however, the only blasphemy punishable by death was that of cursing God by name (cf. Job ii. 9). Here the word is used in a looser sense, but the only element in Jesus' saying that could be considered blasphemous was the affirmation that he was the Son of God; certainly no such blame attached to a claim of messiahship as such. Burkill, *Vigiliae Christianae*, xii (1958), 1-18, has argued that Mark's account is a reading back of the later situation— after the Crucifixion it might have been regarded blasphemy to teach that a crucified man was the Messiah, and Mark's account of the hearing is thus modelled on the martyrdom of Stephen— but this seems doubtful.

(*d*) In any case, the Sanhedrin did not carry out any sentence, even though the Roman authorities did not ordinarily intervene in matters of Jewish law. This may indicate that the Sanhedrin could not act; it had no evidence that Jesus had clearly committed a capital offence against the Law of Moses. Perhaps some members of the court were favourably disposed toward Jesus; at least the Pharisees would have been likely to insist on proper evidence; and, furthermore, Jesus had many supporters among the common people.

(*e*) The account in verses 55-65 involves Mark's basic idea that Jesus is Messiah only in the sense that he is Son of God and Son of Man. This theological colouring raises the question of how well the evangelist was informed. It is often objected that Peter and the disciples were not present at the actual hearing; on the other hand, the substance of what went on could have been learned (however inaccurately) from the servants, and John xviii. 15 speaks of a disciple known to the high priest. John xviii. 19-23, however, contains a very different account of the hearing. There Jesus is questioned about his teaching, and answers that all his teaching has been in public and that its content can be learned from anyone. It is therefore probable that the high priest and his confederates interrogated our Lord in the hope of getting evidence that he claimed to be king of the Jews (xv. 2). This was more likely an informal examination than an actual trial. It is not certain whether the trial before Pilate followed immediately (as in John xviii. 28), or whether Mark xv. 1 and Luke xxii. 66-71 are correct in picturing a morning meeting of the Sanhedrin. If the latter occurred, it may have been to prepare charges for Pilate's court.

(*f*) Pilate unquestionably had the *potestas gladii* and his police powers as governor of an imperial province were very great. cf. Sherwin-White, p. 10. Questions have been raised about the accuracy of the account in xv. 2-15, but xv. 26 shows clearly that the charge was sedition or treason (*crimen laesae majestatis*), i.e. that Jesus claimed to be 'king of the Jews'; the main lines of the story are convincing, and the objections can be answered.

53   The **high priest** at this time was Joseph Caiaphas, who held office from A.D. 18 to 35. Ecclesiastical tradition, which cannot be traced earlier than the Bordeaux Pilgrim (A.D. 333), locates his house in the upper, i.e. western, part of the city, south of the city wall, near Sion Church and the Coenaculum. Such a house would be built around a court with no access to it except through

54 a gate in the wall of the **courtyard.** Peter went inside and **was sitting,** no doubt on the stone pavement, **with the servants and warming himself near the fire,** literally 'the light', of a charcoal brazier.

58   The saying, **I will destroy this sanctuary,** etc., may be an earlier prophecy which came to be attributed to Jesus. Prophecies that the old Temple would be replaced by a new and more glorious one made by God himself are found in Enoch xc. 28-29; cf. xci. 13; Jub. i. 17, 27-28. According to Stephen's speech, God does not dwell in the Temple **made with hands** (Acts vii. 48); for the one **made without hands,** cf. Heb. ix. 24; 2 Cor. v. 1; also the similar idea in Dan. ii. 34. John ii. 19-22 makes the saying refer to 'the temple of his body'; but the idea of John iv. 21, 23-24 is a better exposition of it as understood by Christians; cf. also *Ep. Barn.* xvi. It is, of course, possible that Jesus said, in effect: 'If the Temple is destroyed, the true worship of God can be restored within three days'. The saying in xiii. 2 indicates that he predicted the Temple's destruction; like all Jews, he would have contemplated this with sorrow.

In the face of the charges, Jesus **kept mute and answered** 61
nothing (cf. xv. 4-5). This is entirely possible. What could be
gained by answering prejudiced witnesses before a hostile group
which had no jurisdiction?

The next question of the high priest combines two ideas. **Are**
you the Messiah . . .? If the answer proved to be affirmative,
Jesus could at least be accused of royal pretensions, and this
would have weight in Pilate's court. The addition, **the son of**
the Blessed, i.e. God, had Christological significance to the
evangelist and his readers, but the high priest was unlikely to
have combined the two titles; the Messiah was not often thought
of as Son of God (cf. on i. 1).

From the point of view of the evangelist, Jesus could not 62
answer otherwise than **I AM;** words that imply his deity; cf. on
vi. 50. But he is Messiah only in the transcendental sense of **Son**
of Man, which is further explained: he not only will come on
the clouds of heaven (Dan. vii. 13; cf. on xiii. 26), but will
be **seated at the right side of Power,** i.e. God (evidently a
reference to Ps. cx. 1). It is impossible to tell whether on this
occasion Jesus made such a clear disclosure of the mystery of his
Person, since the phraseology is so bound up with the theology
of Mark, but it should be noted that here he does not identify
himself unambiguously with the Son of Man. The tradition
is that, at any rate, he did not deny his messiahship, and this
figured in the trial before Pilate.

The high priest ripped his garments apart, the proper 63
behaviour for one who heard **blasphemy** (cf. SB, i, 1007 f.).
The gesture is essentially a sign of mourning, and the high priest
was forbidden to use it in sorrow for the dead, but the profanation of God's name was a still greater calamity.

He was mockingly told to **Prophesy** because the Messiah was 65
believed to have prophetic gifts (Enoch xlix. 2; Test. Levi
xviii; Test. Judah xxiv). **Took him and slapped him**: the
translation of ῥαπίσμασιν αὐτὸν ἔλαβον is not certain, but it
cannot mean 'took him into custody with blows'; Arndt-
Gingrich, *s.v.* λαμβάνω, suggest that it is a colloquialism
('treated him to blows') or a Latinism ('got him with blows';
cf. Cicero, *Tusc.* ii. 14. 34, *verberibus accipere*).

The scene of Peter's denial is told in Mark's usual narrative style: note the genitive absolute and the participles ἰδοῦσα and ἐμβλέψασα in verses 66-67; cf. v. 25-27.

66   One of the **maids**: the word can mean a slave-girl, but in any case a servant.

68   Peter **denied** being with Jesus, but this was also to disown him; cf. the special meaning of ἀπαρνέομαι in verse 30. His behaviour is characteristic of the frightened villager confronted by the authorities.

69   **The cock crew**: it has been conjectured that this refers to the *gallicinium* or bugle call sounded by the soldiers at the end of the third watch of the night (the beginning of 'cockcrowing', xiii. 35), but this does not fit with the tradition that the cock crew again (verse 72). Chickens were kept in Jerusalem, and a cock may crow at any hour of the night.

70   **Why, you are a Galilean too**: Matt. xxvi. 73 is no doubt correct in surmising that Peter was recognised by his dialect. The Talmud contains numerous traditions of the linguistic peculiarity of the region; cf. SB, i, 156 f.

71   **He began to curse and to swear,** although Jesus had forbidden oaths (Matt. v. 33-37), and denied him even more explicitly.

72   **And he burst into weeping**: the verb ἐπιβαλών can mean 'began' (P. Tebt. 1. 12); this seems more likely than 'he covered his head' (which would demand some such word as τὸ ἱμάτιον) or 'when he thought about it'.

CHAPTER XV

xv. 1-15. MEETING OF THE SANHEDRIN AND
TRIAL BEFORE PILATE

In the morning the chief priests with the elders and 1
scholars, that is, the whole Sanhedrin, at once reached a
decision, bound Jesus, led him away, and handed him
over to Pilate. Pilate questioned him: 'You are the King 2
of the Jews?' He answered him, 'It is you who say it'. 3
And the chief priests made many accusations against
him. Pilate again questioned him: 'Don't you answer 4
anything? See how many things they accuse you of.'
But Jesus still answered nothing, so that Pilate was 5
astonished.

At the Feast he was accustomed to release to them any 6
prisoner whom they wished. There was one called Bar- 7
abbas, in custody with the insurrectionists, men who in
the insurrection had committed murder. And the crowd 8
came up and began to request him to do as he was accustomed to do for them. Pilate answered them, 'Do you 9
want me to release the King of the Jews to you?' For he 10
knew that the chief priests had handed him over to him
out of envy. But the chief priests had stirred the crowd up 11
so that instead he might release Barabbas to them. Pilate 12
again answered them, 'Then what am I to do with the
one you call the King of the Jews?' They shouted back, 13
'Crucify him!' But Pilate said to them, 'Why? What 14
wrong has he done?' They shouted all the more, 'Crucify
him!' Pilate, wishing to satisfy the crowd, released 15
Barabbas to them, and after scourging Jesus, handed him
over to be crucified.

The old Passion Narrative is now resumed. It is all the more
powerful in its effect because it is so simple and straightforward,

almost objective, using no emotional words and no theological
interpretation. In this it is almost like the Acts of the Scilitan
Martyrs. For the legal background, cf. Sherwin-White, pp.
24-47.

1   **In the morning ... the whole Sanhedrin** could convene;
if this is correct, it was probably not on the first day of Unleavened Bread. They **reached a decision;** συμβούλιον ἑτοι-
μάσαντες evidently means much the same as συμβούλιον
διδόναι: (iii. 6); cf. Arndt-Gingrich, *s.v.* The decision was evidently to bring charges before the Roman governor forthwith.

2   Pontius **Pilate** (the double name is given in Luke iii. 1; Acts
iv. 27; 1 Tim. vi. 13) was prefect of the imperial province of
Judaea, from A.D. 26 or 27 to 36. He began his administration
with the serious blunder of attempting to bring the Roman
ensigns, bearing the medallion of the emperor, into Jerusalem.
Later he took part of the Temple treasure to repair the aqueduct
which supplied Jerusalem with water, and when a demonstra-
tion occurred, his soldiers wounded and killed some of the mob.
Finally he was recalled in disgrace at the end of Tiberius' life,
because of his brutality toward the Samaritans who had climbed
Mount Gerizim to find the sacred vessels supposed to have been
buried there by Moses (Josephus, *Ant.* xviii. 3. 1-2; 4. 1-2).
Pilate evidently showed little tact or wisdom in governing an
unusually difficult province, whose people were proud of their
history and zealous for their religion and culture; but his
governorship cannot have been a complete failure, for Tiberius
kept him in office for ten years. John xviii. 28-xix. 16 shows him
as vacillating, acceding only when accused of not being Caesar's
friend. Josephus' narrative discloses the same combination of
uncertainty and swift, brutal action. Cf. Sherwin-White, pp. 1-9,
14 f.

The charge of royal pretension, whether or not it was based
on a statement of Jesus that he was the Messiah, was now laid
before Pilate. The latter's question, *You* **are the King of the
Jews?** (emphatic σύ), suggests surprise; the Galilean teacher
had none of the appearance of a revolutionist.

Jesus' answer (σὺ λέγεις) must be translated as ambiguous:
It is you who say it, or perhaps a question, 'Do you say so?'
For parallels, cf. J. H. Thayer, *JBL*, xiii (1914), 40-49; Morton

Smith, *Tannaitic Parallels*, pp. 26-27, with AV, RV, RSV, Knox, Basic English, Rheims-Douai, against Goodspeed, Twentieth Century, Torrey, Moffatt and Phillips, who take it as an affirmative. The latter rendering conflicts with Pilate's 4 question, **Don't you answer anything?** though this may refer only to the accusations of verse 3; and it is difficult to suppose that the evangelist would include an utterance certain to arouse the suspicion of the imperial authorities. On the silence of Jesus, 5 cf. xiv. 60-61. F. C. Grant, *ATR*, xx (1938), 116, would restore in verse 3 'but he answered them nothing', with Θ and TR. **Pilate was astonished** because he expected a voluble protestation of innocence, if Jesus was only a simple villager; or, if he was a zealot, perhaps a martyr's testimony. The verb θαυμάζειν may suggest a superstitious dread.

There is no direct evidence that **at the feast he was accus-** 6 **tomed to release to them any prisoner,** but the Talmud contains a rule that a paschal lamb may be slaughtered for one who has been promised release from prison; cf. C. B. Chavel, *JBL*, lx (1941), 273-278. Of course amnesties at festival times are known in many parts of the world and in various periods, particularly at the *lectisternia* in Rome; cf. Livy v. 13.

The Sinaitic Syriac and some Caesarean MSS. of Matt. xxvii. 7 16-17 call the prisoner Jesus **Barabbas;** the *bar* indicates that the name is a patronymic. The **insurrectionists** may have been those who protested against the repair of the aqueduct (Josephus, *Ant.* xviii. 3. 2); Luke xiii. 1 also speaks of an incident in which the blood of some Galileans was mingled with that of their sacrifices, but this may refer to an occurrence in Archelaus' reign (*B.J.* ii. 1. 3); cf. S. E. Johnson, *ATR*, xvii (1935), 91-95. In any case, there was more than one massacre in Pilate's time.

Pilate answered the demand of **the crowd** for Barabbas by 8 asking ironically if they wished the **release** of the **King of the** 9 **Jews.** This would have been wiser politically than to free a dangerous agitator. Furthermore, as John xviii. 38*a*-xix. 6 indicates, he did not wish to yield to the pressure of the high priestly group. The motive of the conspirators is not adequately 10 described as **envy;** no doubt they did not wish such a religious teacher to gain prestige, but the cleansing of the Temple had offended them and they feared the consequences of Jesus' pro-

phetic preaching. The **chief priests had stirred the crowd** 11
up, and if any of Jesus' followers were present they were too few
to prevail against it. Here the rôle of the priests is indirect, and
the pressure on Pilate comes from the mob; in John xix. 6 it is
'the chief priests and the officers', and these are probably the
same as 'the Jews' of xix. 7, 12.

14   It is clear that Pilate bears the primary responsibility for the
Crucifixion, and this is the more blameworthy because person-
15 ally he was convinced of Jesus' harmlessness: **Why? What**
wrong has he done? His motive was political expediency:
wishing to satisfy the crowd, and above all the priestly
accusers, he yielded to popular pressure, thinking it better to
execute an innocent man than to run the risk of further trouble.
The character of his master Tiberius in fact faced him with a
dilemma. The emperor was severe on governors who mistreated
provincials, and Pilate's first fear was that a report of the proceedings might reach him; but Tiberius was also profoundly
afraid of sedition, and in John xix. 12 Jesus' enemies rely on this
well-known fact. Pilate dared not set free a 'King of the Jews'.

A secondary, but almost as heavy responsibility, lies on the
men who forced the procurator's hand. The later gospels increasingly emphasise this (cf. especially Matt. xxvii. 24-25;
Gospel of Peter iii. 6-9; vii. 25) because of the desire of Christians to shift the blame away from the Roman authorities to the
Jewish leaders.

Only condemned slaves and provincials might be scourged.
The **scourging** was an added torture, often inflicted before
crucifixion; cf. Josephus, *B.J.* ii. 14. 9; v. 11. 1. A leather whip,
with pieces of bone and metal set in it, was employed. In John
xix. 1, it is said that this took place before the condemnation.

xv. 16-20a. JESUS IS MOCKED BY THE SOLDIERS

16 **The soldiers led him out of the palace, that is, the Prae-**
17 **torium, and summoned the whole cohort. They clad him**
18 **in purple, wove a crown of thorns and put it on him, and**
19 **began to salute him, 'Hail, King of the Jews!' They kept**
beating him on the head with a reed and spitting on him,

and, bowing the knee, reverenced him. Having made 20
sport of him, they took off the purple and put his own
clothing on him.

Here αὐλή should be rendered **palace,** not 'courtyard', for 16
it is explained as **the Praetorium,** i.e. the government house,
Pilate's home and headquarters on the occasions when he came
from Caesarea to Jerusalem. Archaeologists at one time located
this in the Antonia, at the north-west corner of the Temple area,
because it would be natural for the prefect to be with the soldiers
in this strategic spot, and the λιθόβτροτος of John xix. 13 can be
illustrated here. But P. Benoit has shown, *RB,* lix (1952), 531-
550; *HTR,* lxiv (1971), 135-167, that the *Ecce Homo* arch
and other structures in the neighbourhood of the Convent
of the Sisters of Sion must be dated to the second century.
Furthermore, Josephus tells of an incident in which the βῆμα
or judgement-seat of a later procurator, Gessius Florus, was set
up before the entrance to Herod's palace (Josephus, *B.J.* ii. 14.
8), in the north-west corner of the Upper City where the 'Tower
of David' and Citadel now stand. The authority—and no doubt
the perquisites—of the Jewish kings devolved upon Pilate as the
emperor's representative, and he may have preferred the greater
comfort of this palace; cf. also *B.J.* ii. 15. 5; v. 4. 4; and G.
Dalman, *Jerusalem und seine Gelände* (Gütersloh, 1930), p. 86.
In this case the original *Via Dolorosa* is not the traditional one.
   The **whole cohort** (perhaps the Second Italian Cohort,
stationed in Palestine at this time) had 600 men at full strength;
perhaps only a detachment of it was **summoned.**
   The **purple** is perhaps the *sagum* or scarlet cloak worn by 17
Roman soldiers. Jesus was paid mock-royal honours with this
and the **crown of thorns.** The thorns were not necessarily for
the purpose of torture. H. St. J. Hart, *JTS,* n.s. iii (1952), 66-
75, conjectures that the thorns were upright and intended to
caricature the radiate crown worn by divinised rulers. Such
crowns are to be seen on coins of the Ptolemies and Seleucids
and also of Augustus and Tiberius. The thorny leaflets of the
date palm (*Phoenix dactylifera*) may have been used; cf. C.
Bonner, *HTR,* xlvi (1953), 47 f. Another less likely suggestion

is *Acanthus mollis,* whose leaves were used for honorific purposes and are well known in architectural decoration; cf. E. R.
18 Goodenough and C. B. Welles, *HTR,* xlvi (1953), 241 f. The
salute is a parody of *Ave, Caesar, victor, imperator;* cf. on verse
26. Commentators have often compared this incident with the
mockery of an imbecile named Karabas, whom the mobs treated
similarly on the occasion of the visit of Agrippa I to Alexandria,
in order to insult that monarch (cf. Philo, *Against Flaccus* vi and
Klostermann's note, *ad loc.*).

xv. 20b-21. THE WAY OF THE CROSS

20, 21 **They led him away to crucify him, and they forced into
service a man named Simon, a Cyrenian who was coming from the country, the father of Alexander and Rufus,
to carry his cross.**

21   **They . . . forced into service:** the verb ἀγγαρεύω (cf.
Matt. v. 41) is a Persian loan-word, originally referring to re-
quisition or forced service in connexion with the royal post.
Alexander and Rufus were well known to the church for
which the evangelist wrote; as J. Weiss said, *HPC,* ii, 690, this
shows the intimate, non-public character of this gospel. Their
father **Simon** was probably a Jew who had come from Cyrene
in North Africa; Kyrenia in Cyprus has been suggested, because
of the contacts between the early Church and that island (Bishop,
p. 249; cf. Acts iv. 36; xi. 20;), but the Cypriot city was originally named Kerynia.

Crucifixion was a form of execution by torture which the
Romans had practised since the days of the Punic wars, and it
was inflicted on rebels, slaves and criminals of the lower classes.
At the place of execution there were poles or stakes driven into
the ground, or trees. The man to be slain was usually forced to
carry, not the whole cross, but the *patibulum* or cross-beam
which was then fixed to the upright pole. The condemned man
was stripped, his body supported on the cross by a block, and
his legs were lashed out in an unnatural position. Death some-

times came only after several days, and was due to various
causes: thirst, the cutting off of circulation, exposure and
gangrene. On one occasion the Jewish king Alexander Jannaeus
crucified 800 of his enemies (Josephus, *Ant.* xiii. 14. 2); Varus
crucified 2,000 Jews early in Archelaus' reign (*Ant.* xvii. 10. 10);
and at the time of the siege of Jerusalem in the first Jewish
revolt, the Romans put to death so many who escaped from the
city that 'there was not enough room for the crosses or enough
crosses for the bodies' (*B.J.* v. 11. 1).

The evangelist does not tell why Jesus did not carry his own
cross (contrast John xix. 17); perhaps, because of the severe
scourging he had received, he was too weak to do so.

xv. 22-36. THE CRUCIFIXION

**They brought him to the place named Golgotha, which is 22
translated 'place of a skull'. They gave him wine mixed 23
with myrrh, but he did not accept it. They crucified him 24
and 'divided' his 'garments, casting lots for them', to see
who should take what. It was the third hour when they 25
crucified him, and the inscription of the charge against 26
him was written: 'The King of the Jews'. With him they 27, 28
crucified two bandits, one on his right and one on his left.
Those who passed by shouted insults at him, 'wagging 29
their heads' and saying, 'Aha! You who destroy the
sanctuary and build it in three days, come down from the 30
cross and rescue yourself!' Likewise the chief priests 31
making sport of him, together with the scholars, were
saying to each other, 'He rescued others, he cannot rescue
himself. The Messiah, the King of Israel!—let him come 32
down now from the cross, so that we can see and believe.'
And those who were crucified with him insulted him.
When the sixth hour came, darkness appeared over the 33
whole land until the ninth hour; and at the ninth hour, 34
Jesus cried with a great shout, 'Eloi, Eloi, lama sabachthani?' which is translated, 'My God, my God, why have
you forsaken me?' When some of the bystanders heard it, 35**

36 they said, 'See, he is calling for Elijah'. One man ran and filled a sponge with 'sour wine', put it on a reed, and 'gave drink' to him, saying, 'Let us see if Elijah will come to take him down'.

The story of the Crucifixion, like other parts of the Passion Narrative, is sober and restrained, and no attempt is made to play on the emotions of the reader. The only question is the extent to which reminiscences of the OT have coloured the account. Actual quotations or paraphrases appear; e.g. verse 24 =Ps. xxii. 18; verse 29 =Pss. xxii. 7-8; cix. 25; verse 34 =Ps. xxii. 1; verse 36 =Ps. lxix. 21. Christians would also have seen a parallel between verse 27 and Isa. liii. 12. Other suggested contacts, such as verse 23b =Ps. xxii. 15; verse 33 =Isa. lx. 2, are much less definite. The most probable explanation is that Jesus, in his cry from the Cross, actually used the words of Ps. xxii, his garments were divided, and he was offered wine. This, of course, suggested OT prophecies to the disciples, with the result that the references were included. As the tradition grew, other OT passages were brought in, e.g. in Matt. xxvii. 34 ('gall'), 43; Luke xxiii. 46; John xix. 36-37.

22 **Golgotha** can properly be **translated 'place of a skull'**; the Aram. *galgaltā* means 'head' or 'skull'; and it is usually supposed that the hill had this shape. The place cannot now be identified. The contours of the land have been changed since the first century—at the time of the Jewish War a huge ramp was built against the north wall of the city, and much destruction and rebuilding have gone on since. Jesus is said to have suffered outside the gate (Heb. xiii. 12) and Golgotha was probably outside the second wall of Jerusalem. The traditional site is inside the Church of the Holy Sepulchre, adjoining the Sepulchre itself, which is a rock-cut tomb. The supposed tombs of Joseph of Arimathaea and Nicodemus are in a rock fourteen feet high, west of the rotunda which encloses the Sepulchre. The tradition cannot be traced before the fourth century, but there is some slight archaeological evidence that this site lay outside the second wall. The location of this wall has not, however, been satisfactorily settled, and it is barely possible that it followed the course of the present north wall of the Old City. North

of Herod's Gate is the so-called 'Garden Tomb' or 'Gordon's Calvary', which gives an idea of what Golgotha may have been like, but there is no evidence on which an identification can be based.

They gave him wine mixed with myrrh: SB, i, 1037 f., 23 give evidence from Sanh. 43*a* and elsewhere that incense was put in wine as an opiate to dull the senses of condemned men, and women of Jerusalem often performed this office of mercy. Jesus **did not accept it** because he did not wish to lose consciousness.

The **garments** of an executed man were the perquisites of 24 his executioners. They may have **divided** them even before the Crucifixion.

It was the third hour, approximately 9 a.m.   25

It was usual to mark the condemned criminal with a *titulus* 26 or **inscription** which showed his crime. The words **The King of the Jews** cannot have been invented by the tradition. They show, beyond question, that he was crucified by the Romans and that the claim of messiahship had been twisted to support a charge of treason or sedition. As John xix. 19-22 indicates, this *titulus* was insulting to all the Jews, including the priestly conspirators. In this brutal fashion, Pilate showed the determination of the Romans to destroy anyone who claimed to be king of the Jews.

Nothing is known of the **two bandits,** but there were many 27 such, some of whom attempted insurrections. A tradition about the 'good thief' is given in Luke xxiii. 39-43, and still later traditions give them such names as Zoatham and Camma, Dysmas and Gestas, etc.

The **wagging** of **heads** is an oriental gesture of scorn; cf. also 29 Isa. xxxvii. 22; Jer. xviii. 16. This gloating over the unfortunate was characteristic of the ancient orient but has also been known in modern times. **You who destroy the sanctuary:** cf. xiv. 58. **The Messiah, the King of Israel** could not be a true one if 32 this was to be his fate; or, if he is this truly, **let him come down from the cross,** for he can work miracles.

When the sixth hour came, i.e. noon, **darkness appeared** 33 **over the whole land.** This is understood as an eclipse in Luke xxiii. 45; if this is not a legendary touch, there was a severe storm, or a *shirocco* dust storm that can come suddenly in the spring; Bishop, p. 250, mentions such an occurrence on October 22, 1945.

34 **At the ninth hour, Jesus cried with a great shout, 'Eloi, Eloi, lama sabachthani?'** This quotation from Ps. xxii. 1 is in Aramaic, not Hebrew; Torrey, *ad loc.*, gives the verb form as *shabachtânî*. It is often taken as a cry of dereliction, and it must at least be said that here Jesus is at one with suffering humanity and identifies himself with the ancient Psalmist in his woes. But, as Grant says, *ad loc.*, the centurion (verse 39) recognises that Jesus has died like a great hero, a son of God, and φωνὴ μεγάλη should be translated as above; cf. Ignatius, *Philad.* vii. 1, 'I cried out while I was with you, I spoke with a great voice, with God's own voice'. Ps. xxii, furthermore, ends on a note of hope, not despair, and, as Dibelius says, 'one who quoted a word of the Bible in prayer certainly had not lost faith in God' (*Message*, p. 145). The prayer of complaint, so foreign to modern thought, is an important feature of OT religion, and perhaps the word from the Cross was less a problem to the ancients than to ourselves.

35 **Elijah** was believed to be the helper of the faithful in their distress. But would **the bystanders** have mistaken *'Eloi* or *'Eli* for *'Eliyyâhû*? It is possible that, because of Jesus' agony, his words were not heard distinctly by all.

36 The **sour wine** or vinegar is not the same as the drugged wine offered him at the beginning. Possibly the drink was the soldiers' *posca*, made of water, sour wine and egg, and so was given as an act of mercy; but the evangelist thinks of it as an addition to Jesus' misery (cf. Ps. lxix. 21) and connects it with the remark, **Let us see if Elijah will come to take him down.** The colloquial ἄφετε ἴδωμεν (imperative used as an auxiliary to the hortatory subjunctive) is common in late Greek.

xv. 37-39. THE DEATH OF JESUS

37, 38 **Jesus, having shouted aloud, expired. And the veil of the**
39 **Temple was split from the top to the bottom. When the**

**centurion who stood near, facing him, saw that he had
expired thus, he said, 'Certainly this man was a son
of God!'**

It is not certain whether **Jesus . . . shouted aloud** a second 37
time; the evangelist may refer to the cry of verse 34. He **expired** after six hours of agony, a very short time (cf. verse 44).
Nothing in the account indicates how this release from torture
came so soon, but it should be recalled that Jesus did not carry
his own cross (verse 21).

Josephus describes the **veil of the Temple** as equal in size 38
to the golden doors of the ναός, 55 by 16 cubits, a 'Babylonian
tapestry' embroidered with blue, fine linen, scarlet and purple,
portraying 'a panorama of the heavens, the signs of the Zodiac
excepted' (*B.J.* v. 5. 4, Thackeray's tr.). The reference may,
however, be to the smaller veil in front of the *debir* or Holy of
Holies. The tearing of this veil (ἐσχίσθη) corresponds to the
splitting of the skies at Jesus' baptism (i. 10) and may therefore
have symbolised to Christians the complete and uninterrupted
access to God that men now have through the death of Jesus
(Eph. ii. 14-18; Heb. ix. 1-12; x. 19-25), but more probably the
evangelist regarded it as the divine judgement visited on the
Temple as the punishment of the nation. Josephus tells of
portents preceding the destruction of the sanctuary: the priests
sacrificing in the Temple felt an earthquake and heard a voice
like that of a multitude saying, 'Let us remove hence'; and in
the time of Albinus, a prophet named Jesus son of Ananus, at
the feast of Tabernacles, cried, 'A voice from the east, a voice
from the west, a voice from the four winds, a voice against Jerusalem and the holy house, a voice against the bridegrooms and
the brides, and a voice against this whole people!' (*B.J.* vi.
5. 3; cf. B. Yoma 39*b*).

A centurion (Mark transliterates the Latin word instead of 39
giving its Greek equivalent) commanded one hundred men and
in rank and status can be compared to a non-commissioned
officer in a modern army. This man perhaps headed the detachment which had carried out the Crucifixion. His wonder was
not caused by the destruction of the Temple veil (verse 38 in
fact interrupts the narrative) but by the fact that Jesus **had**

expired thus, with the almost triumphant shout of a hero (cf. verse 34). Such a one was **a son of God,** like Asclepius or the Dioscuri, a saviour and benefactor of mankind; the term was frequently applied to emperors and rulers, and to philosophers like Pythagoras, Plato and Apollonius of Tyana.

xv. 40-41. THE WOMEN OF GALILEE

40 **There were women watching from far off, among whom were Mary the Magdalene and Mary the mother of James**
41 **the Small and Joses, and Salome, who while he was in Galilee used to follow and serve him, and many other women who had gone up with him to Jerusalem.**

40   **Mary the Magdalene** is not mentioned previously by Mark; according to Luke viii. 3 she had been delivered from seven demons, and together with Joanna, Susanna 'and many others' had provided for the disciples, no doubt (as Mark says) **while**
41 **he was in Galilee.** Several MSS., including C D, omit **and serve him;** this phrase may have been based on the passage in Luke. **Mary the mother of James the Small and Joses** is sometimes identified as the mother of Jesus, because he had two brothers with these common names (vi. 3), but it would be strange for the evangelist to mention her in this way if the identification were correct. Matt. xxvii. 56 speaks of these two women but not **Salome.** Mary Magdalene figures in John xx. 1-18 as an important witness of the Resurrection.

xv. 42-47. THE BURIAL OF JESUS

42 **When evening had come, because it was Preparation**
43 **Day, that is Friday, Joseph, who was from Arimathaea, a rich member of the Council, who himself expected the Kingdom of God, came and boldly went in to Pilate and**
44 **asked for the body of Jesus. Pilate was surprised that he**

should already be dead; so he summoned the centurion
and asked him whether he had died some time before.
When he learned the fact from the centurion he granted 45
the body to Joseph. And he [Joseph] bought a linen sheet, 46
took him down [from the cross], wrapped him in the
linen, and placed him in a tomb that was hewn out of
rock, and rolled a stone to the door of the tomb. And Mary 47
the Magdalene and Mary of Joses observed where he
was laid.

Evening (ὀψία) can denote a time before or after sundown; 42
here it must be the former, because it is still **Preparation Day**;
Friday is the English equivalent of προσάββατον. **Joseph** came 43
from **Arimathaea,** perhaps Ramathaim-zophim (1 Sam. i. 1),
about 15 miles east of Joppa. He was **rich;** so Matt. xxvii. 57
correctly interprets εὐσχήμων, which often represents the Lat.
honestus. **Member of the Council** (βουλευτής): not necessarily
of the great Sanhedrin of Jerusalem; perhaps he belonged to one
of the local sanhedrins of 23 members each (Mishnah Sanhedrin i. 6). That he **himself expected the Kingdom of God**
does not necessarily imply that he was a disciple of Jesus, but
merely that he was a religious Jew of the best sort (cf. xii. 34).

Such a person, respected and prominent, might **boldly** go to
Pilate and ask **for the body of Jesus** in order to bury him, for
this was an act of piety and it was customary to bury people on
the day of death (cf. Tobit i. 16-18; ii. 1-8); furthermore, the
body of a man was not allowed to remain gibbeted overnight
because it profaned the Holy Land (Deut. xxi. 23; Josephus,
B.J. iv. 5. 2), and this was felt to be particularly important on the
eve of a high festival (John xix. 31).

Pilate was surprised that he should already be dead; 44
cf. on verse 37. **He granted the body** (πτῶμα, 'corpse') **to** 45
Joseph, and the latter **bought a linen sheet,** not the expensive 46
garments often used at this time for burial (cf. xiv. 51-52),
wrapped him in the linen, and placed him in a tomb.
Several such sepulchres, which had to be outside the city wall,
are to be seen in and around Jerusalem. Sometimes they were
natural caves, but often **hewn out of the rock;** the bodies were
placed in recesses in the walls or on shelves or slabs in the centre.

The opening might be rectangular, with a stone door on pivots; but here a disc-shaped **stone** was **rolled . . . to the door of the tomb.** The 'Tombs of the Kings', where Queen Helena of Adiabene and her family were buried, have a slot at the entrance where the stone could be rolled to close the sepulchre.

CHAPTER XVI

xvi. 1-8. THE EMPTY TOMB

When the sabbath had passed, Mary the Magdalene and 1
Mary of James and Salome bought spices to come and
anoint him. Very early in the morning, after sunrise on 2
the first day of the week, they came to the tomb. They 3
said to each other, 'Who will roll the stone away from the
door of the tomb for us?' They looked up and saw that the 4
stone had been rolled aside—it was extremely large.
They entered the tomb and saw a young man seated at 5
the right, clothed in a white garment, and they were
alarmed. He said to them, 'Do not be alarmed. You are 6
looking for Jesus, the Nazarene, who was crucified. He
has been raised up, he is not here; see the place where
they laid him. But go tell his disciples and particularly 7
Peter that he is going before you into Galilee; you will see
him there, just as he said to you.' They went out and fled 8
from the tomb, for trembling and astonishment had
seized them; and they said nothing to anyone, for they
were afraid.

The Gospel of Mark contains no account of an appearance of
the risen Lord to his disciples, although the tradition was well
known (1 Cor. xv. 3-8), and Mark of course knows and presupposes it (e.g. viii. 31; ix. 9, 31; x. 34; xiv. 28; xvi. 6). The
Longer and Shorter Endings are not in Mark's style, and are
relatively early attempts to make up for what seemed an obvious
deficiency of the gospel and to round it off smoothly. Critics of
previous generations assumed that the gospel had been mutilated and the original ending lost: ἐφοβοῦντο γάρ, at the end of
verse 8, is an abrupt ending for the book; appearances in
Galilee, presupposed by verse 6, are to be found in Matt. xxviii.

16-20 and John xxi; the miracle of Luke v. 1-11, so similar to
the latter, may originally have been a resurrection story; and the
fragmentary Gospel of Peter breaks off just before a contemplated appearance in Galilee.

More recent criticism, under the influence of Lohmeyer,
Galiläa und Jerusalem, and Lightfoot, *Locality and Doctrine in
the Gospels*, inclines to the belief that the gospel originally ended
at verse 8; cf. F. C. Grant, *The Earliest Gospel* (New York,
1943), chap. vi; and Marxsen, p. 55, who holds that this pericope
is intended by Mark as his resurrection story. It is possible for
a sentence or a paragraph to end with γάρ, Mark's style is very
abrupt, and his book begins with no preamble except the opening verse. While Mark does not minimise the importance of the
Resurrection, it is argued that for him this is only a stage leading
to the Parousia which is expected in Galilee after the tribulations of the Jewish War. It is noteworthy that chap. xiii, in Mark
the last great discourse of Jesus to his disciples, looks forward
entirely to the coming of the Son of Man and nowhere alludes
to the Resurrection; nor does the Passion Narrative, with the
possible exception of xiv. 58, for the promise that Jesus will
drink again with his disciples in the Kingdom of God (xiv. 25)
contemplates the coming age.

The matter cannot, however, be regarded as finally settled.
W. L. Knox, *HTR*, xxxv (1942), after a study of abrupt transi-
tions in the NT, concludes that the type of 'dramatic aposio-
pesis' found in verse 8 does not occur elsewhere in the gospels,
even as the conclusion of a section, except in John. If Mark had
ended his gospel so abruptly, says Knox, he would have violated
all the canons of ancient story-telling. It therefore remains possible that the book was mutilated. In this case the 'lost' ending
may be preserved in John xxi or in Matt. xxviii. 16-20 in
rewritten form.

But if Lohmeyer's arguments are sound, the original conclusion of the gospel may have been only a graceful rounding-
off, such as we find in Luke xxiv. 52-53; John xx. 30-31; and
Acts xxviii. 30-31. In this case, one function of Mark's conclusion is to remind his readers once more of 'the promise of his
coming' (2 Pet. iii. 4) and to confirm this by the word of an
angelic visitant or an unknown disciple, almost at the moment

of the Resurrection, when such an assurance was particularly needed.

Other traditions of the Resurrection, beginning with the earliest, preserved by St. Paul in 1 Cor. xv. 1-8, are of an entirely different character, for their witness is that the Eleven and others saw the risen Lord. It is usually said that the story of the Empty Tomb is only secondary and confirmatory evidence, but it is nevertheless Mark's only Resurrection story, and it fulfils the predictions given in viii. 31; ix. 31; x. 34; and xiv. 28. To the evangelist it is a sufficient proof of the Resurrection.

Its historical value is difficult to assess. When compared with its developments in the later gospels, it is seen to be simple and restrained. If the young man in white is an angel, Mark does not trouble to emphasise this. K. Lake, *The Historical Evidence for the Resurrection of Jesus Christ* (London, 1907), pp. 248-252, holds that the story had an historical basis; however, the women, who were in an overwrought state of mind, came to the wrong tomb and were directed by the young man to the place where Jesus was actually buried, but misunderstood his words. The assumption is, however, unnecessary, and—granted the possibility of the bodily Resurrection—the account is plausible as we have it. A more serious difficulty is raised by the statement that the women said nothing to anyone; thus the story gives the impression of being a private tradition which came to the Church's knowledge only long afterward. One motive for its telling may be to teach that the body which the disciples saw had actually left the tomb. This is the tendency of the later gospels, as contrasted with St. Paul, who teaches that the glorified body is not to be compared with the one that was buried (1 Cor. xv. 35-44).

Another motive may, however, be present. The only experience of the Resurrection that Mark recounts is not vouchsafed to the disciples. They have never been more than half-believers. When the second Passion prediction was given, they failed to understand and were afraid to ask Jesus for the explanation (ix. 32); the third prediction was followed by the absurd plea of James and John for places of honour (x. 35-40); in the garden they all fled (xiv. 50), and even Peter denied him (xiv. 71). It was the women, hitherto unnoticed throughout the gospel, who had followed and served him and had the courage to watch the

Crucifixion from far off (xv. 40-41), who were granted the first word that Jesus had risen. On their witness rested the hope that the disciples would meet him in Galilee. The last episode in the gospel is therefore part of the Messianic Secret. What is hidden from the 'wise and prudent', even from the intimate disciples, is revealed to those who seem to be the least. The evangelist has prepared for this climax by inserting xiv. 28 and perhaps xiv. 51-52 into the Passion Narrative.

1   The text of the section is uncertain. D and some OL MSS. omit the phrase at the beginning, **When the sabbath had passed, Mary the Magdalene and Mary of James and Salome,** so that they read 'And they bought spices', etc. The names of the women are not given at this point in the parallels in Matthew and Luke. The first half of verse 4, referring to the stone having been rolled away, is also omitted by D.

The **spices** or aromatic oils were used in embalming.

5   The young man has a counterpart in xiv. 51-52 (νεανίσκος . . . περιβεβλημένος σινδόνα). Here he is clothed in a **white garment;** cf. ix. 3, where Jesus' garments are shining λευκὰ λίαν. It is unnecessary to suppose that because he is dressed in white he is a priest or Essene. Probably he is thought of as an angel, as in Matt. xxviii. 2, but Mark does not stress the super-
6   natural element; the young man's only function is to explain that **he has been raised up** (note the primitive ἠγέρθη: cf. ἐγήγερται, 1 Cor. xv. 4), and to remind them of the promised reunion in Galilee.

7   **But go tell his disciples and particularly Peter:** should be translated thus, not 'his disciples and Peter', for the evangelist could not have thought that Peter was no longer a disciple. Grant, however, argues, *ATR*, xx (1938), 117 f., that verse 7, like xiv. 28, interrupts the narrative and may be an early gloss, based on Matthew. He would reconstruct the text thus: 'But go tell his disciples that they will see him, as he said to them', or perhaps: 'Go tell his disciples, "he has been raised up", and you will see him, as he said to you'. **He is going before you:** cf. on xiv. 28.

When he rose early on the first day of the week, he ap- 9
peared first to Mary the Magdalene, out of whom he had
driven seven demons. She went and brought the news to 10
his associates as they were weeping and lamenting. Al- 11
though they heard that he was living and had been seen
by her, they disbelieved. After this he was revealed in 12
another form to two of them as they went on foot into the
country. They went and brought the news to the rest, but 13
they did not believe the two men. Afterward he was re- 14
vealed to the Eleven as they were at table, and he reproached them for their unbelief and dullness of mind
because they did not believe those who had seen him
risen. [They made their defence, saying, 'This age of
lawlessness and unbelief is subject to Satan, who does not
permit the unclean things which lie under the spirits to
make the true power of God their own; therefore reveal
your righteousness now', they said to the Messiah. And
the Messiah said to them, 'The limit of the years of
Satan's authority has been reached, but other afflictions
draw near; and because of those who sinned I was
handed over to death, that they might return to the truth
and sin no longer, so that they might inherit the spiritual
and imperishable glory of righteousness which is in
heaven'.] And he said to them, 'Go into the whole world 15
and proclaim the Good News to all the creation. He who 16
believes and is baptised will be saved, but he who disbelieves will be condemned. These signs will follow those 17
who have believed: in my name they will cast out demons; they will speak in new languages; they will pick 18
up serpents, and even if they drink something deadly it
will not harm them at all; they will lay their hands on the
sick and they will get well.' Then the Lord after speaking 19
with them 'was taken up into heaven' and 'sat on the
right of God'. They went out and proclaimed the word 20
everywhere, while the Lord worked with them and certified the word through the accompanying signs.

The Longer Ending is omitted by S B k sy⁸ and some codices of the Armenian and Ethiopic versions. In certain Armenian MSS. it is attributed to 'Ariston the presbyter'. This conclusion to the gospel is non-Marcan in vocabulary, syntax and ideas, and is evidently a second-century digest of resurrection traditions drawn from the other gospels and Acts. Its attestation by Tatian and Irenaeus shows that it is relatively early; cf. C. S. C. Williams, *Alterations to the Text of the Synoptic Gospels and Acts* (Oxford, 1951), pp. 40-45.

Codex W includes, after verse 14, a singular interpolation (the so-called 'Freer logion') which, for the sake of convenience, is printed in the text above in brackets. Elsewhere it is known only in Jerome, *Dial. adv. Pelag.* ii. 15, where part of it is given in Latin. Its text is corrupt and many emendations have been suggested. Since its tone suggests the Johannine literature, it was probably written after the collection of the fourfold gospel, *c.* 150–175, but more precise dating is not possible.

9   **When he arose**: ἀναστάς is used here, but ἐγηγερμένον in verse 14. **He appeared**: ἐφάνη is not customarily employed to refer to the Resurrection (contrast ὤφθη, 1 Cor. xv. 5-8), and in Matt. i. 20 this verb is used of a dream vision. He **appeared ... to Mary Magdalene**; cf. Matt. xxviii. 9-10; John xx. 14-17. The phrase **out of whom he had driven seven demons** is derived from Luke viii. 2. In contradiction to verse 8, **she ... brought the news to his associates**; cf. Luke xxiv. 10-11,
11 22-24; also John xx. 18, which does not say that **they disbelieved.**

12   **After this he was revealed** (ἐφανερώθη; the verb is used of the Resurrection in John xxi. 1, 14) **in another form to two of**
13 **them**; cf. Luke xxiv. 13-32. **They went and brought the news to the rest,** but Luke xxiv. 35 does not speak of the un-
14 belief of the disciples. **Afterward he was revealed to the eleven as they were at table,** etc.; cf. Luke xxiv. 36-43.

The Freer logion probably does not belong to the original text of the summary, because it refers to Jesus as ὁ Χριστός, not ὁ κύριος (verse 19); furthermore, it introduces a formal eschatological teaching foreign to the purpose of the passage.

They made their defence: as Mr. J. P. Engelcke remarks, ἀπολογέω is ordinarily used in this sense. I am indebted to a

personal communication from him for several suggestions incor-
porated here.

This age, as in rabbinic Judaism and the gospels, is contrasted with the 'age to come'; for its **lawlessness,** cf. 2 Thess.
ii. 3, 7; its **unbelief,** cf. viii. 12; ix. 19. Here it is formally taught
that the present age is **subject to Satan** (cf. Luke iv. 6; 1 John
v. 19; *Barn.* xviii. 2). The remainder of the sentence is garbled.
Satan apparently **does not permit the unclean things** (neuter
plural) or perhaps 'persons' **to make the true power of God
their own;** on the thought, cf. 2 Cor. iv. 4; Acts xvii. 30;
Hermas *Mand.* v. 2. 7. Here we emend ἀλήθειαν to ἀληθίνην,
but perhaps a καί should be supplied instead: 'the truth and
power of God'. καταλαμβάνω is used with the meaning 'to make
one's own' in Phil. iii. 12-13; Rom. ix. 30.

**The limit of the years of Satan's authority has been
reached** (literally 'completed'). Engelcke notes similarities to
the language of i. 14-15, and remarks also the prominence of
unclean spirits in i. 23, 26, 27; evidently the section is based on
Mark. The **other afflictions** may be the apocalyptic woes of
chap. xiii.

**Because of those who sinned I was handed over to
death:** there is a close parallel in 1 Clem. xvi. 13-14, which
similarly quotes the LXX of Isa. liii. 12. The contrast between
truth and **sin** suggests the Two Ways doctrine of Barn. xviii.
1-2; xx. 1; xxi. 1 and 1QS i. 19; iii. 17-19. The **spiritual and
imperishable glory of righteousness:** the words are all
Pauline; their combination has the form of second-century
Christian rhetoric.

The Longer Ending resumes with a form of the Great Com- 15
mission. Verse 15 is based on Matt. xxviii. 19. **He who believes** 16
and is baptised will be saved: cf. Acts ii. 38; xvi. 31, 33. For
the threat that **he who disbelieves will be condemned,** cf.
John iii. 18.

The term **signs** (σημεῖα) is not used of Jesus' miraculous 17
deeds in Mark, but is common in John, e.g. ii. 11; cf. also Acts
iv. 16, 22. **In my name they will cast out demons,** cf. ix. 38.
They will speak in new (καιναῖς, 'different') **languages;**
the reference is to Acts ii. 4. **They will pick up serpents;** cf. 18
Acts xxviii. 2-6. The NT contains no parallel to the statement

if they drink something deadly, etc., but such a story is told of Justus Barabbas by Papias in Eusebius, *H.E.* iii. 39. 9. **They will lay their hands on the sick and they will get well;** cf. Acts xxviii. 8; Jas. v. 14-15.

19   **Then the Lord** (C and a few other MSS. add 'Jesus') . . . **'was taken up into heaven';** cf. Acts i. 9-11 and the variant reading in Luke xxiv. 51. And **'sat on the right of God';** cf. Acts vii. 55; Ps. cx. 1.

20   The final verse sums up the activities of the first disciples in the Book of Acts. The concept that **the Lord worked with them and certified the word through the accompanying signs** is a good summary of the early Christian view of miracles (cf. Acts xiv. 3).

THE SHORTER ENDING

They reported briefly to Peter's associates all that had been commanded. After this, Jesus himself sent out through them, from the east as far as the west, the sacred and imperishable proclamation of eternal salvation.

This is found in L Ψ and a few other MSS., including *k* of the OL. It evidently refers to Luke xxiv. 10 or John xx. 18 and states in general terms the early Christian belief that the **proclamation of eternal salvation** was due to the commission of Jesus himself.

INDEX OF SUBJECTS

INDEX OF REFERENCES

OLD TESTAMENT

INDEX

GOSPEL ACCORDING TO ST. MARK

INDEX

JEWISH WRITINGS

CHRISTIAN WRITINGS

PAGAN WRITINGS

INDEX